MAN TESTS

THE (MIS)ADVENTURES
OF AN ENDURANCE FANATIC

GRAHAM LITTLE

EBURY
PRESS

1 3 5 7 9 10 8 6 4 2

Ebury Press, an imprint of Ebury Publishing
20 Vauxhall Bridge Road
London SW1V 2SA

Ebury Press is part of the Penguin Random House
group of companies whose addresses can be found at
global.penguinrandomhouse.com

Penguin
Random House
UK

First published by Ebury Press in 2016

www.penguin.co.uk

A CIP catalogue record for this book is
available from the British Library

All photographs courtesy of the author unless otherwise stated

ISBN 9781785031953

Typeset in India by Thomson Digital Pvt Ltd, Noida, Delhi

Printed and bound in Great Britain by Clays Ltd, St Ives PLC

MIX
Paper from
responsible sources
FSC
www.fsc.org   FSC® C018179

Penguin Random House is committed to a
sustainable future for our business, our readers
and our planet. This book is made from Forest
Stewardship Council® certified paper.

In loving memory of two great (and great*) grandfathers, JCL and WM; and in loving anticipation of the futures of three great children, CPP, RJC and IM*

CONTENTS

PROLOGUE

My grandfather had a quip for every occasion. And now that he is gone, I realise he spoke many a true word in jest. Like most of his generation, he was bemused by the idea of running for the sake of running. Every time I was heading off, he'd tell me that if I waited a while I could probably get a bus. He said it so often that I really started to think high-intensity exercise was pointless. By any rational analysis, it is. But unfortunately for me, for millions like me, and probably for you since you've picked up this book, it is both pointless *and* essential.

I've enjoyed a variety of sports for as long as I can remember but there's a marked difference between sport and fitness training. The former is usually fun, and the latter usually isn't. I took up fairly serious fitness training in my mid-teens because I wanted to join the Royal Marines. Dazzled by video presentations from recruiting officers on school visits, I saw a life of *Boy's Own* adventure and comradeship, coupled with the sense of positive self-worth that would come from being a strong and fit fighting machine.

I wilfully ignored the questions of who and what I'd be fighting for and against, and indeed whether I wanted to be fighting at all. I thought it was all just about jungles and gyms, sailing and sit-ups.

At 19, I passed the Royal Marines Potential Officer Course in Devon, as demanding a test of physical fitness as any. But I'd spent the previous year travelling round the world in glorious freedom on a gap year, so enduring three days of being shouted at and told I was slovenly and worthless was a bit of a shock, and the reality of a life in the Armed Forces hit home. I decided that the Marines and I were no longer compatible.

But I'd got hooked on the training. And although I was no longer training to be a soldier, it was very useful for rugby. Then after years of playing the game I loved, it slowly dawned on me that I was beginning to get more out of the preparation than the actual rugby, and that I was better at the fitness stuff than the rugby stuff. The rugby stuff began to feel repetitive and restrictive. I found I didn't really care for passing drills and tackling drills, or any sort of drills. Life had enough rules as it was without having to observe them in leisure time too.

So I dropped rugby as well. That left the strength and fitness training, but with nothing to train *for*. If hours of sweating, striding and heaving every week wasn't a means to an end, what could it be exactly? It had become an intrinsic part of my self-identity; somehow as important for my mental health as my physical health. But why? Given that one of my other big passions was partying, health-wise I was probably only just breaking even. I felt like I *needed* to train hard, I needed to keep moving forward physically, but it was a journey with no destination.

Sometimes we scratch around for answers, for direction, and then it's a seemingly unconnected and completely random sequence of events that shows us the way. Some people call that fate, but in sport we prefer to think that we dictate our own destiny. And I can't imagine that whoever pulls the strings of fate would've been arsed to arrange a transformative experience for me on a wet Saturday on Snowdon.

One
MAN TESTS

My friends and I have always been strict observers of the grand male tradition of leading each other astray. When one of us finds himself with the spark of an idea, the whiff of some adventure, or the taste of some badness, the rest are compelled to follow. This symbiotic relationship, coupled with my own blind devotion to the principle 'better the Devil you don't know' helps explain why in one five-year period, I swam across one of the busiest shipping lanes in the world, ran across the Sahara Desert, and most perplexingly, abandoned my new wife near the summit of Africa's tallest mountain, on our honeymoon.

It's a bit of a stretch to blame my best friend, Slippy, for all of that but it was him that set me adrift on the tide of irrational adventure challenges we would come to label 'Man Tests'. It was an inauspicious start by any reckoning. He phoned me one evening to suggest that we both compete in one of the UK's toughest mountain running races, the Welsh 1000m Peaks Race in Snowdonia. Given that neither of us had ever run up a mountain before, this could be construed as an unusual suggestion, but with the context of the previous summer, when I had insisted he join me at another equally unappealing Welsh event, the World Bog Snorkelling Championships, it seems more orderly.

He'd heard about the mountain running through another friend, Tyvian, a part-timer in the Paras who was helping some of his unit prepare for the event and who had dragged Slippy along to the Brecon Beacons with them one weekend. Being a competitive eejit, it was pretty clear that Slippy had gone to the training just to compare himself to the Paras, but had then been expertly goaded by Ty to go the extra mile and enter the actual race himself. Once he was thus committed, Slippy needed an equally novice wingman. Me.

Of course the sensible thing would have been to investigate what this event we'd never heard of actually entailed before signing up, but as my grandfather again was fond of telling me, among my friends common sense is a most uncommon commodity. I found the race website to book us in and Ty then revealed that he wouldn't actually be taking part himself, which was the first big clue that this was not a challenge to be taken lightly. He's a big lad for running, and he was still trying to get over the postural problems he picked up after sitting in a canoe for 125 miles in the epic Devizes to Westminster race just a month before. But still, I should have thought a bit more about why Ty was happy for us to try it but not him. The second clue about the scale of the challenge was that you couldn't just enter the event automatically. Potential competitors could *apply*, but would then be vetted.

This is because the 22-mile Welsh 1000m Peaks Race, also known as the Snowdonia Summits Marathon, is a proper hard-core trial, and they couldn't have just any impulsive, irrational optimists turning up and getting lost. There are four mountains in Wales higher than 1,000 metres, and in this race competitors have to run up and down all of them. To put it in perspective, that is climbing higher than anywhere in the whole of England four times in a row and then finishing on top of Snowdon. The distance is one thing, but the accumulated climbing is quite another. Reaching *each* summit is the equivalent of marching up the stairs to the very top of London's Shard more than three times. Except that of course there are no stairs on the mountains, and you have to run.

The application form contained a section in which prospective entrants had to list a series of similar events they had successfully completed, including at least one of 12 miles or more. I put down the only Northern Ireland mountain race I had ever heard of and then made a few up. 'The Mournes Fell Race' (13 miles) sounded plausible and was hopefully also untraceable. Other races on our imaginary fell race CV did actually exist but had never been troubled by our entry.

There was also a list of compulsory kit that would have to be carried by all runners and would be checked before the start when race numbers were handed out. Failure to show the correct kit would mean no race number and no entry. Kit included waterproofs, mini first aid kit, hydration tablets, a map and a compass – equipment I had never needed before to go for a run.

I don't remember feeling anything but very pleased when I received an email confirming our entry for the race in three months' time. What I should have been feeling was terrified. I threw myself into running training and loved it.

The freedom to train where and when I wanted was great and I loved the sense of progress. Rugby had begun to feel like training without improving, and after playing badly at fullback during matches I often came off the pitch as fresh as I was when I went on. Now I finished every running session knowing I'd just come through something truly testing.

But getting fit was one thing, learning about fell running or how to find my way in the mountains was quite another. Somebody recommended I speak to a local athlete called Brian who had competed in the Welsh 1000m Peaks Race a couple of years earlier and who was also an expert navigator.

I went round to see him. He had just finished having dinner with his family and smelled faintly of garlic. He was wearing tight, light blue shorts, the kind worn by serious runners but usually only when they're actually running, not when they're eating dinner. He was whippet-lean, without an ounce of fat on long, sinewy legs. He didn't have the powerful athletic aura given off by rugby players or boxers – I'd seen more upper body muscle on supermodels – but had the geeky accidental fitness of the serious orienteer, the kind of person who runs with their glasses on. It was obvious this was a physique and a character ideally suited to running up and down steep hills for hours at a time and not getting lost. Certainly a lot more suited to that type of activity than my own rugby physique and reckless character.

We went out into the garden to talk. Breezily I tried to put across an unaffected air, as if I was in such terrific shape that the prospect of the race was really nothing to me: 'Such a lot of kit and regulations! Is all this really necessary? I'm sure we'll not get lost!'

'Well you very easily could, especially if you haven't much experience,' Brian replied seriously, and slightly contemptuously, I felt. 'All the kit is definitely necessary. Because 22 miles round the highest mountains in Wales is pretty serious stuff actually.'

With a mildly impatient manner he began to take me through the basics of map reading for fell runners. After a minute or two I was hopelessly adrift but nodding repetitively and saying 'mmm, hmm' regardless, lying when he asked me if I'd got it now and if that had been helpful. I left, sensing some disapproval when he suggested I needed another few races before leaping straight into the infamous Welsh 1000m.

I decided that it would probably all make more sense when I actually got into the mountains. This was of course nonsensical foolhardiness. How, under any circumstances, could anything be easier to grasp in the teeth of a gale 1,000 metres up a mountain, than it had been in the comfort of a warm evening in a garden?

I bought a book about mountain navigating and the compass required by the race regulations, but it was all so boring I never really gave it a chance. It was like schoolwork, when all I really wanted to do was the PE. What I lacked in navigational preparation I made up in physical. I put in hours on the roads early morning, up and down as many hills as I could find – and Belfast has plenty of them – then felt charged up and somehow exalted for the rest of the day in work.

I loved the solitary nature of the training, the fact that I didn't have to wait until 7pm for the rest of a team, didn't have to do any drills or specific game stuff, just needed to go out when I wanted, and suffer. I didn't fully understand the suffer aspect, didn't dwell on the irrationality of point-lessly putting myself through a lot of pain, I just somehow found this gave my life some meaning.

And I loved the measurable progress. I could run further and further, harder and harder, feel stronger and stronger. And success would depend only on how hard I worked, and not on the vagaries of fortune, referees and other people in general. This seemed to be sport that was simpler, purer and – at this stage at least – more rewarding.

I bought new kit and my first pair of fell running shoes. These are totally different from normal trainers, with thin-ner but stiffer material that doesn't hold water but does hold your foot firm so your ankle can roll a bit on uneven ground. The sole is solid rubber with no cushioning, but with little studs for better grip on rock, bog and steep wet hillside. Even owning a pair, I felt like a pioneer, boldly going where no rugby player had gone before, namely into an Outdoor Pursuits shop. This was unfamiliar territory. I didn't know any fell runners, other than Brian. I wasn't sure it was *possible* to actually run up a mountain. Was there a secret to it?

After weeks on the hilly roads around East Belfast and on gym treadmills with the gradient tapped right up I decided I was ready for the Mournes and set off with a few mates, stomping up and down the mountains in hiking boots, but not really running. While we were resting on one of the summits, the sound of heavy breathing and the occasional spit came floating up on the breeze, followed by two guys with lycra leggings and bum bags. They were both bent so far into the hillside their noses were nearly touching the grass, their faces were contorted with effort, and when they reached the top they didn't even pause, but ran full pelt across the plateau then bounced with huge leaps like mountain goats down the far side.

'Fell runners,' I said almost breathlessly to my two mates.

'Doesn't seem like much craic,' replied one.

'It's awesome,' I retorted. 'The speed! The views! Up here all the time?' I added, with a broad sweep of my arm out over the mountains of Mourne.

I was hooked, and came back on my own a week later, this time in my fell shoes rather than boots. The going up was tortuously slow, but the going down? Exhilarating! I tried to bounce as beautifully as I'd seen the others the previous week, but my thighs were still burning from the ascent and it felt like my knees would explode. Still, the great ups and downs of both effort and topology beat the hell out of road running or gym work or rugby training, and getting fit in such marvellous territory lifted my soul. I improved my endurance rapidly so that I was able to comfortably run for hours before work. I enjoyed having a focus, a target, something that scared the hell out of me and drove me out of bed and onto the roads or into the hills.

And then it was June, and racing 22 miles in mountains higher than the Mournes with no real prior experience was suddenly both scary and stupid. The only thing that made me feel better was the fact that Slippy had done much less than I had. He had yet to fall out of love with rugby like I had, was still playing and training every week, so couldn't do much extra running and had only been in any hills once since we'd signed up in February. And remember, this was his idea …

He picked me up at Liverpool John Lennon Airport with Ty, who had just finished a tour in Iraq with the Territorial Army section of the Paras. The Devizes to

Westminster canoe race was supposed to have been a kind of celebratory adventure for some of his squadron after surviving Basra, and his stories of both experiences kept us going as we crawled through the weekend traffic into Wales.

I was envious. I didn't want to go to Iraq, it sounded totally shit, but recounting tales of hardship and adventure was a lot of fun. I have always believed in the maxim that sometimes events that are the hardest to endure are the most pleasurable to recount, and Ty had two corkers from the last five months.

I was expecting a good one of my own by the time this weekend was done, but perversely I was also a bit envious of all the other people stuck in the traffic, making their way out of the city for a nice long, lazy weekend. Not for them the pain of running up the highest mountains in Wales on Saturday or the pre-event nerves on Friday. But if this was what it took to explore new horizons, then so be it.

As the name suggests, Ty is Welsh, and boy is that a useful heritage when you're looking for a village by the name of Abergwyngregyn. It would have been nice to have arrived in time to get our bearings ahead of the next day's race, but with the traffic and some eerily prescient navigational errors we didn't get there until after ten o'clock, and it was dark.

At this late hour, choices for pre-race carb loading were somewhat limited. There was a badly lit Chinese restaurant, an old-fashioned pub, a newsagent and a chip shop. Not for the last time that weekend I cursed our lack of planning. I wasn't a nutrition expert by any means but I knew enough to know that a good pile of pasta or potatoes built a big carbohydrate fuel store from which you could take deposits the next day. I also knew that a load of saturated fat was pretty useless, if not actually detrimental.

'If I were you I'd just eat as much as possible, boys, you'll need it,' said Ty once we'd settled on the chip shop being the best of poor options. 'It doesn't matter what it is so long as you're getting food in.'

I was pretty certain this wasn't sound nutritional advice but hoped that Ty's time with the Paras meant he knew a thing or two about endurance, and given that he had managed to *finish* the Devizes to Westminster canoe race while Olympic legend Sir Steve Redgrave abandoned it, he couldn't be ignored. Besides, I was starving.

I reasoned that chips at least contained potatoes – underneath the layers of batter – so I'd go for them only and forego the sausages. Upon such examples of discipline and self-sacrifice are endurance legends founded ... Shackleton would have been proud.

The lady at our B&B seemed genuinely concerned we were heading into the hills the following morning, and in that droll, lugubrious way perfected by many Welsh people she proceeded to read out the local weather forecast. It was not good.

But it was accurate. What a horrible morning. Grey, drizzly, windy, dark and full of foreboding. I couldn't see above the fir trees in the garden, never mind up into the mountains, but reasoned this was probably for the best before trying to heap a load of breakfast onto my butterflies.

Ty gleefully tucked into the best part of an entire hog while I struggled through the muesli and fruit. He was eating for pure greedy enjoyment while we were essentially just fuelling, and his excuse that he was still recovering from the Devizes to Westminster race didn't wash given that it had finished nearly three months ago. His main objective that morning was to see us off and then find radio coverage of the British and Irish Lions match. Slippy and I, on the other hand, were going to suffer, and suffer. Quite unnecessarily. I was definitely jealous now. We found the hotel in which the race registration would take place. It had seen better days, was nearly deserted, and added to the general gloom hanging over us. Other runners eventually filtered in. They were skinny, nobbly, craggy and in their natural environment. Our hearts ached for rugby. Gregarious creatures by nature, we both retreated a little into our shells that morning. Ty laughed.

'I have honestly never heard either of you so quiet. What's wrong with you?'

'Easy for you to laugh, you don't have to do this,' replied Slippy with a slight air of desperation. 'You're just going to sit in the car and listen to the radio – we're going to be wrecked!'

Valiantly I reached out to another runner for moral support.

'Excuse me, we haven't actually done this race before. Have you?'

'Oh yes, a few times.'

'Any tips?'

'Yes. Don't start!'

That was sound advice. Ty was falling about the place laughing by now. We handed our bum bags and kit over for inspection and received our race numbers and course map. I pretended to study it carefully, but within seconds it was all a blur as my eyes glazed over. It might as well have been advanced mathematics.

Slippy's shoes were the same make as mine, but as bright and shiny as a new pin. He had phoned me less than two weeks before, claiming he was just checking some kit details, but I got the feeling he was actually only then getting round to buying the footwear that is a key requirement for any proper mountain race. By the look of his suspiciously fresh shoes he had either done absolutely zero mountain running, or amazingly found somewhere hilly in the UK completely free of both moisture and mud.

But this was not the time to question him; we didn't need anything else chipping away at our confidence. We warmed up a little and took our places beside everyone else in a grit car park. The cloud had lifted slightly, and there were signs of the sun breaking through every now and again. Ty had found the radio commentary and settled himself into the car with his feet on the dash, promising to meet us with food somewhere round the course.

We were on our own. We'd had more than our fair share of adventures by this stage, Slippy and I. We'd travelled right round the world, blundering and bluffing – we'd bobsleighed in Latvia, played elephant polo in Nepal – but there weren't many escapades we'd taken on that caused the cracks in our usual bravado to appear quite so readily.

'Come on, bollocks to it, let's do this, can't be that hard,' I said, suddenly breaking into a big grin. 'Look at all these orienteers, the twats, they have no idea how useless we are.'

His face creased up. He got a fit of the giggles. So did I. Suddenly we were in convulsions, and we were back to our old selves.

It was funny for the first ten minutes. Then we joined a lane that ran past an old farmhouse and started to climb. And climb and climb and climb. The race split into groups and I was keen to stick with the runners just in front of us. I'd been advised by Brian back in Belfast never to follow anyone else, to always know my own route, but he'd said that when he thought I was going to become proficient at map-reading.

I looked round to give Slip a gee-up as we were losing touch with those in front. His face was bright red.

'There aren't many hills in London, G,' he wheezed. That's when I knew we were in trouble. The race was only half an hour old. The group in front soon disappeared off ahead and as we climbed the clouds came down to meet us. Grinding up through the mist we suddenly felt quite alone. There was only the pair of us, and a lone woman about 20 metres up ahead.

'We need to follow her, mate,' I told him. 'If we lose her here we haven't a clue where to go.'

Slippy just nodded, his face contorted with the effort. Neither of us could use a compass nor properly read a map, so once we'd got through the kit checks and away from the race organisers at the start, carrying the map in front of us seemed a waste of time. So it was stuck in the bum bag. In any case, I told myself, with cloud this thick it was impossible to see any landmarks, so the map would have been useless.

Slippy told me later that he'd never stared as hard or for as long at a female bum without ever thinking rude thoughts. Grimly he dug in, realising that keeping that arse in sight was going to save his life and get him up and down a mountain that was rapidly becoming a scene from Michael Buerk's *999* series.

Merely following someone else is of course poor form in a mountain race, where the orienteering aspect is as much a part of the challenge as the running, so we were trying simultaneously to stick to her like glue in the increasing fog, but also keep a consistent, discreet distance. When she stopped to read her map and compass, confused in the cloud, our game was up.

'It's got very thick very quickly, hasn't it?' she chirped with the breeziness of an experienced adventure-navigator. 'Where do you think we are on your map?' she asked.

'Er ...'

It was very embarrassing. I mumbled and fumbled, took the map out of the bum bag, stuttered 'Last time I checked ...' and gestured vaguely with a wide sweeping motion. Miraculously then the cloud lifted slightly and we could see a checkpoint manned courageously by a race official dug in beneath a huge umbrella, just 50 metres in front. We had the good grace to let our saviour arrive there first.

Jauntily we pretended to take a few moments to study the map and select the best course to the next checkpoint, but in reality we were waiting for more of the cloud to lift so we could see more people to follow. And thus the day continued, with intermittent cloud, mist, sun, good temper, bad temper, confidence and worry.

After four hours or so we were both entirely sick of the whole thing. The weather had turned again and the air hung heavily with rain as we ground up another steep climb. We were in full waterproofs at this stage and had long since eaten all our Lucozade energy sweets and the little bag of raisins I had added.

Slip was just ahead of me at this stage; we hadn't been doing much chatting for a while as neither of us really wanted to tell the other how much we were hating the whole experience. It had long ago ceased to be a giddy adventure, and the heavy weather and leaden clouds meant there weren't any decent views to lift the spirits. It was all mulchy bog, heather and rocks. And tired, aching legs.

We tramped on, and below us in a valley we eventually found a car park, the final checkpoint before the climb up to the summit of Snowdon, where the race finished. As we got closer we could see Ty's car and, God bless him, he had a little Trangia stove out and was cooking something. He could tell by our bedraggled appearance and grim faces that our default position of slagging and laughing at each other was not to be engaged at this moment. He was uncharacteristically empathetic in fact, and offered bananas and blissful hot chocolate.

I hesitated again with the hot chocolate, trying to remember some long forgotten sports nutrition laws from my days as a sports science student at Loughborough, but the sterile labs seemed a long way from this dark and wet place in any case. Ty said as much.

'Listen, you need to get some warmth and some energy back in, this is perfect, trust me.'

I did, and I drank it, and immediately felt better. Slip's calf muscles had been cramping up and Ty set to work rubbing them vigorously. I would have said massage, but that would have implied some sort of knowledge or skill was being employed. The sight of these two squabbling with limited knowledge about the ins and outs of muscular contraction cheered me up no end and there were all sorts of crude jokes about Ty rubbing men in remote car parks.

Warmed up and reinvigorated from the sugary hot chocolate, I slapped Slip on the back and felt some of my usual stubbornness return.

'Come on, mate, we can't let this beat us, let's get it done.'

And then Ty said something that really struck a chord. 'It's a Man Test now, lads. Just finish it.'

I got the idea immediately. Finishing the race was no longer about being fit, or a good runner, or map-reading, this was now just about being able to put up with wind, rain, pain and misery. It was a case of grinning and bearing it, surviving. It was, to be precise, about pig-headed, traditional masculine obstinacy; and specifically, being stubborn enough never to let reason get in the way of your objectives. In short, it was about being a man.

With new determination we crossed the car park, pushed through a little gate, and started the long climb to the top of the tallest mountain in Wales. It was miserable, another hour and a half of relentless slog in relentless rain. But we didn't stop, I felt I had more to give if required, and we passed our female friend from earlier on the way up. Once we reached a plateau I demanded that we run the last few hundred metres, and that's what we did, charging up to the summit café to be checked in by a couple of officials and finish the race.

We hugged, in a manly way. 'Thanks,' I said ironically.

'Sorry, mate,' Slip replied. 'That was absolutely horrible.'

'I know. What were you thinking?!'

'I just thought if the Paras could do it we could do it ...'

'Well you were right ... just about.'

I was proud of us for blundering through. We looked at all the people who'd finished before us and remarked wryly that next week we'd take them all on at rugby and see what happened. After being presented with slate medals we proudly wore them into the café, where we were expecting some sort of big post-race after-party but were sadly disappointed. There didn't actually seem to be too many other runners there, just a mix of hikers and day-trippers, and the only revival tonic we were offered was a cup of tea. We collected the bag of dry clothes we'd been asked to leave with the officials at the start and looked round in vain for the changing rooms, before settling for the toilets.

A man came in and started smoking. At this point Slippy's sense of humour finally failed. He huffed and puffed loudly, making it fully clear that this was not acceptable in a confined environment when our lungs had been punished enough over the previous six hours. At that very moment another runner came in to say that anyone who hadn't pre-booked the train couldn't get on it and would have to walk back down the mountain to the village. I need hardly add that of course we were the idiots who hadn't pre-booked.

I started to laugh. Slippy was so pissed off now it was actually funny. My own energy had returned and I had that lovely familiar rush of post-exercise relief and endorphin happiness. We set off down the mountain again on tired legs and an hour or so later were in the car heading back to Liverpool, twitching regularly with awful cramps in our hamstrings.

We met Slippy's dad in Liverpool that evening and ate a monstrous pile of curry with the hunger of the righteous. It turned out he too had completed the Devizes to Westminster canoe race, many years ago, which took some of the wind out of Tyvian's sails. We all traded tales of suffering and adventure, and that night I felt inspired by this recounting of stories and glories. On how many rugby matches would I look back and reminisce, years from now, in this way? This was better, this was more. I was only in my late twenties but already occasionally thought about my old age, reminiscing by the fireside. When my knees were absent friends and climbing the stairs was an ordeal, I'd like to be able to fall back on some past physical triumphs. I'd want to know that I really tested myself when I was at my peak, know exactly what I had been capable of, have some markers to remember and probably to grossly exaggerate.

In years to come, maybe some grandkids would find a dusty slate medal in an attic and ask me about the day I got lost on Snowdon. It wouldn't exactly be Uncle Albert's old war stories, but at least I'd have *something* to talk about. I'd always considered the accumulation of adventure a noble aim, but adding a physical challenge element was even better.

As my favourite sport for 15 years, rugby had given me so much. Most of my best friends were rugby-related, as were most of my modest sporting glories and almost all my immodest drinking stories. But I had long ago accepted that I'd reached a low plateau of ability and that All Ireland League Division Two was as high as I was going. More controversially, I had also begun to suspect that since perfecting a party trick in which I would set fire to my own head with sambuca, my *post*-match performances had reached a peak that only a Byronic death could eclipse. So it was time for a change, for new adventures, new challenges where I could no longer find excuses in the bounce of a ball or the input of team-mates. If I always did what I'd always done, I'd always only get what I'd always got.

Two

MR MOUSE'S FARM
FOR UNFORTUNATES

It was a strange time to make life changes. I was 28, doing my dream job as a TV sports presenter; going out with a fabulous girl who out-ranked me considerably in every relevant dating department; had bought my first house and had expendable income and time to spend it. I was comfortable, and had no real stresses. Perhaps that was the issue. We humans must be the only animals that deliberately seek out stress for recreation. I think we like it. It explains why there are workaholics and adrenaline junkies, and people who get a big buzz out of intense training. My life at that time, with everything seemingly 'on track', was maybe just not challenging enough, too many of life's big unknowns had become known. A few new horizons and ambitions were required to assuage the fear of getting bored or, worse, boring. Running mountains in Wales, kayaking up the Thames to Westminster, these were adventures and fitness tests that I could take on and collect like campaign medals, little extra-curriculars that would make settling for contentment in other areas of life more acceptable.

The fabulous girl was Claire, who is now my wife, and perhaps part of this shift towards fitness fanaticism was a bid to impress her. Before we met I'd been on a solo run of nine years without a proper, confirmed steady girl-friend, but after one too many amorous misadventures had decided that in this department at least, variety was becoming a vice of life. I'm still proud that I got the move to monogamy right first time. Just six weeks after deciding to begin a proper search for the future Mrs Little, I first saw Claire through a camera's zoom lens.

I'm not a stalker, I was reporting at a big rowing event on the River Lagan in Belfast and she was competing. Armed with a professional TV cameraman, I was able to sneakily check her out in the course of duty. When the club captain rang to thank me for the coverage, I replied that getting Claire's phone number would be thanks enough – and, unfortunately for her, I got it. The chase was on.

The early twentieth-century eugenics pioneers would have loved Claire. Tall, blonde and athletic, she won a Commonwealth bronze medal rowing for Northern Ireland, and her sporting heritage includes an Irish champion sprinter for a brother and a father who was for years the fastest pensioner in Britain and Ireland, holding numerous Masters athletics records. Quite what she saw in a short, dark plodder like me is a question for another day, but the salient points are that she was very familiar with people driving themselves demented for sporting glory, and also that she had a history of success and ability that far exceeded my own. She'd also been less than impressed with the various rugby lads she had met through the years, and was quite happy for me to move on both sportingly and socially.

So with her encouragement, I trained harder and harder, ate better and better, drank less and less, bought a bike, and started to consider training as a sport in its own right, with goals like more reps, faster run times, etc. Like a lot of other poor, misguided fools around then I became a disciple of Lance Armstrong, sporting one of his 'Live Strong' wristbands and reading his book, *It's Not About the Bike*. I found his central messages of pride, determination, fitness and the importance of a positive mental attitude inspiring. Of course we weren't to know then that the central message about Lance was that if something seems too good to be true then it generally is.

Having spent most of my life being involved in team sports I was now getting more out of training and competing alone and quickly became an advocate of self-improvement through recreation and every other aspect of life. With a sudden shift from Saturday afternoon rugby and beer to Saturday morning running and wheatgrass smoothies, I felt like a bit of a sell-out and my mates still involved in rugby let it be known that was their opinion too.

Claire and I were out for dinner one evening in Belfast and recognised a friend who had just taken early retirement sitting at a table beside us. We joined his group for a beer and I noticed what looked suspiciously like a tattoo peaking out from under the sleeve of his T-shirt. Assuming it was part of some sort of post-retirement identity crisis, I asked him about it and he revealed it was just a number written in permanent marker, part of the 'branding' of competitors in a triathlon.

I'd long been curious about triathletes. A schoolmate of mine had got really into the sport and become an Irish international before rejecting it at university for less arduous pastimes like the excessive consumption of beer and fried food. His pyramidical transformations from chubby child to international sportsman and back down to corpulent adult convinced me that here was a sport in which the principal ingredient for success was just very hard work. Triathlon had everything I was looking for – a range of sports so I wouldn't get bored, outdoor locations including open water swims, hard and measurable training, a new community and lots of new kit. I headed out confidently one day on my new bike to meet a friend, a former semi-professional rider, who had advised me to go straight into clipped-in pedals and not to look back.

Regular cyclists will be familiar with clipped-in pedals and the terror they induce in the novice. For the rest of you, this is what it's like. Imagine if someone tied your feet together on a big gyroscope and you could only stay upright by spinning at a certain speed. And then suddenly you could no longer go at that pace so stopped spinning and had no option but to fall to the ground. Awful, scary, embarrassing. Now imagine that you are on that gyroscope on a road amid heavy traffic. Well, that's what riding a bike with clip-in pedals is like until you get used to them.

I fell off three times on that first outing. The second time was the most humiliating. Some traffic lights changed just as I got to them, I pulled the brakes, and as I came to a stop suddenly remembered about the shoe anchors. I wriggled valiantly, but the shoes were not coming out of the pedal clips. In what felt like slow motion, I started to tip to one side like a tortoise being flipped on a patio.

Drivers coming the other way had to swerve; drivers behind me had to wipe tears of laughter from their eyes. It was absolutely humiliating. I got up, dusted myself down, adjusted my helmet straight again and tried to stare ahead nonchalantly. There were a couple of toots.

I soon just about got the hang of it and other falls weren't quite so public. But I couldn't believe how quickly the cycling destroyed my legs. After just 40 miles I could barely bring myself to continue. My thighs were aching, a horrible dull throb in which I couldn't work out whether they were happier bent or straight. Meanwhile the area of the body that nobody ever knows the name of (the perineum) was absolute agony, as bruised and delicate as a peach. I got off and pushed the bike for at least a mile. Consider the state you'd have to be in to prefer walking with a bike on a flat road to riding it.

When I got home I lay completely immobile on the couch for a good hour. My legs were cramping, my back and all of my upper body were stiff and sore. I was shocked at the impact one afternoon's cycle ride could have and decided I was far from being a natural and wasn't likely to improve much. But I stuck at it, read from The Book of Lance and entered some short sprint triathlons anyway.

'Pain is temporary,' Lance said. 'It may last a minute, or an hour, or a day, or a year, but eventually it will subside and something else will take its place. If I quit, however, it lasts forever. That surrender, even the smallest act of giving up, stays with me. So when I feel like quitting, I ask myself, which would I rather live with? Whatever your 100 per cent looks like, give it.'

Alright! Go Lance, Go Graham! I wasn't getting close to Planet Armstrong, of course, but I was making changes in my life and noticing changes in my body shape. I'd been busy for the previous ten years putting on muscle and now I was busy shredding it. People kept asking me with a concerned look on their face if I was sick or why I'd lost weight. In Ireland we prefer our people to look well fed – a fleshy chin or two is much less threatening than sharp cheekbones.

I felt the same only fitter, but was definitely lighter, which could only improve the cycling and running. I felt ready for an Olympic distance race – 1.5k swim, 40k cycle and 10k run – and entered the Royal Windsor Triathlon, though I soon wished I hadn't. I had read that it was one of the best organised triathlon events in the UK, and always very popular because of the mix of iconic river to swim in, flat cycle leg and famous land-marks in the town run. Swimming up the Thames and then running round Windsor Castle and Eton College? Fitness tourism. Of course, most people who enter at least live in the same country. I didn't, and got my first lesson on the logistical hassles that come with travelling anywhere with a bike.

To go on a plane, a bike has to be broken down into its component parts and folded into a stupidly expensive holdall imaginatively called a bike box. To the mechani-cally challenged, like me, this is a monumental pain in the arse. It's grand taking the bike apart, but putting it back together is another story. Suddenly things either don't spin or do spin when they shouldn't, don't click or do click when they shouldn't, don't move or do move when they shouldn't. And there is always the fear that you haven't tightened something properly and when you go to pull the brakes while flying down a hill they won't work.

The stress of my first ever bike rebuild was considerably compounded by a delayed flight into Heathrow, an interminable wait for a hire car, having to swap that hire car for a bigger one to squeeze the bike box in, and then queues of traffic all the way into Windsor. So suddenly I was racing against the clock to have the bike rebuilt, signed off and positioned on the rack where it would spend the night before the following morning's early race start.

There is more than a hint of nerdism about triathlon, I decided. Many of the devotees appeared to be only a map co-ordinate away from orienteers on the sport geek spectrum. Equipment and kit seemed to take on an elevated importance. Groups of them were huddled over each other's bikes, spinning wheels, talking in acronyms and digits like some sort of binary code. Many of the bikes had little notes with numbers written on them taped to the top bar. These were power output figures, I later worked out, information that would be displayed on the bike computers and would tell their owners how hard to push and where. Fitted waterproof sheets were pulled over the top of many bikes, which also had a little plastic container beside them with towels, food and clothing inside laid out in neat little piles.

In triathlon, the three individual sports that make up the whole are called 'disciplines', and triathletes speak of 'the fourth discipline' as being the transitions from one to the other. Many of them even train for and rehearse this 'fourth discipline'. Any sport in which competitors regularly practise changing their clothes deserves a place at the sharp end of my sport geek spectrum.

These were all just observations of a group that I recognised as slightly eccentric but which I nonetheless admired and would be proud to join if I finished my first Olympic distance. I say 'if', not because I didn't think I could do it, but because for the past few months I'd been managing an abdominal problem that a scan later revealed to be something called a sportsman's hernia. It basically felt like a very severe stitch, first making its sharp presence felt in the running leg of my very first triathlon, a short sprint distance that I'd really enjoyed except for that excruciating stab-and-twist pain beneath my ribcage.

I'm not sure if it was caused by triathlon, but I'd never had it before and for the next year or so it affected hill runs, 10k races, anything in which I had to dig deep at high pace. So I did have a little anxiety about getting through the whole thing, which I offer up as my defence for an incident that could have been an even bigger threat to completing the race.

The swim leg went well, though the water in the Thames was at record low levels so there were people standing up bemusedly at various points downstream having drifted too far to one side of the channel. Then came my first proper 'transition'. After clambering out of the river everyone dashed up through a forest path towards the bike racks, pulling and wriggling out of wetsuits as they went. It was a strange sight, this half run, half dance, and some were more efficient at it than others.

The lowlight of my bike leg was getting behind a rider who was wearing a tri-suit that was for some reason designed to be see-through at the back. Triathlon rules prevent competitors from cycling too close to those in front so that nobody can steal an unfair 'drafting' advantage, but even the few seconds I spent closing in on this guy were enough to make me feel queasy. It was a particularly hairy arse.

I ran with my bike to my spot on the rack for the second transition, pretty fired up and in the moment by now, but also trying to settle my breathing into a pattern that would leave the hernia less likely to flare up. Suddenly a race official stepped out and raised her arm in front of me like a Gestapo officer.

'Helmet, helmet!'

'What?!'

'You cannot take your helmet off until your bike is on the rack – there are time penalties for that.'

'Ach, Jesus.'

'Swearing at an official, that's an automatic disqualification if you're not careful.'

'I wasn't … Sorry.'

Exasperated, I put my helmet back on for the remaining walk of ten metres to my spot on the rack, and seconds later was in my running shoes and heading for ten or so laps of the old town. I got through the run managing to keep the hernia protests to a mere stitch, and finished the race feeling pretty strong, in a time of 2 hours 20 minutes.

Hours later I was enjoying a solo celebratory lunch in a restaurant as small groups of people shuffled in periodically showing all the signs of suffocating hangovers and a restless lie-in. I could have dipped my chips in my self-conceit as I casually scratched my upper arm to better reveal my triathlon race number.

I enjoyed the achievement of getting through an Olympic distance race, but I wasn't sure that I would ever get swept

up in the triathlon obsession that motivates otherwise normal people to practise changing their clothes and put up with
long hours of repetitive and very specific training sessions. I
didn't feel that shaving minutes off my time in a challenge
I now knew I could complete was worthy of much more
attention to detail or financial investment, and I was never
going to win any of them. There were loads of different triathlon events, all with their own unique environments and
courses, but the essential challenges and boundaries would
have remained the same, and time was always the principal
target. Despite only completing a handful of races, I was
again ready to try something else.

Looking back now, it seems ridiculous to take up a new
sport with great enthusiasm and then decide a year or so
later that it was time to move on, especially when there was
still plenty of room for improvement and I enjoyed it. I
think this was perhaps indicative of my general restlessness
both then and now. If I scratched a little deeper I could
probably dwell longer on the fact that I seemed to feel happier with the role of outsider, which allowed me to dem-
onstrate competence and potential in a new experience and
then leave before becoming disappointed with my limits.

It was entirely in keeping with the way I live life in
general. I've never done the same job for longer than three
years, never liked the idea of being identified solely for what
I did either professionally or socially – never liked being
'labelled', I suppose. My greatest heroes have always been
polymaths or eccentric mavericks, people who combine a
variety of talents or interests without appearing slavishly
devoted to any of them. I love Eric Cantona for mixing
football with poetic quotes about seagulls and trawlers,
and I think the late, great C.B. Fry – England international

in both cricket and football, Barbarians rugby player, long jump world record holder, journalist, broadcaster, nude model, naval reservist, teacher, diplomat and scholar – is probably the greatest Englishman of all time.

We humans are fascinated by identity and labels. We like to belong, we like to be identified in a particular way. It affects where we choose to live, what we choose to wear, even who we marry. We also like to figure out quickly where others belong, what their identity is, and talking about sport can be pretty useful for this. Previously, identifying myself as 'a rugby player' implied certain characteristics, some positive, some negative. I sometimes felt almost apologetic about being introduced this way. I remember once sitting reading the newspapers in a common room in my student halls at Loughborough when a girl I barely knew came up to me and said she was always surprised to catch me reading broadsheet newspapers and novels.

'Everybody thinks you're just an Irish rugby pisshead, but you're not just that, are you?'

It was a strange kind of compliment, but weirdly I have treasured it ever since. I hadn't liked the 'pisshead rugby player' identity very much, but at least it was probably accurate, and now that it was gone I wasn't sure what my sporting identity was. Yes, I had been doing some triathlons, but I didn't feel I had properly become *a triathlete,* which meant something totally different. It's only semantics, but it was an important distinction, and perhaps for me it would have represented replacing one sporting subclass or identity with another.

The annual Tough Guy race is one of those events that resonate beyond its target audience. Many people with no interest in fitness or endurance events, or sport of any kind, have heard something, or think they have heard something, about Tough Guy. And the stories have lost nothing in the telling: people have died, people have been seriously injured, people run it naked, Olympic athletes haven't been able to finish it. It could be summed up as a race over an obstacle course, but only if the World Cup Final could be summed up as merely a football match between two opposing teams. Describing it as an obstacle course is to hopelessly underplay the scale of the monstrous features that make up the challenge.

The eight-mile course features 25 outlandish and ingenious constructions that include enormous towers, a blazing fire, strands of electric wire, underwater tunnels, cold water plunges and 70 metres of barbed wire commando crawling. The obstacles have names like 'Death Plunge', 'Jesus Bridge' and 'Behemoth', and if you're wondering what on earth there is to like, you'd need to ask some of the 5,000 competitors who sign up for each running of the event. Why did I sign up? Well, the sheer anarchic chaos of the thing sounded about as far removed from rugby or triathlon as it was possible to get. It sounded like an adventure, and without doubt a unique new experience.

I found the online home of the event and, curious about what sort of fertile and possibly febrile mind had created this world, read about the Tough Guy founder, a septuagenarian former Grenadier Guards battalion barber who goes by the name of Mr Mouse. It soon became clear that Mr Mouse is a lion of the Man Tests scene, a force of nature who decided in the 1980s that the materialism of modern life was damaging the fabric of society, our backbones had turned to jelly, we'd turned into a nation of unhappy, lazy softies and he needed to do something about it.

His real name is Billy Wilson and his former career is neatly commemorated in the magnificent handlebar moustache he proudly sports, which sets off his sense of purposeful eccentricity. He apparently picked the pseudonym to reflect the ultimate in humility, rather like the smug and dangerous religious fundamentalist 'The High Sparrow' in George R.R. Martin's *Game of Thrones*.

In a video interview on the Tough Guy website he recollects a time back in the seventies when everyone in Wolverhampton appeared to him to be miserable and lethargic. He started trying to change things with community runs in the park, which progressed to army training for the public, which became the monster that is Tough Guy, built on farmland that had been in his wife's family for generations. There he created a parallel universe, a sort of health and safety exclusion zone from where he preached his philosophy of the benefits of exercise, fear, fresh air, nature and teamwork.

And people came in their droves to listen, and to run, jump, climb, wade, shiver and suffer. He built the sort of obstacle course that always features in Pathé news footage of special operations troops preparing for the Second World War, and then each year when people completed the course he added something else to make it harder. Bit by bit over the next two decades the soggy fields of the farm were transformed. The whole thing is a feast of torture and eccentricity, imitated regularly by an ever-increasing cast of rivals, but never equalled. The original race takes place at the end of January, just to add sub-zero temperatures to the sadistic mix, and in recent years they have added a summer edition in which the pain of the cold is replaced by the pain of stinging nettles.

Mr Mouse doesn't like the word 'camaraderie' too much because he associates it with communism. When he does use it he mispronounces it, but it's clearly a central pillar of his philosophy and the 'camaraday' he found when completing the London Marathon for the first time with a group of his Wolverhampton runners reminded him of the kind he'd experienced among soldiers in the army.

'So when I built Tough Guy, I said I would build that magic formula,' he explains in the website video. 'We've got the magic formula. Nobody's going to pinch it. They can copy everything we do, but they can't create that wonderful feeling that is felt by people who come to Tough Guy. It's out there, it's in this ground, it's in this valley. It spreads on Tough Guy Day, and everyone gets a taste of it. It's a magic. A complete and utter magic.'

Being a stickler for tradition I booked in for the winter, when the ground would be so frozen I doubted the magic would get out, and then set about guessing what sort of training to do. Entering the race actually took quite a while because the Tough Guy website is a mesmerising mix of bonkers eccentricity and quasi-evangelical rants. Some of it reads as though it was turned into English from Swahili using an automated online translator. Here is a sample:

Fear joins up the Family of Man. In all historical disaster when materialism has gone, fear sets each group in a concrete form to join the journey into the unknown. As a lump we are more feared to go back we take a communal vision as we grab each others flesh tearing to mingle our blood. We reach a point where fear joins the world of materialism we are leaving behind, together with the serene and beautiful world of death.

That was just a foretaste, for it was once I'd actually entered that the real madness started. I received letter after letter from 'Mr Mouse's Farm for Unfortunates', each one more bewildering than the last. There were 'Jelly Leg Newsletters', constant references to a donkey sanctuary and letters purporting to be from some of the animals themselves at one point, I think. Some packages contained useful things like a registration number and local accommodation suggestions, but the vast majority of the correspondence was utter nonsense, including training tips, which recommended 'exercises' like throwing oneself down a flight of stairs, rolling over a thicket of nettles wearing one's underwear, and grabbing an electric fence.

The whole thing was like stepping into someone's fevered dreams, and although I found the postal packages confusing and almost frustrating, I really couldn't wait to go and see if the reality could possibly be anything like as bizarre as the impression created. Mr Mouse's insistence that he had created a place apart, where the safety helmets and handrails of modern life are left at the entrance, reminded me of the brilliant Two Ronnies sketch in which the world is run by militant women who subjugated men and forced them into skirts and domestic duties. The Two Ronnies, with the help of a mouse, manage to escape over the border to Wales, where a colony of men still live in the traditional fashion, being traditional men.

The anarchic freedom of Mr Mouse's Tough Guy extended to the pre-event preparation of course. What a joy to make the training up as I went along! No more triathlon magazine pullouts, no more schedules, plans or charts, for how on earth could you prepare scientifically and forensically for an event like Tough Guy? There is just no standard physical preparation for the demands of running through electrical wire, swimming through flooded tunnels and scrambling over piles of burning straw. And the best contrast of all in relation to other sports? The fact that the only kit recommended was the worst clothes you possessed, because they would not be coming back in one piece. No expense spent.

I stayed somewhere on the outskirts of Wolverhampton the night before and then followed a printed map, some B-roads and some home-made signs to Madness HQ the next morning. Halfway up a gentle hill I was directed into a field and made to follow a labyrinthine track of straw and mud through various other fields to park the hire car. It was pretty clear even then that the straw was not going to be enough to prevent a quagmire and I was already resigned to getting stuck on the way out. There was smoke and mist rising from the ground of the lower lands, and I walked up another small hill to look down at the battleground.

Mr Mouse's Farm for Unfortunates was exactly as I had imagined it. A sprawling patchwork of boggy farmland; paddocks of weeds grazed by straggly ponies and donkeys; clumps of unkempt woodland; a random mix of outhouses, yards and self-built extensions around a once beautiful old redbrick farmhouse; and, of course, drawing attention from every angle, the acres of enormous obstacles – visible for miles around – spread out over an area called 'The Killing Fields'. There *was* actually an animal sanctuary after all, and in fact this seemed to be the main point of the whole place, when strangers weren't arriving to get electrocuted or hypothermic.

Every rural area has one eccentric rogue landowner who doesn't follow the country code, who doesn't craft neat fields of different hues, who doesn't buy into the pastoral ideals of those who travel through the countryside and expect to realise the visions of farm picture books. It appeared Mr Mouse was the king of all of these outsiders, a man who lived exactly as he pleased and did what he liked with his own land.

I hadn't been able to work out from the avalanche of madness that arrived in the post what was real and what was entirely made up, but it suddenly dawned on me as I stood surveying the scene that *everything* was real, a frightening thought given the content of the mailings.

As chaotic as it all looked at first, the logistics were handled surprisingly efficiently. It was rough but it was ready, and the whole system smoothly handled 5,000 race entrants and thousands more supporters and spectators. Competitors were directed to the 'changing barns', where we could dump changes of clothes for after the race and had to queue to sign 'The Death Warrant' – an indemnity form, Tough Guy style.

By signing the Death Warrant, I agreed to 'bequeath my body to Tough Guy Killing Fields'. I also confirmed that 'if I should die on Tough Guy, it is my own bloody fault for coming' and that I wouldn't make any claim for 'loss or injury suffered by my self-inflicted failure'. I really wished this type of language had been employed on every form I'd ever signed. Paradoxically, it seemed to me to be mature and enlightened. It *was* likely I would get injured, and it would indeed be nobody's fault but mine for placing myself there in the first place.

We were then all penned in like cattle according to our race numbers and previous race experience. Those who had booked early or competed before were rewarded with a place in the front groups, and those who had booked later or were here for the first time were penned at the back and denoted as 'Late Buggers', 'Wetnecks' or 'Dickheads'.

Mr Mouse strode around as the overseer of all, carrying a bone-handled riding crop and looking resplendent in his army shirt, cloth tie, badges and kilt. He was stalked regularly by devotees with cameras. Every so often he would climb up to a turret on a hill beside the last obstacle and gaze out over the battleground he'd spent half a lifetime creating. One of his officers was barking ceaselessly on a megaphone. At one point he shouted, exasperatedly: 'I'm talking important utter bollocks here and no one's listening!'

There was a cacophony of bestial roars every so often as groups of lads, and sometimes girls too, psyched themselves up for the impending release, like the Viking berserkers of old. Each group moved through the pens one at a time until it was their turn to line up at the top of a hill and await the signal to charge. This must be the closest most of us will get to being in a nineteenth-century battle line. In the distance the smoke of the straw bales filled the sky. Cheers and screams blew back on the breeze, people were crawling on the ground, piling up and down the scaffolds, swarming through the ditches and up and down steep muddy hills. And we were about to charge in and join the fray.

There was another mighty roar and with a surge we sprinted off across the fields. People beside me tripped and were trampled by the masses coming behind. Others continued to roar for the first few hundred metres, maddened by fear, noise, cold and excitement and by the exploding smoke bombs, firecrackers and flares placed across the trampled grass.

It had all the ingredients of a charge into battle, except that our battalion included Batman, Superman, the Incredible Hulk, Robin Hood, several Smurfs, a guy wearing armbands and a rubber ring, and even one half of a pantomime horse. Of course *everyone* had at least an element of fancy dress given that we all had our race numbers branded across our foreheads in permanent marker.

Without the explosions and the fancy dress the first few miles could have passed for a fairly routine cross-country run, clearly designed to soften everyone up and spread the groups out before they arrived at the obstacles. The first of those was one of the enormous wooden climbing frames made out of slippery round telegraph poles, and after settling into the steady rhythm of the run, clambering straight up and over such a huge hurdle made my heart slam.

But the ultimate in heart slamming was just ahead. I had read about 'The Tiger' but hadn't quite believed it. It was another massive climbing frame, but this time with a genuine sting in the tail. Remember the scene in *Monty Python's Life of Brian* where the polite Roman official with the ancient clipboard enquires of the unfortunates if they are there for crucifixion, and they equally politely reply 'Yes' as pass they on? Well here, the buzzword was electrocution. Long hanging strips of electric wire in rows and columns awaited us as we scrambled down the frame and meekly took our turn to willingly run through them. 'Electrocution?' 'Yes please.' 'This way.'

This was the warped genius of Mr Mouse: creating a pseudo-religious cult and a world in which his devotees flail themselves on electric wire in the hope of finding some strange enlightenment. In a field in Staffordshire. I managed to avoid getting shocked by the first few rows, but got a bit careless going through the last one and was zapped on the shoulder. I let out a big involuntary yell and my body spasmed. It was captured by a photographer who checked his screen immediately and broke into a sadistic grin.

The sting in the Tiger's tail would sap a lot of people's spirit and stun them back to the cold reality of what they were doing, I reckoned. It felt pointlessly cruel and extreme. I saw a couple of competitors get shocked, swear loudly, throw their hands up and gather for a pow-wow. I didn't hang around to see if they pulled out, but I am sure they at least raised the issue, and once that door was even slightly ajar, the remaining madness would burst it open.

The Tiger was followed by a great human steeplechase, with more telegraph poles or just huge round logs erected at chest height across the route for about half a mile. More clambering, and I realised that one of the great challenges of Tough Guy would be the constant disruption of rhythm. This was as far removed from a 'normal' run as it was possible to be, and would make for much better fitness training if I tried to emulate it at home, without the electrocution.

As if to underline that idea, the next obstacle was a series of hill sprints. Familiar territory for me and I found I actually relished 'The Slalom', a series of eight zigzags up and down a steep hill of trees and dead ferns. As we approached across a valley it was an amazing sight, as from a distance the runners ahead looked like little lines of ants marching in neat formation across the hill.

There was a bottleneck at the bottom. The zigzags were marked out by stakes and white tape, and sections of the hill were rapidly being churned into a mud bath by the plough of thousands of feet driving up and down it.

You wouldn't want to be at the very back with the Late Buggers and Dickheads.

I was totally swept up in the madness of it all, desperate to give my all and get round as effectively and quickly as possible. I had no patience for waiting my turn or using any bottlenecks to get a breather; I was on a mission and skipped past as many people as possible in the tight confines of the mapped course. Repeatedly running up and down the same hill was clearly totally pointless and simply designed to dispirit everyone, but it didn't dilute my zeal in the slightest: I was absolutely loving the whole mad experience.

So far so good. I'd built up a nice head of steam, both figuratively and literally, the body heat generated by the intensity of the exercise compensating for the bite of the January air. But it wouldn't last. The biggest single difficulty with Tough Guy, the principal contributor to the dozens of ambulance cases every year, is the cold. Hypothermia is a genuine concern, and it is Mr Mouse's obsession with water features that is to blame.

The 'Gurkha Grand National' is where we were first exposed to the icy tyranny of the course. This is a series of scramble nets to scamper under, walls to climb over and flooded ditches to wade through. As with the earlier climbing, it was the jolt out of rhythm that struck me first, the slight pauses in which my heart rate slammed harder than my footsteps, and I realised how hard I was working. Just like on the slalom, a lot of this section was zigzagging back and forward over the same stretch of water. In terms of getting from A to B it made no sense whatsoever, but it really didn't do to think too deeply about these things … rationalists need not apply for Tough Guy.

And then my heart seemed to stop altogether as I leaped into the first ditch. The shock of the cold sucked the breath from my chest as I stumbled through the waist-deep water, struggling to keep my feet and falling further forward into the icy grip. I battled to keep my heart out of the water for as long as possible, suddenly and irrationally fearing it would seize in the cold.

The ditches were not wide, and emerging on the other side each time felt like being born again. As my legs ran off the sting of the cold with the next series of running and climbing I felt rejuvenated, strong and determined. Which was just as well, for the next sequence of obstacles was sited in 'The Killing Fields'.

This was the real core of the Tough Guy experience, a series of the most infamous challenges Mr Mouse had created, all grouped together across a couple of acres in a bit of a natural amphitheatre. The approach to this imaginative but barbarous world of pain was again guarded by high walls of telegraph poles – where in the world did he get so many? – that had to be clambered over with the help of knotted ropes. And beyond those, another wooden construction of such magnitude it actually made me laugh.

'The Behemoth' stands over 20 metres high, a bonkers rig of poles, stakes, ropes, nets and platforms, like a giant chimpanzee play area in a zoo. It's not dangerous for them – this is their natural habitat and they haven't been exhausted and rendered hypothermic before playing on it – but for us at that stage of the proceedings it was surely potentially deadly. Pirouetting across swinging ropes, scrambling up slippery poles and picking my way down and across cargo nets I was glad not to suffer from vertigo. I was probably helped by the fact that thick smoke rising from the next obstacle obscured some of the view below.

It was coming from the burning straw bales of 'The Somme', probably the most familiar image of the whole Tough Guy phenomenon. This is a collection of fire pits, mud pits, water pits and barbed wire crawls that batter the senses, pull the strength from the legs and arms, embed deep cold and create some of the most legendary Tough Guy photos so vital to the rise and spread of the brand.

The Tough Guy Death Waiver informs competitors that the event doesn't have insurance. I wondered if they'd ever tried. Can you imagine being the clerk taking that call?

'Does your event include any hazardous activities?'

'Well, apart from electrocuting people and making them run through fire, no ...'

I don't remember being too bothered by the fire running or freezing water pits of The Somme, but scrambling under the barbed wire was a nightmare. The wire was stretched horizontally about a foot off the ground, but the ground at this stage was a squelching, turgid mass of uneven mud, and instinct of course impelled us to lift our heads high above this choking, stinking cesspit. The tearing of skin soon sorted that out, and there was nothing for it but to close my eyes, mouth and nose as much as possible and mole my way through.

I eventually scrambled out the other side, about a stone heavier than when I started, with thick mud clinging to every inch of my body. With an effort I dragged my legs back into motion and ground on to the next swamp run. I stumbled and fell headfirst into the mud with a cry, sinking like I'd been shot. From behind, someone reached under my armpit and helped me up in one fluid movement. It felt almost like a divine intervention, a moment of such soldierly solidarity, such trench spirit that I felt quite emotional. But I didn't want my comrade to think I was weak and so, rather missing the spirit of the whole moment, I took off with renewed vigour to make sure I beat him.

I saw several people hunting for trainers that had been sucked off in the mud, playing some ghastly game of mucky lucky dip for their own shoes, and a little further on, a man lying on his back on one side of the course with a couple of others around him, imploring him to get up.

'Are you alright? Come on, back up!'

'Leave me!' he responded dramatically, and I hoped he'd add 'Save yourselves!' for extra effect, but he didn't.

Just in case there was a fear or phobia untouched by this point, and to continue his journey through military history, Mr Mouse had designed the 'Vietcong Torture Chamber Tunnels'. These are drainage tunnels sunk in the ground, through which we had to crawl on our bellies. Just to add to the fun and the claustrophobia, some were blocked at one end, creating a maze effect and no doubt some serious panic among those unfortunate enough to pick the wrong entrance.

Having once crawled all the way through the storm tunnels under the M1 during an early morning adventure run at university, the Vietcong challenge didn't bother me too much, although I knew the scrapes and cuts I was picking up on elbows, knees and thighs probably wouldn't combine well with the fetid mud.

So the chance of a good rinse in the circular canal Mr Mouse had built in a bog dammed with telegraph poles and mud initially seemed quite welcome. But then the stabs of cold crept into my very core. I was clambering over the poles rather than ducking under them, trying to keep my head out of the water for as long as possible, but still the near freezing water temperature felt like a weight crushing my spirit. My breath came in short staccato bursts and I tried to get warm by pumping my limbs as fast as possible, driving through the water to get it finished.

Full submersion was inevitable at the end of the wading, as that section finished with the 'Underwater Tunnel', a bridge across the canal ridged by four parallel poles under which everyone had to duck, one dive at a time. Sadist spectators and Tough Guy officials gathered on top, shouting at us to go under. There was no way of completing the section without it and I charged straight in, knowing any hesitation would only compound the cold and the dread.

I gripped the first pole and ducked down into the darkness. Ice-cream headache! Pain! A combination of pins and needles and a vice-like crushing of my skull. Horrible. I half swam, half hopped for a few seconds and popped my head up again, panting, struggling for breath with the shock. Then down again, and repeat, each one more painful than the last.

I felt weird after that – woozy, confused a bit, as if my brain had gone on leave for a few minutes. I shook my head to try and clear my thoughts and throw the cold water from my hair, like a dog. My leg muscles didn't seem to respond, probably because they were getting unclear advice from the absentee brain, and it was a mechanical effort to climb up the bank.

There was another short run section when the biting wind did nothing to help the gathering shivers, and then, just when my co-ordination was at its most limited, a vertical climb up more cargo nets and other balance challenges like crossing thin rafts, swinging from ropes and clambering over fences and up muddy slopes. My feet wouldn't go where I wanted them, I had no real grip in my frozen hands, but I did register the careful planning that placed the most dangerous obstacle just at the point where everyone was most severely hampered by the cold.

The 'Death Plunge' was next and would have brought a shudder to everyone if we hadn't already been shuddering uncontrollably. It was quite simply walking the plank and leaping into another deep icy bath. Again, there was the mad ice-cream headache and frantic scramble up the muddy slopes, but seconds later I experienced a great rush of joy, and – whoosh – I was pain and fatigue free, as if I'd had some sort of oil change, or a re-awakening, a re-energising. I charged on through the mire, sinking in places beyond the knees with every step, but feeling absolutely solid, strong. In other words *tough* ...

A final, *Krypton Factor*-style obstacle called the 'Dragon Pool' forced us to cross more deep water about 25 metres wide by sliding over on parallel ropes – an under rope for walking sideways, an upper rope for clinging on to for dear life. As I was crossing they started to bend and wobble, and soon the combination of irresistible body shivering and too many people on the ropes at the same time had me bucking and jiving all over the place. Inevitably, I fell in and swam the rest of the way with frantic, windmill arm strokes.

I scrambled and slid up the other side, crossed more thin planks laid across a swamp and knew I was close to the end. Another horrible section of barbed wire belly crawling called 'Stalag Escape' – this time 30 metres in length – and I'd be nearly finished. I made it through and hauled myself up, trying to get running again. My legs were feeling like two dead weights, heavy and numb, and I was shivering uncontrollably. But with each running stride I gradually regained co-ordination and was soon motoring along on the half-mile or so back towards the barns. I was still fired up, catching and passing everyone in front, really hammering along and wishing I'd signed up early enough to get a place in the front groups and a chance to properly contest the race.

There were more short mud hills up ahead and another brief dip in the water but I was in such a flow now and bizarrely hungry for more punishment that I didn't care what was thrown at me. I can remember feeling weirdly disappointed as I slid down a steep bank of black plastic and into yet another trough of water and realised that was the final obstacle. I was feeling great! I sprinted up through the farmyard and towards the finish line in a huge barn.

It was the first and only time I have ever finished an endurance race wishing it was longer, that the suffering could go on. I began seriously to consider whether I had sado-masochistic tendencies, or whether it was just that the latent sporting talent I had been vainly searching for all these years was actually most manifest in an ability to take on extreme obstacle courses in the middle of winter. It's a real pity it's not exactly a mainstream sport.

A pipe band played us into the barn, where someone solemnly presented me with a medal and said, 'Well done, Tough Guy.' Head bowed as I was crowned, my heart leaped. That was it. I was a Tough Guy. That's why I'd felt so good at the end: I was tough! Wrapped in a big silver sheet that felt like tinfoil, I queued for hot chocolate and biscuits courtesy of the local Women's Institute (how brilliantly British) and then gripped the polystyrene cup with both shivering hands, hoping to stave off the worst of the deep cold that I knew was settling in.

I had to get changed and into warm clothes as quickly as possible. But of course there was mud spread thickly over every part of me, and in every orifice, every strand of hair. I'd heard rumours of showers in one of the barns and followed the shivering masses into a cattle shed. Rows of straw bales only a foot high were the nearest thing to changing cubicles. I had rather optimistically brought shampoo and shower gel, but then I found the 'showers' – cold water dripping from a basic hose structure across some beams. Rough bars of soap were passed around and we took it in turns to catch enough water in handfuls to make some lather. If it hadn't been for the flight home I probably wouldn't have bothered.

Boys and girls were all in together, and some of the men were completely naked, very brave considering the effect of extreme cold on the genitals. We shared the barn with a couple of old Jaguar cars, and earlier I'd noticed an open-sided shed filled with the shells of Citroën 2CVs, an old fire engine and several old Range Rovers, each with the back cut out to create an unlikely 4 x 4 convertible. It all added to the notion that we were all privileged visitors to an eccentric's home, a private fantasy world, as far removed from the sterile set-up of a 'normal' athletics meet as it's possible to be.

I washed as best I could and fought my shivering hands and numb fingers for control of my clean clothes. I looked around the barn. People were helping each other out of destroyed race garments and into clean ones. They were lending each other towels, sharing hot tea, strapping up injuries. Mr Mouse was right: his mad creation *did* in fact promote teamwork and togetherness.

A few hours later I was in a pub enjoying an enormous Sunday roast, continuing my quintessentially modern British weekend and exchanging knowing smiles with others who also had faint numbers written across their foreheads. I wondered how this great nation had arrived at a point where, for hundreds of thousands of people, a weekend wasn't complete without some voluntary suffering, the more extreme or outlandish the better. 'Aren't humans amazing?' I thought. We spent thousands of years learning how to build structures and societies to take us out of mud and danger, and then some of us pay up to 100 quid each to return to squalor and a battle for survival.

Was it all the fault of Facebook and the constant competition to appear more interesting than everyone else in your peer group? I hoped not. I preferred to believe that we were motivated by something deeper. At the airport on the way home I bought a book claiming to be the ultimate guide to life's greatest adventures. I felt inspired by Tough Guy. The whole experience had reawakened my drive for fresh, extreme experiences and reaffirmed my faith in humanity; in the whole mad, curious lot of us. For 5,000 people to arrive at a farm in an unfashionable area of the Midlands and flail themselves in muddy worship at the obstacle altar of one of Britain's great eccentrics was a rare and beautiful thing.

A couple of years ago Mr Mouse announced on the Tough Guy Facebook page that he would soon be stepping down from his role and asked his followers if there were any requests for changes to the course for his final few runs in charge. Specifically, he asked if Tough Guy was now *too* tough. The response was overwhelming.

'Get TOUGHER is what I say!' screamed someone called Julie. 'More shocks, water and cold weather,' responded another. 'Harder the better,' said Karle. Someone even asked, apparently without irony, for flame-throwers to be considered. Kevin replied simply that he wanted to feel more pain next year.

So is Tough Guy a form of group sado-masochism?

'I'm not a sadist, I am a provider,' insists Mr Mouse. 'A provider of fear. Fear is the most magical thing. Anyone who has experienced fear will realise that it is the greatest thing to join us all together, because in fear, we cling together.'

He's right, there is no doubt that fear has a peculiar fascination for us humans; we love to get a fright in a controlled environment. That's why we have a multi-million-dollar horror film industry, ghost trains and rollercoasters at theme parks, and all manner of madness at Halloween. I think that the apparent irrationality of this is related to the apparently no less irrational idea of choosing suffering as a pastime.

Basically, it's all in our blood, our evolution, our history. Temporarily frightening ourselves gives us a jolt of adrenaline, a jag that reminds us we're conscious beings. It brings us temporarily to a powerfully unpleasant place so that we can return to our previously pleasant place with a new appreciation of its benefits. Just like high-intensity exercise.

I hadn't really thought much before about *why* I was getting such a kick out of completely exhausting and endangering myself on a regular basis. Why did I feel so alive when I was probably close to collapse, and why was there such a 'rush' after a bout of self-inflicted torture? One theory put forward by various scientists is that our distant ancestors derived benefits from moments of intense clarity during and after exposure to severe stress. With a heightened sense of awareness when they were being chased by a bear, for instance, they were better equipped to select the correct evasive action and were more likely to survive. Consequently we evolved to come through moments of intense activity or stress more alert and in tune with our surroundings.

A clearly very wise person called Solomon (a sports scientist and not the ancient King) put forward a theory for why we usually get a big rebound towards pleasure when intense activity stops and the pain is over. He said it was because of the 'adaptational benefit associated with the removal or termination of a noxious or aversive stimulus and the return to affective equilibrium'. In easy speak, we learn to really appreciate getting rid of the threat to our health caused by over-strenuous activity by 'over-enjoying' the return to base levels of breathing and muscle strain.

By generating equal measures of fear, stress and intense activity, Tough Guy did indeed include all the elements prescribed by evolution for the perfect exercise rush and post-event wellbeing. They should write a science paper on Mr Mouse.

Three

MAN V HORSE

I didn't plan it this way, but it turned out that after a cathartic and muddy day in a donkey sanctuary the next event that really grabbed me was the annual Man v Horse Marathon in the mountains of mid-Wales. It wasn't that I was deliberately trying to take a trip round the athletic eccentricity of the UK, but I'd known about the Man v Horse for years and Tough Guy had confirmed that, for me, the more off the wall, unpredictable and adventurous the event, the better.

If Mr Mouse is the first person inaugurated in the Man Tests Hall of Fame, Gordon Green should be the second. He lives in Llanwrtyd Wells, officially the smallest town in Britain, and unofficially surely the most eccentric. Concerned about falling tourism numbers in the late seventies when he was running the town's only hotel, he and several other locals devised a series of outlandish events that would encourage people to come and stay.

The Man v Horse Marathon was one of the first, spawned like many a great idea from a late night discussion at the hotel bar, but others include the Mid Wales Beer Festival, which lasts for a liver-busting ten days; the Real Ale Wobbles, where participants mountain bike around the hills of the area with real ale being served at every checkpoint; a Carriage Driving Championship; the Bog Snorkelling World Championships, and a whole series of inter-related Bog Snorkelling derivatives including a Bog Snorkelling Triathlon.

The Man v Horse is the most 'serious' in terms of the athleticism required of the human competitors. The basic principle is simple. Could a human beat a horse over a long distance if the terrain was bent in his favour? One can only imagine the nonsense spouted when the concept was first mooted in the bar, so the fact that it has evolved into an intriguing contest in which the gap between the leaders of each species is often less than a minute, is testament to the unique drive and logistical acumen of Gordon Green and his friends.

I felt I had unfinished business with hill running in Wales after the mixed success of the Welsh 1000m Peaks Race a few years previously, and I was, for reasons I can't quite explain, tremendously excited about the opportunity of testing myself against horses. All in all it was certainly worth a few months of hard training. I was living in the shadow of Cavehill, the 400-metre-high mountain that looms large over Belfast, so had the perfect environment in which to prepare, and working as a freelance presenter I was often free during daylight hours for a gallop up and over the mountain while below me the other citizens of the city went about their daily business. I was starting to resent the amount of weekends I lost to work at Sky Sports, UTV and elsewhere, but the flexibility I had for training and mini-adventures during 'school days' was fantastic.

When the online entry form for the Man v Horse arrived, I found it impossible to determine what was serious and what was a joke. 'Runners must be 18 or over, Horses must be 5 or over' … 'Confirm entrant is Human or Horse'.

I wondered whether the 'Free race memento and free pasta supper' were available for both humans and horses, debated how to identify my 'Breed', and hovered my pen over the three boxes labelled Mare, Stallion, Gelding.

Speaking of stallions, since I owed him from the last time, I tried to persuade Slippy back into the fray. 'No chance,' came the blunt reply, albeit expressed in a less polite pair of words. He hadn't been as captivated by the whole concept of big Man Test adventures as I was after the Welsh mountain run and was still enjoying rugby. He loved the camaraderie and social aspect of his club in London, and one painful, rainy Saturday in Wales hadn't changed that. (A few months later, however, he wished he'd given up the game when I did; he ruptured his Achilles tendon just before his wedding day. His wife is one of the most forgiving people I know, but the addition of a huge plastic 'air boot' and a pair of crutches to the expensive wedding photos did not go down well.

I tried telling him that this run didn't require any map-reading, but he still didn't bite, so I prepared to go alone. And then another potential wingman appeared. A wingwoman actually, for it was my wife-to-be who quietly volunteered for hours of inter-species torture. Just a year earlier, Claire had run the Belfast Marathon in under four hours, so I didn't doubt for one minute that she had the *potential* to take on the Man v Horse, but she hadn't had to run up mountains before. We were getting married later that summer and in the final stages of planning the wedding, and Claire was also busy running her family's furniture retail business, so I thought she'd struggle to squeeze in the training. I patronisingly re-told the story of my previous Welsh mountain run, identical in distance to the 22 miles of the Man v Horse Marathon, and also arrogantly pointed out that I had since inched my way up to a much higher level of competitive fitness. She said nothing but quietly re-asserted that she'd like to go.

I left her to her own training devices and pounded away on Cavehill every spare morning or evening.

When you get fit enough to climb without blowing your heart out of your chest wall or coughing up half a lung, hill running must be one of the most inspiring forms of exercise in the world. The views, the off-road sense of leaving the real world far beneath your feet, the exploration, the solitude, the sense of tangible achievement that comes from making each summit – all combine to forge the perfect fitness activity.

Since the Snowdonia Summits experience, I had a few more years of hard training and events behind me and felt terrific on my hill training runs, much better prepared than I had been for that first Man Test, and confident of taking on most two-legged opponents if not the four-legged ones. I'd been in the Mournes a good few times and joined a pair of champion fell runners on a couple of 12-mile training runs. I felt ready a good few weeks out from the actual race. Claire, on the other hand, had barely set foot on Cavehill and, from her tetchy response to gentle questions, wasn't entirely confident of doing so too regularly before we left for Llanwrtyd.

The right preparation for any big endurance challenge has as much to do with timing as training. I was physically ready weeks before the event but the fortnight immediately before it could hardly have been better designed to undo everything I'd done. One of the problems with being an enthusiastic amateur as opposed to an unenthusiastic professional is that you have to do your best to fit in training and events around existing work and social commitments. Your sport can't always take precedence – there is a fair amount of diary shuffling and squeezing to manage. That was a particularly busy summer since we were getting married halfway through it, so there was pressure both work-wise and fun-wise to squeeze in as much as possible before the big day and subsequent three-week honeymoon.

The two weeks leading up to the Man v Horse were unusually busy. I had a run of shifts at Sky Sports News since the regulars all took off as soon as the football season ended, and I had also, with monumental temerity, agreed to no fewer than three stag parties. Two of them were epic weekend benders involving a day's travel each way, and they would run on consecutive weekends immediately before the Man v Horse.

The days in between were filled with more travel between Belfast and the Sky studios in London and a series of late-night presenting shifts. In one memorable 24-hour period I finished presenting at half past midnight, flew from London to Belfast at 07:30, got the boat to Scotland at 11:30, drove to Hawick for 17:30 and was in the pub preparing to play a very full part in their Common Ridings festival by 18:30.

I'd prepared perfectly up until then, fitting my training around a very varied work schedule. Running is a fantastically accessible sport in that it can be done virtually anywhere, although admittedly fell running adds an extra topographical dimension, and I'd put in the hours where and when I could. But the total alcohol immersion of a stag treble, coupled with the late night work schedule, took some of the wind out of my sails.

So I was heading to the race with, potentially, a shattered immune system. During that mental two weeks when I'd been raiding my reserves of health and fitness with partying and work, Claire had been building hers by quietly plodding away in the hills, so we arrived in Wales with roughly equal levels of confidence and trepidation. She did go a little quiet on the back roads to Llanwrtyd, though. It was either travel sickness or the sight of the peaks and valleys of the surrounding area, the arena in which we'd be tested the following day. The question of how on earth a race between man and horse could ever be even is answered by the terrain, and it was a fact not lost on either of us that if ground was too steep or rugged for horses, it wasn't likely to be easy for humans either.

That area of mid-Wales is stunningly beautiful, but it could have been designed to shred the thighs and calves of runners. By the look of the 22-mile course marked out on a giant map in the Neuadd Arms Hotel, we'd be constantly up hill and down dale, through forest and along river. It looked a fantastically varied, classic cross-country fell race, but my God it would be hard.

Reading through the rules and chatting to some veterans in the hotel bar, where it had all started three decades before, it was clear that the organisers' top priority was the wellbeing of the horses. Humans could take care of themselves. The two-legged do get a 15-minute head start, but this is so that the horses don't get nervous at the sight of the tight mass of people on the road. There is a compulsory veterinary check at the halfway point, where all horses get a once-over and a cool water rub-down, and the time spent here is then subtracted from their finish time at the end. So the horses get a recovery break, basically. There is no such facility or concern for humans.

Possibly because of this additional help to the equine competitors, there have only been two occasions in the 30-plus years of the race when one of them hasn't been first home. It ran for 25 years before the first human winner. Bedford runner Huw Lobb proved the neigh-sayers wrong and also saddled race sponsors William Hill with a massive £25,000 bill. They had put up a grand every year if a human could beat the horses, and this accumulated into an amazing windfall for Lobb, running the race for the first time and taking home prize-money that would be the envy of most professional runners.

I didn't expect to get close to matching Lobb, who had run the 22 miles up and down mountains in a scarcely believable two hours and five minutes, but I did really want to beat *some* of the horses, even if I couldn't beat them all. What a boast that would be.

It was the first time I'd travelled to a big endurance event with Claire and I can't imagine I was good company. I was tetchy and a bit tense. It was a combination of tiredness from the past few weeks, the usual post-binge demons still making their way out of my system, and pre-race nerves. Not for the first or last time, I asked myself why on earth I was taking this on, that summer of all summers.

Next morning, the mid-June sun streamed through the thin white curtains of our B&B and woke us at around five.

It was going to be a hot day. We ate breakfast mostly in silence. Claire was her usual chirpy self but I was fairly monosyllabic in reply. She is one of the most open people I have ever met, selfless and generous to a fault, and mostly level of personality and mood. By contrast, under pressure, I'm a bar chart of highs and lows. I retreat into myself to work things out, which must be confusing for someone as gregarious as Claire, especially when it was just the two of us on the trip. I'm the first to admit that in our relationship some stereotypical characteristics of the traditional masculine–feminine identities are reversed. Claire is the easy-going pragmatist who can build flat-pack furniture; I am the temperamental sentimentalist who can't tell one end of a spanner from the other.

We walked in to the centre of town after breakfast and found the place totally transformed. It was suddenly a hive of activity. Horseboxes lined the sides of the narrow roads and traffic was backed up on each of them. It was a hilarious conflation of two sporting worlds, demonstrated most effectively by the smell of fresh manure mingling with that of Deep Heat. Runners jogging and stretching gave wide berth to horses being reversed out of their boxes or prancing excitedly as they got saddled and bridled. Claire is nervous of animals at the best of times and was still more than a little apprehensive about the prospect of sharing a running route with these jumpy beasts whose iron shoes scored the tarmac and sent echoes round the town.

We had only briefly discussed our running plans, primarily because mine involved leaving her on the first climb and running off on my own. As a former competitive athlete and after going out with me for the previous three years she expected this, but I was feeling a bit guilty given that horses would be galloping towards us soon after the start.

About 400 runners were corralled into the town square for the mass start, while the 50-odd horses were held further back up the street. The 15-minute head start would allow the race to thin out before the horses got going. Music and excited chatter filled the air as everyone made their final stretches and checks. I gave Claire a kiss and a squeeze and agreed we'd run together for the first sections out of the town and towards the first hills. It was already hot in the town square, but I told her the horses would feel the heat much more than we would once we all got going.

The pace was a bit mad from the start. I couldn't believe so many runners could possibly sustain that for the whole distance, unless the Man v Horse Marathon had somehow attracted a field of the most elite fell runners in the world. It was hard to ignore everyone else and settle into our own rhythm, and Claire soon let me know we were going off too fast. I responded a bit snappily – she is like my conscience speaking out loud, which I both recognise and resent at the same time – but did slow down slightly.

Once we were off the roads and on to farm lanes everyone settled down and the pace was more realistic, and I was glad to see the majority of people who had stormed ahead beginning to blow a bit and then slip behind us. A few minutes later came the sound I'd been waiting for. My heartbeat quickened and Claire gave a little excited yelp as the unmistakable thunder of hooves – surely one of the most evocative sounds in the animal kingdom – got closer and closer.

The hurried rules briefing at the start line that morning had reminded everyone that one of the principal safety regulations is that humans give way to horses when they're on the same path by pulling over to the left to let them pass. But the thunder of hooves and the sensation of being hunted down scrambles the brain, and all around us people jumped and darted to either side of the lane. Even Claire drifted right until I grabbed her arm and pulled her to the left just in time for the smell of horse sweat to envelop us as a big chestnut mare cantered past, with its rider's shout of 'Thank you!' left hanging in the air.

I just about resisted the ridiculous notion of giving chase and tried to settle again to run my own race, but each time another horse came thundering past it grew progressively more difficult. I'm sure I wasn't the only first-timer battling to subdue growing resentment of the riders who only had to sit and make someone else do all the running, but their unfailing horsey-person chirpiness made them hard to hate.

As a slightly tubby little pony scampered past at the bottom of the first big grassy climb, I could stand it no longer. Claire was red in the face and puffing as I looked over half apologetically. 'On you go,' she panted, 'I'll be fine, just taking a bit of time to get into it.' I nodded and gave her a little bum tap as I accelerated into the hill.

Halfway up that first steep climb my heart was really thumping, but I kept up a solid rhythm, passing lots of the runners who had hared off at the start, and feeling pretty good. There was another small group of horses behind me but they were not gaining, and I began to see how the terrain could tip parts of the route in our favour. Horses aren't good going up or down anything steep, especially not with someone on their backs. They also aren't too good in the heat, and this was easily the warmest day of the year so far, mid- to late-twenties I guessed, without a breath of wind.

Far below me runners were bent low into the hill, hands on knees, grinding their way up; some horses were picking their steps slowly and carefully, and others seemed to be taking a longer route round the outside of the hill. There was such a glare from the sun I really wished I'd brought sunglasses and resolved not to look further than the ground in front again.

Up the first hill I followed other bipeds through a gap in a fence and grinned as I saw the horses having to trot down to a far corner of the field and an open gate. I was fairly punctured after what must have been a solid 20-minute climb and was glad of the water station just to the side of a bumpy farm lane. I grabbed a plastic cup as I ran past, threw most of it over my head to cool me down and then flinched slightly as a breeze pressed my newly cold, wet vest to my hot skin.

The lane ran along the top of the mountain and I soon recovered from the climb and started to really enjoy the run. It was a beautiful place: mountains, valleys, farmland and forest as far as the eye could see, which wasn't that far given the glare of the sun. I could feel the heat of the rays burning my shoulders and heating the top of my head as the water dried off, and wasn't surprised to see a horse pulled in up ahead and its rider standing alongside.

'Is he struggling?' I asked with a smile as I ran past.

'*She*,' came the frosty reply. 'And no, she's just taking a breather.'

'I know the feeling,' I replied, to which the rider responded with just the thinnest of smiles. It hadn't occurred to me that the riders would be taking this just as seriously as many of the runners – I'd forgotten there was still the matter of a £1,000 prize for the first finisher, be it man or beast.

Just like in the Welsh 1000m Peaks Race, I was running with a small bum bag of first aid kit and food. In the interim period I'd learned a little more of the theory about the nutrition required to finish these events, but not put much of it into practice. I had a small and rather random collection of gels, energy bars and Lucozade sweets, but found that I was so hot and out of breath I could only really stomach the sweets.

At the halfway point, on top of another hill, I felt really strong and pleasantly surprised that 11 miles was up already. In the shade of the edge of a pine forest, horses were lined up and being given a bucket and full cold-water baths as vets checked them over. Their human pilots looked on anxiously.

'Do you have to have four legs for that treatment?' I shouted over, probably the hundredth time the vets had been asked that. It really didn't feel fair that horses got to take time out with the clock paused, while humans, with only half as many legs, had to plough on without stopping.

The lane turned into a rough trail snaking down through the hills and from behind me again came the thunder of hooves, but also on occasion a runner showing a remarkable turn of pace for this stage of the proceedings. One in particular coming from behind me pissed me off and, ignoring my own pace-setting rules, I gave chase and stuck with him until he settled down to a more manageable speed. It slowly dawned on me that his race number was a different colour to mine. Idiot. This was a *relay* runner. That's why people had charged off so recklessly at the start: many of them were only running five or six miles!

Once I thought about it, this was a good sign; most of the runners I could see ahead of me had yellow numbers, unlike my own white one. I was probably doing quite well in the main race, and since the half-time break fewer horses had been coming past than in the first few miles. Encouraged, I pressed on and even overtook the relay runner as we splashed through a river crossing.

So far, so good, but still the sun beat down, and my jauntiness gradually left me. I passed a horse and rider on a steep downhill section through some ferns and over rutted earth, and didn't have the energy to respond to their cheery 'Well done!' with anything more than a muted 'Thanks'.

I hadn't eaten or drunk enough, I thought. I tried to force one of the gels in, but the gloop covered my hands when I tried to open it on the move, and everything just felt sticky and turgid. I swallowed what I could slowly, but got the sensation of it gathering in globules in my stomach, which made me feel a bit queasy.

I reached the edge of a forest where humans would follow a trail over a fence and through the trees while the horses had to take the long way round. I was really glad to be out of the sun for a while as I was beginning to feel a bit over-heated and lethargic. I thought enviously again of the horse cold-water bath and force-fed myself another few energy sweets.

Gradually but very definitely, my condition was worsening. I can't think of another occasion when I was able mentally to chart my own physical decline so clearly, stage by stage, step by step. That I was sliding slowly to exhaustion first became obvious when I realised I was no longer feeling better on the downhill slopes or in the shade. I wasn't recovering, just felt shite all the time, running on empty whether going up or down. Coasting down in neutral wasn't an option any more; gravity could no longer help because my legs felt so wobbly that I couldn't trust them to keep me upright.

I tried to retreat inside myself, ignore my surroundings, pain, feelings, and just run down the clock, because it had to be over soon. I'd run the first 11 miles in about an hour and 20 minutes, so I reasoned that I'd be well on the home straight after two and a half hours. I banned myself from checking my watch for a while to see if I could make the time move quicker, but when I came stumbling down another hilly, narrow track and saw a couple of officials waiting at a stile, I sneaked a look and saw that the two and a half hours was indeed up. I was pretty confident that the end was nigh and I might just have enough fuel to limp over the line in a really good time.

You can probably imagine my disappointment therefore when, after a brief consultation as I jogged past, they told me there was still another three miles to run. In fact, the first official said four miles, but this was later rounded down to about three.

'What?! I thought I was nearly finished! Are you sure?' I pleaded pathetically, almost angrily, as if it was the fault of these two officials that I was knackered.

'You *are* nearly finished, just another few miles. Come on, keep going. There are no more big hills, it's all just down through the woods now.'

But my heart had dropped; in fact my whole body had almost dropped. Suddenly every step was a challenge, my legs felt like two tree trunks, and I almost resorted to lifting them along on each step with my arms. How could there be another three miles to go?! They must be wrong.

I plodded on, shocked at how much of an effort it had become to do something I had always taken entirely for granted. Now the simple act of running had become an enormous challenge, and when the little shaded lane through the woods ended and I was directed up a long, steep slope on a grassy hill, I nearly gave up. This was probably the worst I'd ever felt on any fitness challenge, and the closest I'd ever been to not being able to finish a race.

It was a dire situation. Ordinarily I'd have loved to charge up a long grassy slope – I trained for this, I relished running up hills faster than most people. But right now, I was completely unravelling. I wasn't just exhausted and dispirited; I was scared. I can remember looking around, wondering if there was any way to find a short cut, any way of avoiding the hill. I was half demented, irrational and desperate for a way out.

There was no short cut. I cursed the officials who told me there were no more hills, raged that they'd wronged me, and used the rage to try and help myself up. But it soon petered out and I was still in the nightmarish situation of having miles to go and nothing left to give. I finally gave in to the temptation to lift my legs physically with my arms on each climb, hoping that they'd remember the piston-like action required to move up steep hills. In this erratic, unorthodox style I moved slowly and mechanically to the top of the field.

I was in a world of pain by now, confused and still overcome occasionally by the mild panic of running completely out of gas so close to the finish. I'm sure I expended a good bit of my last energy reserves on this pointless anxiety, but I couldn't help it. I trudged on, painfully slowly, overtaken at one point by a man at least 30 years my senior,

I reckoned, and breezy with it. I checked his race number and was crestfallen to notice it was white. He'd run the whole distance too and appeared in a much better state than I was. What the hell was wrong with me?

I was practically hallucinating – everything was a daze. I remember picking steps down through some trees, and then there was a river crossing where I was so shaky I slipped on the rocks and fell forward. The cold water did nothing to revive me and on the short hill on the other side I seriously felt like I was going the wrong way up an escalator, such was the effort to keep moving forward. But once up that slope I could hear music and the race announcer, then there were people along some tape on both sides of a grassy straight, and this was it – the finish. With a final effort I broke into a lumbering trot, raised my arms halfway above my head and slumped over the line. Two hours and 55 minutes.

I collapsed in the corner of a refreshment tent beside a tea-urn and lay in a heap for I don't know how long. I was utterly spent. I normally recover pretty quickly from exercise but this was different. I could hardly find the strength to lift myself off the ground and sit up. My legs ached, my shoulders and upper back ached, and I felt sick and faint. I just lay there, sipping water and waiting for whatever natural healing process would bring me back to the real world.

When I finally managed to stagger to my feet I found a table of sandwiches and began nibbling bread while the world slowly stopped spinning. I hunkered down again to be closer to the ground and tried to focus on taking big breaths and how the food would set me right again. A few minutes later I set off to find an official to ask them what happened when runners couldn't go on. I was suddenly worried about how to get Claire back, because I was sure she wouldn't make it all the way round. The race had been much, much tougher than we'd feared and I felt guilty for encouraging her to take part.

While I was waiting to speak to a guy with a clipboard, someone grabbed my elbow. 'Hi, baby!'

I was genuinely shocked. Claire had finished just half an hour after me, and was in much better order. In fact she was so chirpy I thought she must have bailed out and got a lift back to the finish, an accusation she didn't appreciate, unsurprisingly. I was so proud of her, and we chatted happily as we staggered back up to the B&B.

'I can't believe you finished that. I'm telling you, that is some of the worst I have felt in any of the big challenges I have done. That was bloody hard.'

'Did you not expect to see me so soon?' (That was about as close to self-satisfaction as Claire ever gets.)

'Nope. I was seriously about to go and ask how they round up people who don't finish! Well done, Sweetpea.'

She smiled, squeezed my arm and we walked on a bit. I was slowly coming round but still felt like my brain was only half working, and my body ached. It felt a bit like flu actually, a faint headache and zero energy. I was relieved it was over, of course, but there was still a nagging little pang of regret or disappointment about something. I couldn't quite place it.

A cold shower revived me and we went back into town to check the results and get some food. I had beaten 36 of the 41 horses in the race, which cheered me up no end, and was 27th runner to finish. Claire was 179th, and also beat at least 10 horses. It was a pretty good performance, but I just knew that I wasn't 100 per cent right; I should never have disintegrated that badly at the end. I put it down to the impact of the previous two weeks' extra-curricular activities, which was a bit annoying after all the training I'd done before that. It was also the first time I started properly to consider what I'd been eating and drinking. Or rather, what I *hadn't* been eating and drinking. I was pretty sure I was very dehydrated by mile 18, and running hard for nearly three hours was bound to be impossible without proper fuel. Food for thought.

Still, to have got round in under three hours and beaten most of the horses was great, so what was this nagging little negative feeling dragging me down a bit? As we walked into town for dinner it suddenly dawned on me.

'Were you surprised with me, Sweetpea?' Claire asked me again. And then the killer blow. 'Did you think you'd beat me by more?'

Sucker punch. I did, actually. I was torn between pride at her doing so well, and a feeling that after all that training I should have been on another level entirely. The fact that Claire had finished in such apparent comfort, while I had felt close to death, proved that I wasn't. I raised a smirk and replied that to be fair, half an hour was a sizeable gap, and if I'd been half an hour quicker again I'd have won the whole thing and we'd be thousands of pounds richer.

'I know, I'm just teasing,' she said, squeezing my arm again.

The race was again won by a horse, Duke's Touch of Fun getting round in 2 hours 18 minutes. But it was close, one of the closest finishes ever in fact – with just 30 seconds separating man and beast. John McFarlane was the quickest human, and I can only imagine the excitement during the last blast through the forest with Duke's Touch of Fun hunting him down before the end.

*

I really enjoyed Llanwrtyd; it felt like a little quiet hub where local and visiting eccentrics could mingle for whatever mad event was in season, and as we walked round the town next morning I was suddenly quite depressed at the thought of having to go back to London for work that afternoon. Claire dropped me off at Bristol railway station on her way to the airport, and I really felt quite sickened. I hardly spoke all the way there, which was so far removed from my usual post-event euphoria as to be quite alarming.

Normally I was on a bit of a high for days after a big challenge, feeding off a feeling of achievement and also relief that I didn't need to do it again or train for a while. But this sudden depression was strange. Looking back, I think it was just the fact that I wasn't going home with Claire to Belfast but straight to work at Sky in London, with all the stresses of live television; and also the whole previous mad month catching up on me. There was an awful lot happening at once in our lives and it would have been nice to have had a breather and take stock for a bit, rather than repeatedly lurching from one mad commitment to another.

I'd get one on honeymoon of course, for which we'd booked three weeks off in Africa. But not if I decided to squeeze in another epic challenge while I was there … Which of course I had. Even to me, it now seems ridiculous that we would attempt to shoehorn climbing Kilimanjaro into a honeymoon, but again, Claire was willing. If her choice of husband wasn't enough to call her judgement into question, her choice of honeymoon certainly was.

Four

ON A HIGH IN AFRICA

Getting married, or staging a wedding more accurately, was not unlike taking on a big fitness challenge, I found. You make the commitment; it seems very far away; there is so much preparation you wonder if it's worth it for one event; it dominates your life for too long; you perform in public, you think it's a big deal, and then it's over and life continues as normal.

Claire did the vast majority of the heavy lifting, which is why everything ran very smoothly, but it seemed to dominate most of our time together, which was limited anyway given the nature of my irregular life. One beautiful sunny afternoon, before I headed to a Sky Sports News evening shift, we were walking in Kew Gardens enjoying one of those infrequent but special snatched 'couple moments' we found it harder and harder to find.

My phone buzzed. It was Robin, an old rugby mate from Loughborough that I was still in touch with. Not your typical university rugger bugger, he was more earnest and sensitive than most of us, and he and I became friends during the first big fitness test for our Freshers squad, which was unfortunately held on the Monday after the big drinking test. In both of these sessions, everyone was out to prove themselves to a new group and it got messy.

We were put through a 'bleep test', the mere mention of which will strike horror in many readers familiar with squad fitness sessions. A bleep test is painfully straightforward. Everyone has to complete a series of 20-metre shuttle runs in time with a series of 'bleeps' pre-recorded and (back then) played on a CD. Every minute the bleeps get closer together, so you have less time to complete the 20 metres. It gets harder and harder obviously, and at the end you get a comparable score that is used to estimate your 'VO2 Max', or the amount of oxygen you can process during exercise. In other words, the score tells everyone how fit you are.

That Monday evening in one of Loughborough's many sports halls, as all around us young men were making themselves sick and keeling over, Robster and I silently did battle. When it got to about Level 14 we were the only two left. There was much at stake. Being the fittest person in a squad at a place like Loughborough was a worthy title.

The bleeps got faster and faster, and as everyone else recovered, the cheering got louder and louder. The hot stale air felt thick to breathe, thick to run through, and the spills of sweat on the polished gym floor made turning at the end of each length treacherous. I can still remember the dead weight of my legs and the building nausea as I fought for a breath and a break. The whole room swam from the perpetual motion, and still Robster clung on.

I think 16.1 was the score at which I eventually collapsed, and I have been proud never to see that matched anywhere since. Except by Robster that evening. I think that stubborn bastard actually went one further, which is both admirable and – even 15 years later – immensely annoying.

We hadn't spoken in ages, so I wanted to answer and Claire didn't mind – she does that to me all the time.

'Robster! Hello, boy.'

'G ... long time no chat. How are you, boy?'

We caught up for a minute before I told him I was out walking with Claire and couldn't chat long, which is friend code for 'get to the point'.

'Listen, there's something I have wanted to do for ages. Ever heard of the Marathon des Sables? The Sahara race in Morocco, 150 miles across the desert? Doesn't have to be raced, though, just finishing it is the main challenge. I have read about it so much, I just really want to do it but I don't think I could do it on my own. But I reckon you could do it, we could try together. I'd really love it if you'd be my wingman. What do you think?'

'Waoow. Marathon des Sables. Yes, I have heard of it, of course, it sounds mental. I'd love to.'

'Seriously?!' Robster sounded elated. 'It's years away, there's a big waiting list and everything but I reckon we could get on it and we'd need all that time to train anyway.'

'We could definitely do it, course we could, let me call you tomorrow and we can chat it through.'

I hung up and waited for the most difficult part of the challenge to begin, thousands of miles from Morocco.

'What was that about, Sweetpea?'

'It was Robster, you remember him, one of my Loughborough mates?'

'Yes, I think so, what were you talking about?'

'Ah, he just wants me to help him run something, wants me to go with him to an event some time.'

'What event?'

'Eh, the Marathon des Sables. Just this run thing in the Sahara Desert. We were the fittest in our team, used to play together, were really close, I'm quite touched actually, he wants me to …'

'When is it?'

'Oh, it's years away, there's a big waiting list, not for ages. Oh look, a rhododendron.'

I did a bit of Googling while on air at Sky that night. Little two-minute bursts between story links or ad breaks. The Marathon des Sables seemed to have attained the status of 'hardest footrace in the world'. There were literally hundreds of blogs, articles, books, photo essays and videos on the event, and dozens of forums for aspiring and veteran runners. It was a big one.

Robster and I chatted it through the next day and committed. He is incalculably more organised than I am, and I did worry a bit about how thorough his preparations would be and how pissed off he'd get about mine. He knew that the next release of race places for UK citizens was the following Wednesday at 8am, and insisted we man the phones from 7.45.

I laughed. 'Robster, there are hundreds of places available, I can't imagine there will be that many idiots clamouring to sign up for a masochistic run across the Sahara in two years' time.'

'You'd be surprised, G. I have read all about it, places are gone in minutes. We need to be phoning and on the 'net just clicking "Enter" from 8am on the dot. OK?'

And we were. But still we didn't get in. Incredibly, there actually *were* hundreds of others as desperate if not more desperate than us to sign up for running 150 miles across a desert in temperatures of around 40°C, and to pay £3,500 for the privilege. Three and a half grand! To risk exhaustion and heatstroke all day, eat food that bounces about in a rucksack for the best part of a week, and sleep on the ground in a camel-hair shelter. The world had gone mad.

And so had we.

'I hit enter enter enter non-stop for 15 minutes, G, and I hit re-dial on the mobile flat out, but it was always engaged. It's a fix,' complained Robster.

I wasn't sure how or why such a system would be fixed but I was frustrated too. We called the company that looks after the UK entries and hounded a poor girl called Sarah who only worked there one day a week. She said the next stage was for us to go on the waiting list and promised to make sure we were near the top. A week later she was in touch to say we were numbers 12 and 13 on the waiting list, and that was virtually a guarantee of entry.

'Why?' I asked, confused as to why someone would go through the hassle of registering and training, part with a hefty £500 non-refundable deposit and then pull out.

'We get so many drop-outs,' said Sarah. 'Injuries, problems finding the money, the realisation of how tough it will be, the size of the commitment, lots of things. You two will definitely be in, I promise.'

That was good enough for Robster, who immediately threw himself into the preparations, both logistical and physical, even though we still weren't officially entered and the event was nearly two years away. I found it harder to get that set for something so far in the future, and there was plenty more fun to be had in the meantime, including the small matter of climbing Kilimanjaro. Oh yeah, and getting married ... which was easy in comparison.

We had a proper traditional Irish hooley, with much mention in the speeches of our prior adventures and hobbies, and bemused looks from older aunts and uncles when mountain races against horses came up. Their confusion only deepened soon after when it was revealed that our honeymoon plans included an attempt to climb the highest mountain in Africa.

It takes at least six days to get up and down Kilimanjaro, not including the travel time to and from that part of Tanzania. We had allowed for only four, because there was so much else we wanted to do, including a week in Zanzibar and a stay in that most obvious of honeymoon destinations, Rwanda. If this all sounds unforgivably counter-romantic, you should also know that one year we ended up in Auschwitz on Valentine's Day, so I suppose anything is an improvement on that.

We grossly underestimated Kilimanjaro, which I know sounds ridiculous. Underestimating the highest mountain in Africa? A land mass six kilometres high that towers over an entire continent? Yes. We knew a few people who had climbed it, had heard of celebrities we didn't exactly respect as athletes making the summit for charity, and felt that if they could struggle up it, a pair of mountain-running veterans like us would be up and down without any bother in a couple of days.

And so, after a week recovering from the usual wedding madness in Zanzibar, we found ourselves in Moshi, a small town on the lower slopes of Kilimanjaro, meeting our mountain guides and sorting kit in a fairly basic motel. We had brought our own hiking boots, but needed thick mountain sleeping bags, waterproofs, padded jackets and a rucksack.

The chief guide, Muti, repeatedly stressed the challenges of the mountain, and told us that our timescale of four days was ambitious to say the least, but could probably be done if we followed the advice of the guides at all times and took things slowly on the ascent. I should probably have paid more attention, but I felt I already knew about altitude sickness. It happens because at higher elevations the atmospheric pressure is less, presumably because there is less air pushing down, and the concentration of oxygen in any gas is dependent on a calculation involving atmospheric pressure. Obviously less concentration of oxygen in the air is bad news for humans, especially if we don't allow our bodies enough time gradually to adapt to it. Muti cautioned that it is impossible to predict how different people react to altitude, and that being fit is largely irrelevant. Actually, some smokers tend to fare better than non-smokers because their lungs are used to dealing with variance in oxygen supply.

I'd experienced it before, on one occasion in particular that was pretty horrible, though hardly surprising given our approach. I was on a whistle-stop tour of Bolivia, and in one day we drove from the sea level of the salt plains to over 4,000 metres. And then went for a hike. Walking out was grand, but once we'd turned back, after seeing the flamingoes we had come to see, everything changed.

I presume it was a gradual process, but I just remember suddenly feeling like I was wading through treacle, like someone had dumped a massive hangover on me without the fun part before. My head thumped, I felt as if I could trace the blood flowing round my temples and it was carrying something pointy, which clattered round in my veins. I was really nauseous and my mouth filled with saliva constantly as if I was about to throw up. But above all, I was completely knackered, struggling to even shuffle back to our base. Once there, my two mates and I just collapsed on the bunk beds, but sleep was hard with a body crying out in protest. I never forgot the overpoweringly heavy effects of altitude; it was quite shocking to realise that very slight changes to the oxygen content of the air we breathe can render us sick and totally useless.

The weird thing about altitude sickness, a bit like morning sickness in pregnant women, is that it seems very random in terms of who it affects and when. There are no specific factors that increase the likelihood of getting it; some people do and some people don't, and even if you weren't sick at a certain height one time, it doesn't mean you won't be sick at that height another time.

Claire and I were still riding the wave of the Man v Horse and our decent general fitness levels. We were also both a little impatient to get this out of the way and get on with the rest of the honeymoon. Then we were introduced to Minja, the guide who would spend the next three days taking us to the final camp before the summit. He was stinking of drink and languorous in the extreme. The die was cast. When Minja started like a tortoise up the track through the rain forest in the mountain park, we hared off in front. When he told us off, and repeated his mantra 'Pole, pole' – Swahili for 'slowly, slowly' – we sniffed that there was no reason for the rest of us to go at his pace just because he was hung over.

We had joined with a PE teacher from England called John, who was also proud of his own fitness and more than a little sceptical about the state of Minja. The mountain park fees included porters to carry food and cooking gear, so at the end of each day there was a hot meal to look forward to, which we ate hungrily in a communal wooden cabin in a forest clearing that evening. Minja didn't eat much but was still smelling strongly of drink, and we began to suspect that we had acquired an alcoholic mountain guide, which wasn't ideal. We debated going to find Muti to tell him we weren't happy, but given that Minja had done nothing wrong so far, bar walk slowly, we thought we'd give him another chance.

That first camp, Mandara Hut, was at 2,700 metres, three times the height of England's highest mountain, Scafell Pike, and really we were only just starting. Colobus monkeys gathered in the trees around the wooden huts, the little white rings round their black faces giving them a spooky, unearthly quality in the half-light of the late evening.

It got quite cold at night, even in the wooden huts in which eight of us were crammed into bunks, and we were glad of the proper sleeping bags. The others in our cabin seemed slightly appalled when they learned we were on honeymoon; they said they felt guilty about intruding so would do their best to give us as much privacy as was possible in an eight-berth wooden shack no bigger than the average domestic garage.

'Pole, pole' (pronounced pollay, pollay) was the key objective for Minja the next day too, and again we tried to gee him on a bit by walking ahead. We followed another forest trail for a while, then said goodbye to the monkeys as we headed up and away from the tree canopy and onto more open moorland. Thin, wiry grass, rocks and an unusual array of bulbous spiky plants that looked as if they'd been planted upside down made up the terrain, and every now and again when the hazy clouds parted, we'd get our first glimpses of the flat white top of the mountain, which glinted in the sun and seemed so far away as to be in a different time zone.

The second camp, Horombo Hut, was pretty cool; a collection of even smaller huts than the previous day, dug into the sides of the hill, with little pointed roofs like mini Alpine chalets. We'd been hiking for about five hours so the bowl of hot water waiting for each of us at the huts was really appreciated; a little hot wash was a great revival.

I really liked Horombo. It was still very hazy but we could see out over the valley and up towards the summit, and the air was fresh and cool like a British autumn morning. There was also noticeably less oxygen. I got out of breath walking all of ten metres uphill to the toilet, and we soon became aware of every little thing taking more effort than normal. It was more of a novelty at this stage than a concern, but at 3,700 metres there was no doubt we were operating well outside conditions with which our bodies were accustomed.

Optimistically, I felt that a night's sleep would accustom my lungs or heart or blood, or whichever internal organ needed to learn how to cope with the reduced oxygen supply, and when we set off the next morning I felt grand. We *all* professed to feeling good, though I did notice that the morning's porridge was much more difficult to stomach. I wasn't hungry at all but I put this down to the watery, bland and generally unappealing qualities of the porridge rather than anything else.

We were making for Kibo Hut, the final camp before the summit on this particular route up the mountain. It was at 4,700 metres so we had to climb a kilometre straight up on this day's hike, and the majority of it would be across a barren, windblown desert, the 'saddle' between the two peaks that make up the approach to the cratered summit of Kilimanjaro.

We reached this dusty, exposed plain shortly after leaving Horombo, and I felt like I needed some music to lift both the monotony of the scenery and the effort. It helped, but I felt selfish shutting myself off and offered Claire an earphone as we walked beside each other. She hadn't spoken for at least an hour. Every time I asked if she was OK she just nodded and tried to be chirpy with an upbeat 'Mmm hmmm.' But I could tell she was struggling.

I was beginning to feel it too. First there was the lack of appetite from this morning continuing when I tried to eat some of the packed lunch; then a slight constriction round the temples slowly sliding into a headache; and then a growing nausea and lethargy. I knew a good dose of altitude sickness was definitely on the way and just wanted to try and get to the camp and lie down, as quickly as possible.

Twenty minutes later we had to stop and Claire was sick behind some rocks. I again offered my headphones and one of my training playlists to try and help her on, but she just shook her head and grimly set off again. 'Pole, pole,' I whispered, but she could only manage a thin smile.

Kibo is a stone-built cabin of 60 beds in various dormitories, and compared to everything else we'd experienced on the barren and lonely day across the saddle, it was a hive of activity. Porters walked to and from the cabin and other outhouses, and there were even young children and animals running round kicking up the dust. It felt like a Western frontier town, a hub of local supplies where people would come and go in various states of exhaustion after trekking up en route to the summit, or on the trek back down.

I couldn't figure out how on earth this was a good place for kids, how they'd got there, or how they could run gaily around while I could barely put one foot in front of the other. *We* had arrived in total silence. John was white as a sheet and Claire went straight in to find an empty bunk. I tried to stay outside for a while, hoping that the fresh air and some deep breaths would help me adjust. I met some German girls who were on their way back down. Only half of their group had been well enough to even attempt the final climb. One of them had some anti-sickness pills and insisted I take a couple.

'I'm a nurse,' she said, 'and you'll seriously need these. They really helped me.'

'Did you make it to the summit?'

'No, but I felt a lot better after taking the anti-sickness pills and I feel like I can hike back down again now.'

Sheesh. If drugs were required just to get the energy to walk back down, this was pretty serious. I put them in my pocket and tried to tough it out since I didn't really know what the pills were and knew even less about the person who'd given them to me.

I felt worse and went in to lie down. Restful sleep is nearly impossible while heavy with altitude sickness. It's like having a fever. Random thoughts slam in and out of your mind, the same imagery is repeated over and over and it's impossible to get comfortable.

But I was nowhere near as uncomfortable as Claire. She had been gone from our cabin room for 20 minutes and it was starting to get dark, so I struggled off the bunk and went to investigate. She was bent over a drain at the side of the hut and had been retching almost constantly since we arrived. She looked dreadful. I didn't know what to do. I knew this was just altitude sickness, but puking for half an hour non-stop was quite serious, and she also now had a bleeding nose.

Muti arrived, alongside Minja, and looked gravely down at Claire.

'I don't think this is good,' he said with classic under-statement. 'She will need to go down. It's the only way to get better with bad altitude sickness.'

'Pole, pole,' added Minja with a shake of his head. I would have throttled him if I'd had any energy. But to be fair, he was probably right. Maybe if we'd listened to him and taken it a lot easier on the way up we'd both be feeling better now.

'I might be OK,' Claire offered, unconvincingly. 'I'm sorry, Sweetpea.'

'Don't be silly, it's not your fault you're being sick like this,' I replied.

My mind was racing. I felt dreadful too, but I really didn't want to have got this far and not have a go at the summit. I didn't know if we'd *all* have to abandon now, or what the etiquette was either while climbing mountains or being on honeymoon … Did Claire have to go straight to the bottom? Did we have to hike all the way back down and then climb back up again? We had no more days, so I'd have to do all that non-stop, and then try to reach the summit, while feeling shite. Muti took control.

'OK, we can get you down to the last camp,' he told Claire. 'You will be fine when you drop to there. I get one of the guides to go with you, he has a torch. We will be back down in the morning and see you.' He turned to me. 'So you still want to go to the top?'

I hesitated and looked down at my new wife.

'Yes, yes, of course you must go on, a hundred per cent,' she said, stuffing a tissue up her dripping nose. 'I'll be fine, I just need to get down a bit, don't worry.'

On the plane on the way over we had briefly discussed the possibility of one of us not making it to the top, but we hadn't seriously considered the prospect of splitting up. It seemed like an unhealthy portent for a new marriage. I certainly hadn't considered the prospect of leaving Claire to walk down the mountain in the dark alone with a guide she didn't know and only one head-torch between them. We had no phones or way of communicating once she went down and I went up. But on the other hand, I was 12 hours away from getting to the top of the highest mountain in Africa …

Claire had tears in her eyes as we kissed goodbye. 'I'm sorry,' she said again, 'I just feel so weak. But I'll be fine, please don't worry.'

I have to be honest and admit that once the decision was made, I *didn't* spend too much time worrying about it. Partly this was because Claire is more than capable of looking after herself, but mostly it was because my own condition worsened so much that I couldn't think of anything apart from the pain in my head and the sickness in my stomach. In desperation I took one of the anti-nausea pills. It seemed to get stuck halfway down my gullet. Maybe I lay down before it was fully swallowed, or maybe I took it too late, but for whatever reason, the anti-nausea pill's only contribution was to make me feel considerably more nauseous.

The 'toilet' was a rough wooden shed built around a hole in the ground outside the main hut, and I visited twice in the dark with increasingly violent results. The second time I was so weak I could hardly make it back to my bunk. I forced myself to wash my teeth and down a bottle of water, and pretended I was going to bed for a proper night's sleep before the next day's big summit push.

Muti shook me awake at midnight. 'OK? Now we go.'

There seemed something different about him. He wasn't as laidback or cheery as normal. It was as if everything was about to get serious. He left a plate of dry, broken biscuits on my bunk and advised me to eat as much as possible. I nibbled a couple but felt so nauseous I wasn't sure they'd stay down. I pulled on my tracksuit bottoms, my boots and the thick padded jacket and tried to shake myself awake. It was cold and I was stiff, and feeling rough. The thought of a six-hour mountain climb was awful. I looked over at John. He hadn't even been able to get off the bed yet.

Muti came back to hurry us up. He looked at us quizzically again. 'OK guys? We need to go.' I didn't dare mention how sick I'd been in the evening. He was definitely much more business-like now, and I felt he was assessing whether we were in a fit state to start the summit climb, so I tried to inject myself with a bit of false bravado. 'Never better,' I lied. 'Let's go!'

It was very cold outside, and the air felt crisp and clean. I took some long, deep breaths through my nose and felt a little better. The sky was magnificent, with hardly a cloud, a tiny moon but millions of bright stars. Minja emerged from nowhere wearing a balaclava and began checking that our head-torches were working.

Ahead of us, an enormous and ominous grey mass hung over everything. Somewhere above and beyond that lay our destination. It was probably just as well that we couldn't make out much of the detail. Head-torches on, we moved in single file behind Minja. Me, John and then Muti at the back. All was silent apart from the grating of boot against grit, and the sound of our increasingly heavy breathing. After the first solid mile or so we hit the scree slopes, which made climbing even more difficult. Every step forward was accompanied by a bit of a slide back down, which would have been disheartening had I been thinking straight. Luckily I wasn't.

I felt a bit dizzy and faint, and had long before tried to banish all thoughts of what time it was, how far we had to go, or the fact that I was supposed to be on honeymoon and had abandoned my wife with a random Tanzanian the evening before. The other, blaring fact I tried to ignore was that altitude sickness obviously got worse the higher you went, and I was getting higher with every step.

There was a groan from below and John sank to his knees, vomiting. When he'd finished, he tried to get back to his feet but stumbled and Muti caught him. He told him to sit with his head between his knees for a while. I was glad of the chance to do the same. I had a Snickers in my bag and managed to eat half of it before feeling again as if something was stuck in my gullet.

'This is why we say four days is not long enough,' Muti grinned up at me, while John just continued to groan and spit in the ground. He tried again to stand, but once again didn't have the energy.

'OK,' said Muti brusquely. 'You need to go down now, it's too much to go on.' John didn't complain. The urgency in Muti's manner made me think about my own position. Was I right to continue in such a state? 'I will bring him down and you can go to top with Minja. OK?'

Minja grinned down at me. Oh Jesus Christ. I would be alone on the high slopes of Kilimanjaro, feeling like death, with only Minja and his limited English for company. I swallowed. Fuck it. I wasn't going back now.

'Sure,' I said. 'Just you and me, Minja. Do you know the way?!'

'I know way,' he replied solemnly.

Muti took John's arm and they set off slowly, criss-crossing back down to the hut. Minja adjusted his balaclava and stepped into the mountain again. I fell in behind him and started tapping out the steps, swaying slightly in his rhythm. 'Pole, pole,' I said to myself.

Not long after, I knew I was going to be sick and told Minja I needed to stop. I threw up the half Snickers and bits of dry biscuits. Christ, this was a dreadful experience. What on earth was I doing?! I was supposed to be on honeymoon! I fell back on the slope and looked up into the sky. What a sight. My head cleared a bit, I took a few big breaths and washed my mouth out with some water. This was all ridiculous. It was half past one in the morning, I was puking up here, Claire was puking somewhere down there; neither of us knew how the other was. And we'd only been married a week. Actually it was quite funny. I took another big breath and resolved to go on. When we went home and I had to explain myself, I'd at least need to produce a summit photo to justify abandoning her.

'Now you have new power,' Minja growled.

I laughed. 'Yip. Let's go.'

I did feel a little bit better. I was far from 100 per cent, but at least now I was somewhere above 10, at which I'd been hovering for the last 12 hours or so. I was still battling through a haze of nausea and weakness but I wasn't going to stop. I'd gone too far for that. We plodded on, settling into a rhythm of slow but sure upward progress and regular stops, when I would lie down and try to get my breathing under control. This felt like proper mountain climbing alright. We were about five and a half kilometres up by now, the highest I'd ever been other than in a plane, and I thought I could sense the thin air with every breath. With hindsight, it was probably just the bite of the cold.

I needed to be sick again, and threw up while Minja looked on. He kept saying, 'After Gillyman easy, after Gillyman easy.' It took me a while to work out what he meant. Gilman's Point was at the top of the really steep slope that we were climbing. It was on the rim of the mountain and although the true summit – Uhuru Peak – was at least an hour's hike from there, the worst of the climbing would be over. So 'Gillyman' became my focus.

Because it has a big flat top and you can get up without any rock climbing or mountaineering experience, people think reaching the summit of Kilimanjaro is easy; and maybe, compared to Everest or McKinley or Aconcagua or any of the other highest peaks, it is. But trying to do anything at all, never mind anything physical, at five kilometres up in the sky is far from easy if you haven't got your body used to the idea.

I knew from the moment we arrived at Kibo Hut that I hadn't taken it remotely seriously enough, and that without the proper acclimatising it was going to be a real struggle. But I also knew that family history would only record whether I'd made it up or not, without setting out the reasons why, so even if Minja had to carry me all the way back down, I was getting to the summit.

This is probably exactly the sort of bullshit thinking that leads people to go the dangerous extra few miles and die on Everest when everything has been telling them to back off. I can easily imagine how difficult it would be to turn back before the summit, if things started looking a bit ominous, when you'd spent an absolute fortune and prepared for years to get to the top of the world and it now seemed so close. Turning back would of course be the smart thing to do, but when the air is thin and the desire to reach a goal has become an expensive obsession, reason goes out the window.

Only about 40 per cent of those who take on Kilimanjaro reach the summit, which is a failure rate 10 per cent greater than for Tough Guy. I imagine that the vast majority of those who turn back are forced down by altitude sickness.

The knowledge that it was a common and natural phenomenon helped me cope: if others struggled through it, I knew I could too. I had focused so intently on hauling myself to Gilman's Point that as soon as we got there I took out my camera for a photo with Minja and told him I was happy now and ready to go back down. It was still pitch dark, probably about four in the morning, I was exhausted, and this was the rim of Kilimanjaro. I was happy at that moment to insist that this constituted climbing the mountain.

'No, no, no!' protested Minja with great alarm. He pointed towards a trail between huge rocks. 'Uhuru, Uhuru. Easy.'

I sat thinking about it for a few minutes. He was right. I had to do this properly. How could I undo three and a half days of hiking with a calculated piece of self-deception that would unravel as soon as we caught up with Muti back at Kibo Hut? That terrible old sports cliché popped into my head: 'Pain is temporary, glory lasts forever.' We set off along the trail, climbing over and through some rocks that formed a natural tunnel, and then out into a more open section that gradually revealed itself as the great rim of Africa's highest mountain, as the sky drained from black to dark blue, and then to dolphin grey with an orange glow.

We were walking along a vast rocky ridge, skirting around a centre filled with bright white snow, the most incongruous sight I saw in Africa. What mad explosion of geography created this huge lump housing a frozen secret just kilometres above some of the driest, dustiest plains in the world? The sun rose further and the whole of Africa appeared below us. It was incredible, a once in a lifetime experience that I may have enjoyed if I hadn't at that moment been feeling close to death.

The little lift I'd felt at Gilman's Point was a distant memory. It was now over an hour later, and I was feeling as sick and as weak as ever. Worse, in fact. I was dizzy again and crouched down on my hunkers to try and stop my head from spinning. Minja thought I was just looking for a photo and motioned that he would take it. I shook my head, smiled weakly and motioned back that I was going to be sick again. And then was, almost immediately.

I rinsed my mouth out again, moved away slightly and then thought that me crouched down at that spot would actually make quite a good photo, so handed over the camera. Minja laughed. We were bonding. He's not a good photographer, but I treasure that slightly blurred pic of me crouched above the frozen core of Africa's roof. I love it because I'm smiling, you can't see the vomit, and people still think a picture speaks a thousand words.

We plodded on round the ridge as the dawn glow turned to the full brightness of a new day, and then suddenly there was a plateau and loads of people. Some of them were even smiling, laughing, taking photos, *enjoying* themselves and not apparently on the point of exhaustion. These were the smart ones who had taken different routes, and taken time to do it slowly, as the guides suggested. But this was it, finally, the summit. The specific highest point is marked by a wonky and battered sign: an inauspicious landmark after such a struggle, but familiar to me from dozens of pics I'd seen of charity fund-raisers, former professional sportsmen and celebrities, all leaning in triumph against it.

We trudged over to join the queue. I was really feeling desperate now, very weak and not enjoying the moment at all unfortunately. I kept thinking of the refrain I'd heard so often from proper climbers of properly dangerous mountains, who all said that you only really celebrate a summit when you get right back down to the bottom, because when you reach the top the challenge is only half over. I'd made it up, now I wanted just to get my photo and get the hell off there.

Jesus, some people took ages at the sign. I was really getting impatient waiting for our turn, hunched down hoping I wouldn't faint or spew again, with Minja standing patiently by. At last it was our turn, I hurriedly and probably rather rudely gave the camera to someone else who was waiting for their moment to pose, just about held a grimacey smile for long enough and then started marching back down the path.

'You want go?' said Minja, catching me up.

'I have to,' I replied through gritted teeth. Getting dizzy again, I was determined to move as fast as possible.

The difference in altitude between Uhuru Peak and Gilman's Point is only 200 metres, but I swear by the time we got back there I was a new man. Within minutes of retracing our steps around the rim of the Kili crater, I started feeling better. It was as if every stride that brought me lower than the 5,900 metres of the peak absorbed some of the nausea, gave me a little more energy.

I was almost giddy when we reached Gilman's, and the view out over the mid slopes of the mountain was brilliant. Suddenly I remembered that somewhere down there was my wife, hopefully safely sleeping in a little wooden hut and no longer bleeding or boking. I quickened the pace and soon it was Minja who was struggling to keep up.

Cavorting down the loose scree was great. I took huge leaps, half sliding, half running, and the tortured progress of the climb up the same slope just hours before seemed like a different day. Gradually I was able to make out more of the features of the Kibo camp as we dropped further and further off the high slopes and closer to the mid plains.

My thighs burned a bit from holding back my weight on the steeper, solid sections, and of course from the six-hour climb to the summit, but I felt great apart from that, almost giddy with extra energy after such a long time feeling horrendous. I guessed this must be what it felt like to be properly acclimatised. After all, we were now at the same height that just 12 hours before caused me to vomit violently and nearly faint.

Muti came out to the bottom of the slope to meet us with a big smile and a high five. 'I knew you'd be the one to do it,' he said, and I felt genuinely proud. I smiled back. 'It wasn't easy, I felt really terrible. Thank God for Minja, he kept me going!' I clapped him on the back and he smiled bashfully.

'What about Claire?' I asked him.

'She is fine. I radioed down to the next camp and they got there and she felt much better. She is in a hut with some other girls. But we should go when you have had a rest.'

I told him I felt fine and would actually rather just get on down to join her. John came out of the hut looking unnecessarily sheepish. He still felt a bit rough and hadn't slept much, he said. But as soon as we started down the mountain across the plains, he also began to feel better. It was another epic hike, probably three hours or so at a good pace, and I reckoned by the time we got back to the Horombo Hut camp I'd been on the go more or less non-stop for 14 hours.

Claire bounced down the steps of one of the huts as we arrived. She was totally fine and chatting excitedly about her trip back down the mountain by torchlight. We shared our adventures, I met the girls in the hut who had looked after her when she arrived back in the dark, and we spent a nice few hours recovering. I fell fast asleep early that evening with my thighs twitching in the sleeping bag and didn't wake until the next morning, when we trekked all the way back to the mountain-park entrance.

Muti presented me with a summit certificate, and I learned they gave out two – a green one for those who made it all the way to Uhuru Peak, and a red one for those who got to Gilman's Point. That would never have done. I thanked Minja with a big hug. 'Pole, pole' was my parting shot. He nodded his head and smiled.

Five

RACE AROUND IRELAND

By any measure, that had been a big year. Three big adventure challenges, three stag parties, a wedding and then in November, a pregnancy. It had all happened rather quickly. (The progress from honeymoon to impending parenthood, I mean, not the act of conception itself ...) In her usual fashion, once Claire had set her mind to the idea of having a child, she approached it methodically and determinedly. It wasn't the most romantic time of my life but her mating by numbers technique sure was effective. In my naïvety I was determined that parenthood would not change our lives too much, and things that were important to us – like the pursuit of pointless but essential fitness challenges, say – need not suffer from the arrival of a new life.

So when I sat down the following January to think about what else I wanted to do that year, I was still focused on finding the next big test. I did make one allowance for the expected birth: the baby was due at the end of July, so I decided to pick an event that was to take place in Ireland, in the hope of reducing the time away from home and the hassle of getting there. What a mistake that was.

I'd heard about a new ultra-endurance cycle event starting that year, called the Race Around Ireland, which would act as a qualifier for the epic and infamous Race Across America. The RAI was 1,350 miles non-stop, either solo (as if) or as a four-man team. It started in Navan, just a few hours down the road from Belfast, and was in September, by which time I reasoned the baby would be at least six weeks old and I'd have had loads of practice at coping with no sleep. Perfect! I signed up.

Claire coped brilliantly with the pregnancy. Not sick at all, she was very tired at times and a bit fed up not being able to train or run around quite as much as she used to, but nothing like the pregzillas I'd read about. The only issue was that the baby was breech – turned round with its head up under mummy's ribs and its feet pointing down towards the escape hatch, as if it was ready to kick its way out. By the start of July, a month or so from the due date, this became more of an issue because it was likely to be too big to be able to get turned round again. We tried all manner of homeopathic new age nonsense to correct it, including a strange hour in a therapist's front room as she lit incense sticks and chanted all round us, but the baby was not for turning. This meant it had to come out through the sunroof, and a Caesarean section was booked. It's a major operation, amazingly performed only under local anaesthetic, and Claire had never spent as much as an evening in hospital before, but it had the advantage of giving us an exact slot for the birth: 23 July at 9.30am.

She was taken in to the hospital the night before, so I had a last night of contemplation on my own. Almost every single person we spoke to about impending parent-hood had whistled through their teeth, shook their head and told us our lives would change massively. I was deter-mined this would all be managed, that our proven fitness and determination would help us sail through, and that the baby would have to fit in round our busy schedules and not the other way round.

Determined to start as we meant to go on, I set the alarm for 6am so I could get up and do a couple of hours on the bike before heading into the hospital. Unsurprisingly, I found it hard to focus. I couldn't escape this mad, irra-tional thought that getting knocked down and killed that morning would mean I missed seeing my first-born by a matter of hours. I was wondering how to convey my impending dad-hood to all the other road users in the hope of making it less likely they'd run me down. Was there an 'Expectant father' sign like the 'Baby on board' ones? Would they go ahead with the Caesarean if I didn't turn up? Would they tell Claire before or after? Was there a morgue in the same hospital? Horrible thoughts, and I was relieved to get back.

I couldn't quite place this irrational anxiety. The baby wasn't even out yet and was already making an impact on my wellbeing. Was I going to turn into a paranoid parent, perpetually fearful for the safety of the family and myself? How would this affect my adventurous spirit? The end was nigh!

Apart from driving home from the hospital with Claire and baby Christian a few days later at no more than ten miles per hour, I didn't experience much of this again. I didn't have the time. I had imagined I'd enjoy some times of proud introspection, gazing lovingly over the cot and considering the circle of life, but the reality was a whirlwind of new tasks that removed completely the whole idea of 'spare' time and left me too exhausted to think about anything other than the next feed, nappy change or bottle wash.

Christian weighed in at an impressive nine and a half pounds and with an appetite to match. He needed very regular feeding, and if he didn't get it, he knew how to let us know. Parenthood is a full-time job, but there aren't many people these days who have the luxury of making it so. Balancing those early baby days with work would have been manageable and almost fun had it not been for the amount of time and energy I also had to find for sorting the Race Around Ireland, a commitment I now seriously regretted. Finding a team of cyclists good enough and stupid enough to cycle non-stop for nearly three days, and enough volunteers to drive support vehicles, navigate and babysit the four exhausted cyclists, was a hell of a challenge. Trying to pull together the massive logistics of that event was like having an extra job at a time when I really didn't need an extra job.

Trying to get through the training for the RAI was one thing, but organising the campervan, race van, communication system, support crew, route maps, food, etc. was something else. It was overwhelming in fact, and in a summer when time and energy were absolutely at a premium, this absorbed an inordinate amount. By hook or by crook I had eventually press-ganged enough people through various contacts to at least get a team and support crew to the race start in Navan. Our official entry identified us as 'Team No Prior Experience'.

I was kicking myself for taking on a team event when the whole point of my adventures up until now had been about simply challenging myself and taking all other reference points out. Now I'd managed to enter something that had already been more hassle than everything else put together. Success would be judged not just on my keeping going or giving my best, but on how I got on in relation to my team-mates and how we as a team got on in relation to the opposition.

I tried to remember why on earth I'd thought it a good idea. Believing the event would be less hassle just because it was in Ireland now seemed ridiculous, but that was the deciding factor. I had also thought that zipping about Ireland through the night on a bike with some mates would be good craic, and subconsciously maybe I was missing the general camaraderie of team sports. But the crucial difference between previous team experiences and this one was the fact that this time I was not just a team member, but also team captain, manager, sponsor and secretary. The actual cycling would probably be the easy bit.

The first selection I made for the cycling quartet was Simon, one of my oldest and best school friends. He had rowed for Ireland at schools level and for Great Britain as a postgraduate student at Oxford, but had recently converted from boat to bike. And in typical Simon fashion, he had leaped in with both feet, trading one absolute obsession for another. Like me, he had recently become a father for the first time, but he wasn't letting a trifling little life change like that hold back either his manic training or his work as a surgeon.

At that time he was without doubt a general over-achiever, combining great intelligence and natural talent with a ruthless, tunnelled focus. He had always been all or nothing in everything he did, so how he was combining huge commitments to sport, work and family I wasn't sure, but I suspected it was in descending order.

He had pulled in a university friend of his, Rob, who shared his cycling passion and had cycled across the Pyrenees earlier that summer. That made three of the four-man team. Another couple of choices turned me down, and by mid-August, with just a month to go to the start of the race, I was concerned. Christian was only three weeks old, I was very busy with both presenting and production work, but bizarrely, the commitment giving me the most stress was a fecken cycle race that I'd taken on entirely voluntarily. I turned in desperation to the race organisers, who suggested a guy from Meath who'd been in an Irish team that successfully completed the Race Across America the previous year. His name was Colm, and when I contacted him he was slightly cagey at first, as he thought we weren't taking it seriously enough.

He was wrong, but it wasn't until we all got together a few weeks later for some laboratory testing that I could prove it. There was a sports scientist from Dublin doing a study on ultra endurance and testing one of the teams throughout the whole race. We were offered the chance to have our pre-race performances tested in a controlled environment and, curious, I'd agreed to it as a means of getting our four cyclists together for the first time and to see if we were any good.

Simon's stratospheric performance especially was enough to convince Colm that we could be serious contenders. But the team would only be as good as the support crew, and recruiting *them* had been an even tougher job than getting the cyclists. I only finally completed the crew five days before the race start, and would be meeting half of them for the first time ever at the event itself …

*

So I was a little anxious as I drove to Dublin the night before in a hired van with John, the guy who had taken me out for my very first proper cycle ride when I fell off at the traffic lights in the middle of town. John hadn't seen me cycle since, so he couldn't have been expecting much over the next few days, but had gamely signed up for crew duties anyway.

We were staying in a hotel outside Dublin, near Colm's house, where Simon and Rob were sleeping on a spare mattress. Colm had decreed that everyone would need an early night, but I'd been delayed getting away, and it was nearly 11 o'clock by the time I got near the hotel. Near, but not near enough. We ran out of petrol on the dual carriageway. Colm was not amused to be getting out of bed and driving down to meet us with a petrol can, and he let me know it. My logistics having failed before the race even began, I am sure he had grave concerns about how things would pan out once we started. And he wasn't the only one.

The racing rules were quite straightforward. Teams had to follow the exact route laid out by the organisers; four racers had to be registered but only one had to finish; when 'handing over' from one rider to the next, wheels must overlap; and it was up to each team to decide on which racing combinations to try, there were no set times or set distances per rider. However, there were loads of regulations about crew cars, campervans, lights and riding at night and it became clear that I hadn't a clue how to go about this. The race was due to start at 8pm, just to throw the extra challenge of night cycling in from the off. So we had the whole day to sort ourselves out, which was just as well.

My original strategy had just been for the four cyclists to take it in turns to do two hours each, but Colm unpicked this pretty quickly and decided that we would operate in pairs, with each pair doing four-hour shifts and half-hour turns on the road within the four hours. So half an hour on the bike, half an hour off. While one pair travelled with the support van doing their half-hour cycle repeats, the other pair would be with the campervan, which would drive to a new rendezvous point for the end of each four-hour shift. The short cycling shifts would preserve energy, Colm said, but it meant that every transition had to be seriously smooth to avoid losing too much time.

The rest of the support crew arrived at various points throughout the day. Apart from my cycling pal, John, in our eclectic crew we also had a Jon from Cork, whom I'd never met but who had been recommended by a mutual friend; Ian, a happy-go-lucky friend of Colm's who had recently lost his job and must have been bored; Chris, an mixed martial arts promoter I'd worked with who used to be in the merchant navy and who declared himself a 'joiner-inner'; David, a mild-mannered 76-year-old who had recently lost his wife and nearly pulled out two days before the race started; Liam, an Irish League football manager and former motor mechanic who I knew had the boundless good humour to keep us all going; and Brooksy, a former university housemate of mine who had just retired injured from professional rugby and who had a Masters in sports nutrition. He was the cook. So a crew of seven, plus four cyclists, spread over a six-bunk campervan for sleeping, eating and travelling, and another van for carrying bikes and following the racer on the road.

There wasn't one person on the crew who knew more than one other person. It was a gamble from the start, and looking round at the team of strangers as we gathered together for the first time in a pub just outside Navan, I couldn't quite believe they'd all agreed to come.

I assigned a few roles, and Brooksy took himself off with my credit card to get supplies. He arrived back with enough food to comfortably feed a Roman legion and began to pile it onto the campervan, stuffing it into cupboards, drawers, under tables, anywhere. I was seriously worried the van wouldn't be able to move. John, Jon and Ian set to work on a proper logistics plan, poring over a map and breaking the 1,350 miles down into sections. Like the cyclists, the crew would split time in the campervan and the support van, except for David, whose main duty would just be to drive the camper.

The clock ticked ever closer to 7pm, when we had to be ready for inspection in Navan town centre. The race would start at eight, with teams rolling down the ramp at five-minute intervals. At half six we were still waiting for some food we'd ordered in the pub, a last proper meal before three days of Brooksy specials cooked on the move on a tiny gas hob.

Just as 11 portions of shepherd's pie arrived at our table, Ian burst in looking shocked.

'Shit, lads, the bikes have gone!'

We sat there looking at each other.

'I'm serious! They're gone!'

'What do you mean? They're out the back of the pub.'

'No, they aren't! Have they been nicked?!'

Jesus Christ. I couldn't believe it. We ran out behind him. No bikes. Recriminations. Splits in the crew already.

'Who was meant to be with them? Did someone just leave them here unattended? Ah, fuck's sake. What do we do now?'

Silence. It was horrible. All that work, all that planning, all that training ... Jon came walking round the corner swinging a supermarket bag. He stopped in his tracks, staring at our glum faces.

'What's up, lads? No dinner yet?'

'The bikes have been nicked.'

'No! Are you sure?'

'Well, they have gone. When we were inside.'

'But I locked them in the campervan before I went to the shop.'

'You did?'

'Yeah. Didn't you look there?'

I was over in seconds, looking through the window. There they were. Christ, what a relief. But what a shambles we were, Team No Prior Experience. When we eventually made our way into Navan my nerves were shot. The 11 other teams were all set, and the first rider off the ramp at 8pm on the dot was a guy called Padraig Marrey, the captain of a team from Connacht and a multiple Irish long-distance cycle record holder. We were to go off five minutes after him, and Colm was first for us. He and Rob would be one pair, and Simon and me another.

The plan was for us all to watch Colm start and then the support van would take Rob and two of the crew to follow him, and the campervan would take the rest of us on the main roads towards Belfast where we would do the first swap four hours later. Simon and I spread out along the road to cheer Colm on as he set off in pursuit of Marrey after a big countdown from the MC and the crowd. Everyone was really pumped up and Colm set off like a bat out of hell. Si and I roared him past and finally the race was on.

And then David roared past us in the campervan and disappeared up the road.

'Hey! Hey! Wait for us! Hey, David!'

We charged up the road after him, laughing nervously. What if he didn't stop?! When would we finally get our act together?! Thankfully someone in the camper eventually realised they'd forgotten half the team and they pulled in and waited while we sprinted up.

'Things can only get better, right?' I asked Brooksy with a smile. He knew me well enough to know that this sort of chaos was par for the course. 'Well, maybe not,' he replied. 'I can't get the cooker to work.'

I didn't want to know. I'd had just about as many frights and setbacks as I could cope with and the race was only ten minutes old. I wanted only good news from now on and settled down in a bunk to try and relax as much as possible before our shift. I was wired up and so was Simon. It would have been better to have gone off first, rather than have this hateful waiting period after such a mad rush of excitement and build-up. Starting a serious endurance challenge at midnight after a stressful few days wasn't ideal.

Simon was feeling it too; he'd been to the campervan toilet three times by the time we reached the agreed rendezvous point, and when the first update came through the race radio I thought he was going to combust. We were leading! Colm had got ahead of the great Marrey really early on and he and Rob had maintained the lead. We found out later that the Irish police, who'd been tasked to escort the first rider out of town, had guided Marrey down the wrong road. By the time they realised their mistake and turned onto the proper route, Colm was ahead.

My heart started thumping. Jesus, we were in front. I could be cycling into Belfast in the race lead with someone on my tail. This was epic! Time flew by and soon Simon was peeling on a skinsuit he'd bought on eBay, getting ready to go. He also had a pointed aero race helmet we were going to share, which made him look like a character from *Spaceballs*.

We waited nervously in the lay-by for the support van to arrive, with either Rob or Colm taking their final turn of the first shift. We were just off the main road to Belfast but still at least 15 miles from the city, and everything was quiet. It was a completely clear night, with hardly a breath of wind. Simon and I stretched and hopped about in silence as the clock ticked towards midnight and the four-hour change of shift. Brooksy had worked out how to use the oven and the smell of onions and garlic wafted out of the campervan. David had the radio on and we could hear the low buzz of some chat through the windscreen. I took a big breath and felt strangely proud. I'd at least got things this far. It was a moment.

An intermittent glow appeared in the road behind us, faint at first but becoming sharper. It was the lights of the support van. Less than a minute later we could make out all the details and Colm was advancing smoothly towards us, silhouetted by the headlights of the van, which had to be no more than 20 metres from the nominated rider at all times during the night.

All the bikes were travelling on a rack at the back of the van, and as soon as they pulled up Simon sprinted round to start yanking his free. Everyone piled out of both support van and campervan and there was an orgy of excitable shouting, ordering and tripping over each other. Our lead was about 15 minutes, which added to the general excitement and pandemonium, but Colm again was the voice of reason and experience as he told us how to achieve the smoothest possible changeovers.

His sage advice was entirely wasted on Simon, who was on his bike and away up the road before the van was properly in gear and everything was packed. John was on the radio and following the route map, Liam was driving, and I leaped into the back.

'He's flying,' said John, pointing at Simon, lit by our headlights. 'He looks fantastic but he's going to burn himself out.'

'You can try and tell him, if you like,' I replied. 'But I wouldn't waste your breath.'

We each had radios clipped to the top of our cycling tops so we could receive orders or advice from the car. John, or whoever was map-reading at the time, would tell us about forthcoming turns and junctions.

'Simon, take it easy, it's just the first shift, long way to go, mate, over,' said John through the radio.

There was no response and certainly no slowing down of the rhythmic motion from our skin-suited friend.

'Simon, if you can hear me, just nod. Just checking the communications, over.'

The pointed helmet bobbed up and down.

'OK, there's a right turn coming up in the next few hundred metres, you need to take it. Going off this road and onto a back road over some small hills. Coming up shortly, when you get to that sign up ahead, turn right. OK, there it is, turn right. Simon … Simon!'

He flew straight past it, his speed apparent from the length of time it took him to stop and the heavy braking line as he slid up the road, both legs dangling as he frantically clipped out of the pedals. We had to follow him and hope there was nobody coming the other way, and as we drew up alongside he apologised as he clipped back in and took off again. I could see the whites of his eyes – they were out as if on stalks, he was so pumped up. My heart was hammering again. I'd be on soon and I'd better keep this up. No way I wanted to be the dickhead who lost the lead.

All too quickly Simon's half-hour was up and we pulled over on the ring road in Belfast. Simon had spit all over one cheek, his skin was shining with perspiration, his chest was heaving. He was a man possessed.

'Go for it, go for it, just hammer it,' he said, 'it's only half an hour.'

I didn't need a second invitation. I knew I couldn't possibly match his speed or rhythm on the bike, but I was damned if I was going to get caught from behind going through my home city. I forgot everything John had said about pacing and flew down into the city, past bars and chip shops spilling the detritus of student Freshers' Week onto the footpaths. They whooped and hollered as I blasted past and the lads tooted in the van behind. My heart was smashing in my chest. I had been handed the lead and I felt the pressure. No way was I losing it on my first shift.

'Good stuff, Graham, keep the focus,' said John. It was weird to be hurtling up the road, the wind blasting in my face and ears, and then hear a clear voice speak from within my top.

'Turning left up here.'

It was a complicated junction, but one that I drove past every day on my way home and should have recced properly had the previous two months not been the most hectic of my life. I hadn't cycled a single section of the course, even though it twice passed within a mile of my house, which I really regretted now. This was a back road up Cave Hill, very steep, but I tore into it, and a minute later Simon was hanging out of one of the windows roaring me on, his voice echoing round the silent streets.

My half-hour was up in a flash, and Simon and I exchanged high fives and hugged as he headed off. I threw myself into the back of the van.

'Well done, son, first class – great effort, mate, well done. Get a drink,' said Liam, in his strong north Antrim accent. He positively sings when he speaks and I could imagine what it felt like to be one of his footballers. He has the knack of inspiring people. I felt amazing, more awake than I'd been at any stage since Christian was born, really alive inside, buzzing. And it was one o' clock in the morning.

Our four-hour shift finished at a big car park near the Giant's Causeway. The news came over the race radio that our lead was now out to more than 25 minutes. Simon and I were ecstatic.

'Good job, mate,' he said as we shook hands after seeing Rob and Colm on their way. They seemed in great spirits too, and once we got back into the campervan we knew why. Brooksy had recovery drinks and huge hot bowls of pasta waiting for us on the little table, and stewed apple and raisins on the hob for afters. I couldn't believe it.

We ate happily, munching and chatting at a hundred miles an hour, high on both relief that we hadn't lost the lead, and exhilaration that we'd actually increased it. Ian had set his watch when we arrived, and when we pulled out half an hour later the Connacht team still hadn't arrived, so actually the lead was *more* than 25 minutes. We changed quickly from cycling gear to recovery tights and tried to lie down and rest. But we were both buzzing, so sleep was impossible. And it would be, for the next two and a half days.

It's amazing how little we actually know about ourselves, the things we think are facts, until some experience proves them otherwise. Before fatherhood, and before the Race Around Ireland, I thought I knew roughly how much sleep I required to be a fully functioning human. I'd have said it was almost impossible for me to go much more than a day and a half without sleeping at all. But I don't think I slept between Wednesday morning and late on Saturday night. I must have dozed for ten minutes or so here and there, but that was it. I still can't quite believe that now, but it happened.

And speaking of how little we actually know, how had I cycled for several years without knowing that you're not supposed to wear pants under your shorts? On the second day I was considering washing a pair and trying to find somewhere for them to dry, when Colm asked me why I was wearing them in the first place, scornfully describing that as 'a bit of a newbie mistake'. It certainly felt better without them.

The four-hour shift cycles worked a treat, and for the whole of that first full 24 hours we were always more than half an hour ahead of the chasing Connacht team. The organisers had picked the most sadistic route imaginable, steering a course for every mountain range in Ireland, and without Brooksy's titanic hot meals we'd never have recovered.

It was both incredible and heart-warming to see how quickly a team of random strangers could pull together and form a slick, supportive unit, and also incredible, but not heart-warming, to see how quickly we could all go mildly savage. By the morning after our first night the toilet was out of action. It had spilled out over the floor of the tiny cubicle that served as a bathroom. Not pleasant. So everything had to be done outside. Everything. And it never cost me a thought. There was a race to win.

Our changeovers were soon running almost like clockwork and I couldn't believe how well everything was coming together. I had never ever imagined we could actually win this thing, but if we kept this up we could. But the threat of something going wrong, of the vehicles or our bodies breaking down, hung over us all the time. We were maintaining our lead, each race update reported either a small gain or a small loss, but we were only ever a navigational or mechanical error away from losing it. So there was this constant pressure, and by Friday evening, over 40 hours after the race start, the strain really started to show.

Simon and I were on shift when we got down to Mizen Head. I'd never been at the very southern-most point of Ireland before, so it was cool to cycle right down to the tip, especially since only 36 hours before, Colm and Rob had been to Malin Head, the most northerly point. There was only one road down to and back from Mizen, and heading away again we got a terrible shock. We saw the Connacht team coming the other way, much closer than we'd been led to believe at the last time check. We'd been told they were about 40 minutes behind us, and even that they'd had a puncture in their support car, but this now looked like less than 20 and there was no way they had closed the gap in that time and also stopped to change a car tyre. It meant we'd been getting duff information and someone was out to get us, or else the Connacht boys had found their form again. Either way, it wasn't good.

I panicked. I had been struggling a bit with the rolling roads to and from Mizen and now I just felt sick. They were closing rapidly. They must have saved loads of energy until now. Maybe they'd taken a short cut? I tried to shake the fuzz from my head and some energy into my legs. We were still in front, I only had to finish this half-hour and then do one more before we handed over to Colm and Rob again, so I would just bury myself now and hope the other lads did the same to see if we could pull away again.

Having come this far, being so close actually to winning something – not what I'd ever expected from any of these challenges – there was no way I could face losing it now. Grinding away on the pedals I began chanting to myself.

'Nobody's taking this off me. Nobody's taking this off me. Nobody's taking this off me. Nobody's taking this off me …'

I'd been in some pretty dark places in the cause of physical challenge, but this was different. There was an enemy in this one. A competition. Massive pressure. This wasn't just me versus myself, this was a proper race, and the success of other people depended on me sticking with it, pulling more out of myself to pull us further ahead.

Dark places bring dark thoughts. I began exploring what I'd do to win this. I came up with the unlikely scenario of Lance Armstrong arriving at the race with his full chemical war chest. With a shock I admitted to myself I would strongly consider taking whatever was on offer. I am still disgusted by this, but that was the point I was at. If adversity reveals character, I'm not sure what this says about me and it's not nice to dwell on it, even years later.

I had never previously thought of myself as a 'win at all costs' guy, but with a return to team sport had come a return to old motivations, and success in this particular challenge would now only come from a demonstration of superiority over someone else, namely the Connacht team. Everything had changed.

It was dusk when we handed over to Colm and Rob. According to the most recent official reports and some intelligence Colm picked up from another, unrevealed source, the gap was back to about half an hour, but the Connacht team had lodged an official but totally specious complaint about us not sticking to the route. That really annoyed me, since the crew had been absolutely meticulous in following the route, and the couple of times when they did make a mistake and we'd found ourselves on the wrong road, it had actually cost us time doubling back.

'They're just getting desperate,' said Colm. 'They're making one last big effort to try and catch up, and unsettling us is probably part of their plan. We're fine, don't worry about it.'

Well, if that was their aim, it had worked in my case. I had emptied myself on each of the last two half-hours, and was now wrecked. Exhaustion enveloped me and I could barely bring myself to eat, which was a real shame because chef Brooks had somehow rustled up a salmon risotto. I forced in as much as I could, along with big spoonfuls of the stewed apple and raisins, but every mouthful was an effort to chew and swallow, and both Simon and I sat slumped over our bowls.

Much of the jauntiness and manic energy of the first two days was long gone; there wasn't much chat from anyone by now. The crew were all getting by on the same pitiful snatches of sleep as we were, of course, and the effort of concentrating on map-reading, driving and cooking had left them all exhausted. But an incredible sense of camaraderie had built up in just three days among a team of men who didn't know each other, and by now each and every one of us was focused solely on winning.

But mistakes were going to happen as the effort and lack of sleep took their toll. I was lying in the bunk trying to ignore the snatched bits of conversation I was hearing from the driver and passenger seat in the campervan until I could ignore it no more. Brooksy and Chris were poring over a map with a torch, checking something off against the route notes. There was a whole lot of head shaking and chin scratching going on.

We were lost. I was angry. We were supposed to be meeting the support van to swap with Rob and Simon again somewhere just outside Cobh, and a small loop around that area seemed to have totally confused the lads.

'We should have been through Cobh by now is the issue,' said Chris.

'About 20 miles ago probably,' agreed Brooksy. 'We must be on the wrong road.'

'But we *were* in Cobh! I remember it,' I said exasperatedly. 'I got out of the van and took a piss in the harbour, don't you remember?'

'That was Cobh?'

'Yes! Where the hell did you think it was? Big harbour, big town with big signs everywhere saying "Welcome to Cobh"!'

'We thought Cobh was meant to be just a small village,' said Brooksy defensively.

I looked from one to the other, trying to quell the rising panic within. If they had stopped in a historic big town like that without noticing what town it was, we were in trouble. It couldn't be long now until Simon and I were due to take over cycling again, so this needed to be sorted.

'Can't you just find some road signs and go back into Cobh and get back on the right road?' I asked.

'Look, we'll sort it, don't worry, you need to go and try to get some sleep.' Chris was one quarter suggesting, three-quarters telling. I stood for another few moments trying to look grim to underline how serious this was, and then climbed back into my bunk.

Minutes later they'd made a decision and got David to restart the engine and drive off. There was an almighty crash. He had driven straight into a large overhanging branch and ripped the whole window out of the passenger side of the campervan. Suddenly everyone was up and fully awake. That had blown the tiredness away both metaphorically and literally, as a cold breeze now swept into the van. Poor David was so embarrassed he was almost in tears. We set about clearing all the glass from the seat and laughed it off.

Chris and Brooksy finally found the route and the rendezvous point and we swapped roles with Colm and Rob. They looked both elated and exhausted, and Liam told me they had put in a huge effort to try and increase our lead again and break the spirit of the Connacht team. They were all glad to see the camper, if not the missing window, and we did a full crew swap.

It was another incredibly still and silent night, and cold too until I was well into my half an hour and had built up

115

enough body heat. Everything was mechanical at this stage and I felt like I was robotically spinning my legs in a half-dream. My body was on the bike but my mind had drifted off somewhere else. John spoke through the radio a few times to advise me to change gear as I was spinning easily but not going anywhere. I wondered whether it was possible to fall asleep on a bike.

Suddenly a huge rat ran across the road ahead of me. A brute. I have a weird phobia of mice and rats. The mere idea of them makes my heart leap and the blood slam in my head. This was a timely jolt. What a burst of energy is adrenaline! I shuddered, was wide awake again and back up to speed in seconds.

'Jesus, did you see that?' laughed John. I nodded and looked round to the van behind with a big grin. 'That must have woken you up!' I nodded again and pushed on, rejuvenated.

Some of the toughest sections of the whole route were coming up, tiny back roads, often little more than farm lanes, narrow and uneven, and very steep. The darkness added to the challenge but also added more adrenaline as night creatures poked their heads out of hedges, startled sheep scattered across the road. We swapped over and Simon absolutely flew up the thin tracks, high up into the hills. John told us these were the very roads that had forged the iron legs and will of the great Sean Kelly, former world number one cyclist and an Irish sporting legend.

'Aye, but I doubt he ever rode up them at two in the morning,' I responded.

'You wouldn't know,' said John. 'He was a savage on the bike.'

But surely no more savage than Simon. What an effort! He disappeared into the clouds and the van really groaned and whined trying to keep a steady speed behind him as we hit the steepest sections of the climb. This was a standout moment for me, one of those snapshot parts of a great adventure that I'll always remember. We were all gunning for him up that hill, willing him on and shouting across the radio. For some reason this felt like a watershed. We knew that if we got up and down this section without a major issue, we'd be well in front and odds on to win the following day.

Finally he stopped, and we were at the crest of a hill. He was utterly spent, and I hopped out to take over. We hugged and I could feel his chest heaving with the effort. It took quite a while for my eyes to adjust to the half-light, the cloud was thick as I began to descend the narrow track and I almost overshot a number of hairpin corners. There was no grip on the uneven surface, and John warned me several times to go easy. An accident up here would be very costly. A puncture was inevitable, and sure enough I heard a pop and felt the bike shudder beneath me. I heaved on the brakes and managed to control it while unclipping my feet and hanging my legs out to show the boys something was wrong. John leaped out and fitted a spare wheel in seconds.

It was a tough four hours and I was counting down the minutes before seeing the campervan again. We were back on the main roads and I came round the corner and there it was in a lay-by. But something was wrong. The camper was in darkness, there was nobody outside it, the door was closed, there was no sign of Colm or Rob. We pulled up to make sure it was the right van, but there was no mistaking the missing window. I had no option but to keep cycling. We left Simon banging on the door and I headed off up the road cursing and shouting. What was going on?! Where were they?

Inside the camper, Liam was the first to wake. He later told me that in a sleepy daze he'd opened the door to an irate Simon in his light blue skinsuit, and thought he was looking at Bananaman. They'd got to the meeting point early, lain down for an hour and all passed out until Bananaman began thumping on the door.

The last day dawned with us comfortably in front. We were now heading for Wicklow and still had to drag ourselves up and over the Wicklow Mountains, but it looked like we'd finish some time later that Saturday afternoon, and hopefully at least 40 minutes ahead of the next team. Colm had trained a lot in those mountains, and decided we needed a slightly different approach to get through. So for a couple of hours all four of us took short turns on the bike, with changeovers down to about every 10 or 15 minutes, or whenever we could go no further.

The scenery was stunning, we were closing in on Navan and on victory, but everyone was close to being totally spent. We had another set of hills to negotiate south of Dublin and then we'd be on the home straight. We were back to the routine shifts by now and Simon and I were about to take over again just before the last hills.

He was asleep, sitting slumped over the table, head resting on his folded arms. I shook him awake. His eyes rolled in his head and he looked confused, as if he didn't know where he was.

'Come on, mate, last set, let's go,' I said, trying to pump him with enthusiasm. But I was slurring, and felt dizzy. Everything felt a bit hazy. Together we pawed at our kit like drunks being woken from a sleep in a bar, and half stumbled down the campervan steps and onto the road. The van was pulled over beneath some overhanging ancient oak trees. This was a beautiful part of Ireland, near Powerscourt, but very hilly and the last big challenge before some flat sections into Navan.

The fresh air roused me a bit, but Simon just stood there, leaning against the side of the van. Right then he was a hollow man, present physically but not mentally. His eyes were sunken in his head, devoid of all spark, as if someone had dimmed the lights, and he was mumbling, 'Shoes, shoes, shoes.' I looked down and saw that he was still in his socks.

'Can you put on my shoes?' he asked, confused.

Somebody fetched them from the van and dutifully I went to bend down and put them on. I toppled over slightly, just about getting my hands out before my head hit the road. We were a mess. Chris bounced out of the van with a couple of cans of Red Bull and forced us to neck them before Colm came riding into view. Amazingly, he still looked fresh. Rob heaved himself out of the support van and smiled. They'd been told our lead was over 50 minutes now; the Connacht team seemed to have abandoned the chase. Our tactics in the Wicklow Mountains had worked.

'You guys OK?' asked Colm, suspiciously.

'Yip, sure,' I said, swinging my leg over the bike. 'Let's get this finished.'

'Want me to ride in the support van? I feel totally fine …'

'We'll be OK,' I said through gritted teeth, slightly offended by the implication. I set off, and he got into the van beside Simon anyway.

I was pedalling, I knew I was pedalling, but I didn't seem to be going anywhere. I felt as if I was on a treadmill. The road didn't look steep, but the hedges and edges seemed blurred so it was hard to tell. Why wasn't I moving? Was I moving?

John came through on the radio. 'We're going to do 20-minute pulls just to get through this hilly section, OK?' I nodded. 'So just another couple of minutes and we'll swap.' I didn't argue. I felt really weird. Overwhelmed with exhaustion, I was having this strange out-of-body experience, my head was in the clouds, as if I was drunk. Was I moving at all?

John told me to pull over at the next junction. Simon stumbled out and John helped him onto his bike. He pushed him off but he couldn't clip into his pedals. Now Colm jumped out and wouldn't take no for an answer. He gently pushed Simon aside and pedalled off. It was the right call and there was barely a protest from Simon as we bundled him back into the van. He had given everything.

I reasoned that Colm taking an extra turn was only fair after he'd made me ride for longer the night before while he slept in the van, and said so as we changed over 20 minutes later.

'No wonder you're so fresh!' I laughed. 'You slept half the night.' I was feeling better as the Red Bull kicked in and the road levelled out. We came out of the hills, Simon did the next turn, and we were headed for the finish. I couldn't understand the peaks and troughs of my performance. How I could be confused and exhausted one moment and then revived the next: weak as water and then strong as a bull. It had been that way the whole race, and now, after four days with no sleep, had Red Bull suddenly given me wings or was my body making another big self-adjustment to get us to Navan? Where did the energy come from?

Mum and Dad arrived from nowhere in their car and followed us in, tooting the horn. I was absolutely elated by this point, really going hard. I felt like I could ride forever and I cycled along looking over my shoulder at my parents, grinning and punching the air. I pulled in at the entrance to an industrial estate where both support van and campervan were waiting, and all four riders changed into the same Race Around Ireland official kit. Colm wanted us all to ride into town and over the finish line together.

What a moment it was. What an unlikely victory. We finished on Saturday afternoon, in a time of 2 days, 19 hours and 27 minutes, over an hour ahead of the Connacht team in second. I was so proud of us all. Claire was there with baby Christian and I was almost afraid to lift him in case I passed out. My hands were shaking, my vision was still a bit hazy and everything just felt dream-like. The race organiser made a speech and presented us with our trophies, and then I responded with a speech of my own, probably delivered at bewildering speed as my mind was racing.

We all congratulated each other, took swigs from a champagne bottle and posed for photos. Simon disappeared and passed out in the camper, Liam had to go to catch a train home, Brooksy hitched a lift to the airport and the rest of us couldn't really put off the clean-up operation or the wind-down logistics any longer. I was afraid the manic energy might run out any minute, so we set to it, sweeping, wiping and peeling the detritus of three days' sport into bin bags. Someone bravely took on the task of sorting the toilet, which left just the broken window as irreparable. Not a bad return for victory, I felt.

Anyone still awake headed for a celebratory dinner that night. Simon hadn't moved for hours, so after checking his vital signs we left him sleeping in the van. The next morning Colm dropped him down to the port to catch the ferry back to Holyhead. Unfortunately the zombie then fell asleep in the toilets of the terminal and was woken by a cleaner after the ferry had left. He had to wait four hours for the next one, arrived home in the early hours of the following morning, and missed work the next day.

I didn't have that luxury. After negotiating the cost of the damage to the broken camper van window I drove back to Belfast on Sunday afternoon and had to start preparing for a live football match I was presenting on Sky that Monday evening. It took all I had not to fall asleep live on air. The producer asked me why I was so tired. Now that it was over, I couldn't even find the energy to describe it. The Race Around Ireland was something else. Coming through three days of that, not to mention the build-up before it ... I felt like I'd reached somewhere new. A different plain. I felt like there was nothing I couldn't at least consider.

Six

FRONT CRAWL TO ASIA

For years, Claire's sports-mad family have spent each Christmas and New Year at a resort called Club La Santa in Lanzarote. It's a sports and activity resort, like a Butlin's for fitness fanatics, and since I was now part of the family I got to join them. The resort has top of the range bikes for hire so I packed my gear and proudly wore my Race Around Ireland cycle top on the first day during a spin round the island. My German brother-in-law, Philip, read the race overview on the back of my top and in typically Teutonic fashion queried the organiser's claim that the Race Around Ireland is 'Europe's Toughest Endurance Cycle Event'.

'How could it be Europe's toughest endurance cycle race?' he asked. 'What about the Tour de France?'

'Well, they're very different events,' I began. 'The Race Around Ireland is non-stop for a start. In the Tour de France they race in stages, resting every night. And they're professionals.'

'But yours was a relay, so you had rest too?'

'Well, a little bit, yes, but no sleep for nearly four days,' I bleated, almost pleadingly.

Philip wasn't being deliberately antagonistic, just applying the kind of clinical analysis he used in his day job as a financial wunderkind, but in the process he was casually stripping away the mystique and wonder I had allowed to build around the epic that was the RAI.

'Do you think you could do a Tour de France?' he continued, 'if you can do a Race Around Ireland?'

'Well, ahem ... those guys are at a bit of a different level!'

'But I mean could you do the course, not necessarily at the same speed as the professionals?'

'Well, funnily enough ... there is a day when amateurs can ride the toughest stage of each Tour de France every year, with closed roads, feed stops and everything, and ... maybe ...' I tailed off as Claire had arrived beside us. I didn't want to spoil her holiday by announcing another big challenge, so quickly changed the subject.

I had already read about the following year's 'Étape du Tour', one of the biggest annual 'sportives' in the world, and it just so happened that as a result of their sponsorship of British Cycling, Sky were organising a big trip for employees and contractors the following July. Philip's unwitting intervention sealed it. As soon as I was next in London after our holiday, I booked.

But the Étape was nearly seven months away so there would have been nearly a year between that and the Race Around Ireland. I had itchy feet. I've never been a good long-term planner, I'm much too impatient, and something seven months away didn't scare me enough to force me out on the bike in all weathers. I like goals that are fairly immediate and I'd worked out by now that about three or four months of training for the one event was plenty; any more than that and I started to get a bit bored and also ran the risk of getting fatigued with over-training.

If I could find the right events at the right time, I could aim for about three 'Man Tests' a year, one in late spring, one in mid-summer and one in the autumn. It would be our first full year as parents, and it was important to me that I continued to have the odd adventure and didn't succumb to the sense of put-upon resignation I'd seen all too often in other family guys. But there was no doubt that having a child squeezed everything. Time, energy and sleep were all in much shorter supply, so if I was going to add to the pressure with a few perfectly pointless physical adventures, they had better be worth it.

Capitalising as usual on our collective January self-improvement urges, one of the Sunday papers ran a list of the ten most inspiring physical challenges to take on that year. I read it one gloomy afternoon when Claire was out and it was too wet to take Christian anywhere. If ever there was a moment for escapism that was it. I actually felt my eyes widen when reading about something called the Hellespont Swim, which crossed from Europe to Asia. You could really *swim* from one continent to another?! Oh the romance!

The Hellespont, now more commonly called the Dardanelles Strait, is a thin strip of water linking the Aegean Sea to the Sea of Marmara, or – when you add in the Bosphorus in Istanbul – the Mediterranean to the Black Sea. That strip of water divides European Turkey from Asian Turkey; it splits the long finger of the Gallipoli peninsula from the rest of the country and was the scene of infamous carnage in the First World War. Going back further, this was the home of Troy; it hosted the Trojan War and the famous wooden horse; it witnessed invasions by Alexander the Great; it is a region rich in history and famed in Greek mythology. The mad, romantic notion of swimming across the strait instantly grabbed me. And, at a distance of four or five kilometres, it was definitely achievable.

According to one of the Greek myths, Leander swam nightly across the Hellespont to be with his beloved Hero, a priestess of Aphrodite. She lit a lamp in a tower each night to guide him over, but one evening a storm blew the lamp out. Leander lost his way and was drowned. On hearing the news, Hero threw herself out of the tower to join him in death. A charming tale, and one that inspired the absurdly romantic poet, Lord Byron, to take on the role of Leander and complete the swim in a bid for glory on 3 May 1810. Byron's clubfoot limited his opportunities to impress anyone with his athletic prowess, but he was a strong swimmer and he survived to write about the experience later in a poem imaginatively entitled 'Written after Swimming from Sestos to Abydos', comparing his crossing with that of Leander.

> For me, degenerate modern wretch,
> Though in the genial month of May,
> My dripping limbs I faintly stretch,
> And think I have done a feat today …
>
> 'Twere hard to say who fared the best;
> Sad mortals thus the gods still plague you!
> He lost his labour, I my jest;
> For he was drowned, and I have the ague.

It took two attempts, but he later claimed in his journal to have done it 'with little difficulty'. He was more than a little proud of himself, saying: 'I plume myself on this achievement more than I could possibly do on any kind of glory, political, poetical, or rhetorical.'

This year was the 200th anniversary of Byron's swim, and although they normally now hold a mass crossing attempt every August, there was to be an extra event to mark the poet's achievement on the very day he managed it, the third of May. The timing was perfect for me; I'd be able to train for that challenge at the start of the year, and then for the Étape du Tour, which took place in July.

I checked the calendar. Ah. My cousin was marrying one of my best friends in Belfast the first weekend of May. Shit. I had introduced them, was down to be an usher, and missing such a momentous family occasion having played so major a part in its beginning was unacceptable. But the 200th anniversary of the Byron swim? That seemed just too good to pass up …

The wedding was on Saturday in Belfast, the swim was on Monday in Çanakkale. I pored over an atlas. There must be a way. Swimming the Hellespont had it all: history, identity, natural environment, romance, danger, and a proper hard, physical challenge. I *really* wanted to be there. Of course I could always do it another year, but I couldn't wait. Much of Byron's writing and identity is associated with impractical, absurdly romantic adventures, and putting myself at the centre of an event commemorating what he regarded as his greatest achievement suddenly became really important to me. I tried to accept that it wasn't possible, but I couldn't. It felt like a failure not to try, as if I was accepting that I was now constrained by family and other practical responsibilities, and chasing adventurous dreams round the world was no longer an option.

I did try to force myself to accept that the weekend would be spent drunk and then hung over, and I'd be back at work on Monday instead of floating between Europe and Asia. But I also looked at flights into Istanbul, flights into Bulgaria, charter flights to İzmir. I checked out hire cars in Plovdiv, ferries in Alexandroupoli. I reluctantly concluded there was no way for me to get there except to fly from Dublin to Istanbul via Paris at 6am on Sunday. So basically to go straight to the swim from the wedding, which would be as raucous an affair as you'd expect from a Scots-Irish matrimony and far from ideal preparation for a 20-hour journey followed by 2-hour intercontinental swim. But fleeing a party and embarking on a mad dash across the continent was entirely in the spirit of the thing. I liked to think it was exactly what Byron would have done, though he would probably also have eloped with the bride. Especially if she was his cousin.

The die was cast, but I then had to break it to bride and groom that I wouldn't be honouring their union with my usual total social immersion. In Ireland a skinful of drink is one of the ways in which you pay your respects to the married couple; especially if your prior friendship with the groom has been based largely on ferociously competitive bouts of drinking. So there are usually two types of people at a party – those pretending to be *less* drunk than they really are, and those pretending to be *more* drunk than they really are. Neither group fools the other, and being visibly pregnant is about the only acceptable excuse.

I felt a weird mix of guilt and defiance telling them I had to drive to the airport in the early hours and would not therefore be joining them at the hotel bar at midnight. Guilt because I knew they could interpret this as somehow selfish or disrespectful, and defiant because since becoming a father I was probably even more protective of my right to the odd adventure, and I was doing my absolute best to fit in both duty and diversions.

I spent the evening of the wedding being harangued by friends and family for my shameful sobriety and felt distinctly unpopular. Clearly I was not visibly pregnant, but that would have been more believable than the fact that I was going straight from the wedding to swim from Europe to Asia. That was off the chart in terms of inventive excuses. In the early hours of Sunday morning, I slipped out of the wedding chaos, folded my inebriated wife into the car, and drove home. Half an hour later I was showered, packed and on the way to Dublin Airport. I squirted cold water in my face at intervals down the motorway to keep me awake, and then slept for a rejuvenating 40 minutes on the ground in the terminal. Two connecting flights, some brief naps and a whole day later I arrived in Istanbul as the evening sun hung low over the city. And there the loose threads of what could not even optimistically be called 'the plan' began to unravel.

The swim was organised for UK people as a package tour by a company called SwimTrek. Everyone else had arrived together on Saturday as a nice manageable tour group and had even been for a practice swim that afternoon. None of them was at a cousin's wedding in Ireland on Saturday night, and none of them arrived in Istanbul on Sunday afternoon with a vague notion of getting a local bus to Çanakkale, six hours away down the Gallipoli peninsula.

SwimTrek had insisted this should be straightforward. It wasn't. Every bus heading along the peninsula was full of locals, all getting away for the public holiday. There wasn't a single spare seat. Nor were there any tour operators, nor any SwimTrek people answering their phones. In 15 hours' time I was supposed to be in the water, and I was still six hours away from the start point, with no transport prospects and having not been to bed for 36 hours. I was beginning to look like a Byronic hero before even getting to the Hellespont.

There are many positions that the adventure tourist should endeavour to avoid. One of these, wherever you are in the world, is being totally at the mercy of local taxi drivers. In the unlikely event you find yourself in Istanbul bus terminus in need of a taxi to Çanakkale, know that the starting price for negotiation is £300, and £200 is the lowest any driver in the area will go. It was one of those moments to be mindful of the difference between cost and value. Having come that far, I would have paid double to complete the journey and get a crack at the swim.

That said, being far too tight to accept any of the first ten offers, my price research took an hour. Once we were finally underway in an alarmingly creaking car of indeterminate origin, the appointed driver scared the shite out of me by pulling into an estate of high-rise flats on the outskirts of the city to pick up a rough-looking companion.

The rough-looking companion was clearly an accomplice – digging a grave was too big a task for one. At this point my options were to either leap from the car and run blindly through the high-rise flats, or sit politely where I was and send a series of potentially final texts to friends and family informing them of the current situation. At least then future TV documentaries charting my disappearance would have something around which to build narrative and conjecture.

After an unsatisfactory pre-swim carb-loading meal of Nutri-Grain bars and oat crackers, I tried to stretch out a bit in the back seat and sleep, while also looking out anxiously for road signs. There was a coastline at least, which was reassuring. I tried to block out the nagging suspicion that we were at the wrong side of it. Eventually, five hours after leaving Istanbul and nearly 24 hours after leaving Belfast, the taxi stopped at what looked like a deserted ferry terminal.

I was now certain that I was at the wrong side of the peninsula. I found a map on an information board. It looked like it had been drawn by either Andy Warhol or the winner of a primary school colouring competition, but Çanakkale was marked clearly enough ... on the opposite side of the water from where we were.

After a full five minutes of increasingly wild gesticulations and the full gamut of facial expressions, the taxi driver and his friend had managed to inform me that a ferry was imminent and I should pay them and get on the boat to complete the journey. *Not* paying them was the only ace I had left, a message I tried to convey by another round of gesticulating and facial contortion.

Eventually, a large moving constellation of lights came close enough to be indeed identified as a ferry. As the terminal began to show some signs of activity and there was now a chance I was after all going to make it to Çanakkale, I headed for a cash machine. The driver enlisted one of the terminal staff to join in the charades, and with a flourish he produced the ferry timetable. Whether by accident or by design I'll never know, but we had arrived 20 minutes before the last sailing of the night to Çanakkale. I embraced both driver and companion and made the action of a swimmer, while shouting 'Tomorrow, tomorrow' and pointing towards the sea. They shook their heads solemnly and pointed towards the ferry.

Including me, there were three passengers on a ferry with a capacity of 300, and I was fairly certain I was the only one that would be repeating the journey across the following morning without the boat. I stood at the bow, as far forward as I dared, and watched the lights of Çanakkale come closer. There was hardly a breath of wind, but the air had a spring bite. It was a clear night and the stars were bright as I fondly imagined myself the hero in my own epic film scene, triumphantly crossing the Hellespont at last and about to enter some historic city on the eve of battle after overcoming the hazards of the long journey. I was silhouetted against the dark outline of the coast, accompanied, in my head, by an orchestral soundtrack from James Horner. Getting off the ferry with no idea where my hotel was, the soundtrack changed to Benny Hill's 'Yakety Sax'.

I found the swim briefing next morning and was finally in the warm embrace of the SwimTrek organised tour. They had persuaded a real-life descendent of Byron to try and repeat the feat two centuries later, so The Honourable Charles Byron was in town and I sat beside him at the briefing. He was just 20, strikingly similar to his illustrious ancestor, with wavy dark hair, pale skin and blue eyes. One day he will be Lord Byron, and given that he claimed to have come straight to Turkey from a nightclub and done very little swim training, he appeared to be a chip off the 200-year-old block.

An hour later we were all filing on to a ferry which would take us across to the terminal I'd arrived at the night before. The strait looked wide, deep and choppy in the unforgiving glare of morning light. I bought a dreadful coffee served in a shot glass and tried to take it all in. The Gallipoli peninsula, the Hellespont, the Dardanelles, two continents split by a narrow stretch of sea. Leander, Byron, me. Me. Swimming between two continents. That morning.

The ferry crossing took a good half an hour, a fact not lost on those who would shortly be returning under their own steam. They then bussed us further up the coast and pulled up at a rocky beach, where we tugged on our wetsuits and began our individual preparations. There was a frisson of nervous energy. Excited chatter and black humour. An Australian in his late fifties had written 'Asia or Bust' across his chest. He told me he'd recently had a heart operation, so the 'bust' was quite likely. He didn't know what he was doing there, hadn't thought much about it until that very moment. This was not the time.

I took a long, deep breath and closed my eyes. I had made the start line. I was happy. The rest would be easy. Suffering is gloriously uncomplicated and requires neither thought nor planning. It is liberating, and provided you have done the training, the body can cope better than most of us will ever know.

The briefing had been comprehensive, but as usual I hadn't taken it all in. We were basically to zigzag our way across in an attempt to avoid the currents that would take us all the way to Istanbul if we got it wrong. Large buoys and several boats were marking the course. Unfortunately, a late change enforced by the local authorities, none too happy about shutting down one of the busiest shipping lanes in the world for a few hours, meant we were already further down the coast than originally planned.

Details, mere details. I just wanted to get going. I could do it. I was suddenly confident and relaxed. Another deep breath with my eyes closed as I centred myself in the challenge. An air horn blasted and we charged in. Some screeched at the first bite of the cold water. We were soon a great human soup of thrashing arms and legs and coloured hats swimming beside, beneath and on top of each other. Slowly this dispersed as we moved further out into the strait and became more of a thin line than a shoal.

Waves disrupted my rhythm and swamped seawater down my throat if I was taking a breath at the wrong time. At random intervals I lifted my head to make sure there were still people in front of me. The glare of the sun through my goggles and the swell of the sea made it increasingly difficult to see anyone, but I was headed for the first buoy. Every so often the top of a safety boat would rise into view before sinking again behind the next set of waves.

The greatest challenge of open water swimming is ignoring what lies beneath. For a generation brought up post-*Jaws* and in the sterile confines of a tiled swimming pool, the notion of not being able to see the bottom takes some getting used to, as does the idea that if you *could* see the untold creatures lurking down there you wouldn't want to see the bottom anyway.

Occasionally, even for seasoned veterans, a sense of panic sweeps over, especially if you think you have just seen or brushed against something else in the water. It happens regularly to me, and I basically tell myself to settle down and wise up. On the plus side, such fleeting panic also injects the body with a flood of adrenaline just when you need it most.

Time moves slowly when you're swimming. Perhaps it's the limited field of vision, or the effort required, or a combination of the two. After 45 minutes of thrashing through the Dardanelles Strait, I stopped to adjust my goggles and tried not to notice that I was drifting alarmingly towards Istanbul. There were no other swimmers. I could see nobody else but those in the safety boats, too far away to pick out individuals. Where was everyone else? Was I leading? Probably not. Was I way off course? Probably so. When would the ships be allowed up again? How close would you have to be to get sucked into the engine? How long would it take to swim across the bow of an oil tanker? Could my arms keep this up?

Questions, concerns, and then suddenly a moment of pinpoint clarity. A moment of what is now termed 'mindfulness'. What the hell was I doing?! I was right in the middle of one of the busiest shipping lanes in the world. I was completely alone, completely exposed, and completely responsible for my own survival. I could see myself bobbing up and down, miles from land between two continents. I have rarely felt more self-aware, more alive. I looked around, and I smiled.

I thought of my grandfather. Ninety-two years old, and a pragmatist to the last, he would simply be shaking his head. He was a hard-working farmer. Farmers do what has to be done to survive, and constantly strive for ways to make a hard, physical life easier. They carefully balance input and output of energy and effort. Farmers don't go to gyms. And they certainly don't deliberately and pointlessly swim into the middle of the busiest shipping lane in the world.

I actually laughed out loud. My grandfather would not understand. But I felt as if I was beginning to work it out. As one of the lucky generation who don't have to put in hard physical effort to earn a living, I can get more out of life than the survival balance of energy input and output. I can afford pointless quests of adventure, safe in the knowledge that I can always rest when I go back to work the next week. And because of this great good fortune, it is almost my *duty* to explore and squeeze more adventure and challenge out of an otherwise sheltered life. I need to experience these moments of jeopardy, exposure and struggle; I need the mindfulness to be found in extreme situations. And that's why the swim was more important to me than the wedding.

That also explains why so many people deliberately incapacitate themselves with drink: they don't just *enjoy* getting completely and utterly plastered, they *need* to get completely and utterly plastered. We have to occasionally escape from things making sense. Humans imposed order on themselves, but it's not natural, and it's not always good for us. We evolved through millennia of disorder, chaos, fights, hunts and daily life or death struggles. Experiencing and coping with physical stress is part of our genetic make-up, but these days we can survive without ever even getting out of breath.

But not when we're treading water in the middle of the Dardanelles. I swam on and had another moment of bright clarity as I settled into a rhythm. The sea doesn't give a shit about us. When you're in the sea, you're in a really hostile environment. I was quite literally in much deeper than I had been on any previous escapade. When things started to unravel on the Man v Horse I could have just stopped running. At Tough Guy, there was a St John's Ambulance on hand if I needed it. But here … between continents … stopping meant drowning. The sea doesn't care if you have family back at home, work to go to on Monday, friends to meet that evening. The sea is a huge malevolent force quite unmoved by the suffering it can inflict simply by being. It can drown you, smash you against rocks, drag you out, throw you in, toss you round, make you puke. And it doesn't care. It doesn't even notice.

I was suddenly taken with the idea that the sea wouldn't notice if I drowned in its cold embrace. In fact, at that point nobody would notice, nobody could do anything about it, except me. 'I am the master of my fate; I am the captain of my soul.' I was inspired by the fact that my survival depended entirely on my own physical capacity. And I was going to complete the swim.

It was hard work. For almost the entire crossing I saw no other swimmers. A human is not a significant marker buoy in a choppy sea. I could rarely see above the next hump in the swell, so mostly I only saw the top half of the hills miles away on each side of the strait, and occasionally the top of one of the safety boats. Had I dwelt too long on my position, I'd have been completely overwhelmed. Looking back now, it is terrifying.

It was predicted that most of us would be finished in about an hour and 15 minutes, which is a long time to swim continuously. After an hour I was still way off, and stuck in one of the infamously capricious Dardanelles currents. They are something to do with the two seas that the strait connects, the Marmara and the Aegean. Our route had been designed to counter this, but I knew by now that the enforced change of the start point had disrupted things. This swim was now much further and harder than the 4.5 kilometres advertised.

After an hour and a half I was finally in the bay of Çanakkale and completely Çan-knackered. The last, cruel current was holding me out and I had to swim in an arc to get towards the huge red balloon on a pontoon that marked the end point and a successful crossing. Finally I was close enough to grab the ladder. Two marshals pulled me up. I wobbled at the top and almost fell back into the sea. My head was spinning, my legs weren't ready to be vertical again and I felt completely unbalanced.

I pulled off my goggles and swim cap, loosened my wetsuit and sat down. As my breathing returned to normal and some of the swaying subsided, I felt better and, pretty quickly, elated. There were others lying down, struggling out of wetsuits, sitting hunched with their heads in their hands. I could see small coloured hats spread out across the bay. It had taken me an hour and 45 minutes to get across. I was the 15th swimmer home out of 150.

The winning time, by Channel swimmer Colin Hill, was 1 hour 27 minutes. Given that the organisers had previously said an hour and a half would be the cut-off for everyone to finish, it was pretty clear that something had gone wrong. It may just have been the conditions – the water was an uncharacteristically cold 13°C – but I'm sure it had more to do with the sudden change of start point and the extra distance against currents.

It had been a struggle. A number of people hadn't made it. They were hauled out of the water with large black hammocks in the way marine biologists transport whales and dolphins. The shipping lane was to reopen after two hours, so some swimmers had to be lifted out to clear the strait again. Those of us who had finished and recovered now gathered with a drink and tried to warm up in the afternoon sun.

It was a disparate group to say the least. Travel writers; adventurers; the curator of a Byron museum; Charles Byron himself, who finished in a very respectable two hours; lawyers and financiers; all united now by the post-challenge throb of self-satisfaction. We chitchatted contentedly about the only things we knew we had in common – an adventurous spirit and a feeling of achievement – before going back to our hotels and reconnecting with folks back home and a life more ordinary.

One American gent working in finance in London was straight back onto a Blackberry as we sat and relaxed, barely half an hour after finishing the swim. I hoped he apologised for delayed responses earlier in the day with an out-of-office reply along the lines of: 'I will be back in touch this afternoon if I survive the swim from Europe to Asia.' It is a sad reflection of the pressures of the modern world that a man cannot even take an afternoon off to recover from swimming between continents, but as an illustration of the lengths one has to go to these days to have or rather *do* it all, this was mighty impressive.

Next day I joined a group visiting the First World War battlegrounds and graves of the Gallipoli peninsula. Swimmers of the previous day were identifiable by a red ring around their necks, a result of two hours of wetsuit rubbing. It was handy to help us stay together as a group but was bloody painful when bathed in sunscreen.

Like the Somme offensive, the Gallipoli campaign has become an emblem of the utter futility and senseless waste of the First World War. In eight months of turgid and inconclusive battles following an Allied invasion of this small, arid peninsula, around 130,000 soldiers were killed. The peninsula guarded the Dardanelles Strait, which gave access to Istanbul and on to Russia, so was considered of great strategic importance.

It was hot and dusty while we were driven round the various battle sites and mass graves, getting educated about the acute suffering on both sides. The steep cliffs of the peninsula made it easy for the Turks to dig in and defend, firing down on the battalions of British, French, Antipodean and other colonials who were trying to land.

There was a regiment from my own hometown, Enniskillen in County Fermanagh, who fought at Gallipoli, and a patchwork of streets housing the men from this regiment was thereafter known as The Dardanelles, so it was a bit of a pilgrimage for me to find out what had happened to them and pay my respects.

There were dozens of Inniskilling Fusiliers gravestones. Many of their dead were teenagers. I thought of the sodden fields of our western county and the journey those young men had made. From there to here and on to eternity. From the poverty of damp Irish backstreets to the horror of a dusty Turkish shooting gallery. Such a narrow life experience, such a tragic waste.

On one high point on the peninsula we gathered as our tour guide identified key naval positions in the waters below. My mind wandered as we stared out over the huge expanse of sea. Had I really just swam across this historic and strategic channel? And why? Even then, with my neck still bearing the scars, it seemed somehow unlikely. From Belfast wedding to Istanbul to dangerous sea swim to historic battlefield tour, all in less than three days.

Immersed in history, the joys of the present struck home. This was the twenty-first century, where the scale of adventure is limited only by our imaginations, and we should be thankful. Unlike the men of my town 100 years ago, I can *choose* to suffer on foreign soil or in foreign seas, pretending that perfectly pointless physical challenges are somehow worthy; I can broaden my horizons, safe in the knowledge that I will return and not lie for ever after in a shallow distant grave; I can travel a thousand miles from home and back in a couple of days; I can earn a living sitting on my arse.

The very next evening that's exactly what I was doing. There I was, presenting Sky Sports News with the red ring around my neck hidden under a trowelling of make-up, looking back on what became the perfect adventure: a brief physical, intrepid interlude along the physically unchallenging and unadventurous journey of modern life.

Seven

TACKLING THE TOURMALET

After the chaos of getting to Gallipoli, I was relieved that my next intrepid interlude shaped up more like a package holiday. Albeit a package holiday that involved tackling one of the longest cycling climbs in the world. The stage selected for that year's Étape du Tour, from the 21 to be ridden by the professionals, was 185 kilometres long, from the city of Pau to the Col du Tourmalet. I had heard of Tourmalet before, vaguely thought it was a big mountain, but foolishly didn't bother learning any more before signing up. Turns out it's a high mountain pass – the highest in the French Pyrenees. And the Tourmalet, being preceded by two other mountain passes, the Col de Marie Blanque and the Col du Soulor, was basically just dessert in a three-course meal totalling 4,000 metres' climbing. Just to be clear, this meant that over the 185km we would be climbing two and a half miles straight up in the air.

The good news was that I would be travelling as part of a group, with all logistics handled by a sports event company hired by Sky. All employees (including me in my capacity as a freelance presenter on Sky Sports) were given the chance to apply to take on the Étape, part of Sky's sponsorship of British Cycling. They would organise event entry, accommodation, bike and human transport, everything. They even offered to organise our training. Everybody got a training plan, nutrition bulletins and a general support network. The only thing we had to do was follow that plan – training by numbers.

Problem was, my irregular life made following someone else's general plan a bit tricky. Spending so much time away from home inevitably meant a lot of time away from my bike, so I just adapted some of the information from their schedules and fitted in what I could when I could. The training plan was quite specific in any case, and sticking rigidly to someone else's timetable was hardly the self-regulation that had been the biggest bonus in moving from team sport to individual.

There was useful information on heart-rate training, which was pretty new to me – the idea of spending time in different 'zones' in which you could vary efforts fairly precisely. Having the heart rate on a cycling computer in front of me meant I couldn't pretend to myself that I was working harder than I really was; your heart doesn't lie. It wasn't exactly a free-wheeling adventure, but it was a new approach for me and worth exploring.

The irregularity of my working life was made a whole lot worse one morning when a volcano in Iceland decided to dump all over my normal schedule. Looking back, I still don't know how we all coped when the volcanic ash cloud grounded all flights in the UK and Ireland. It sounds pathetic, since the world functioned perfectly well for millennia without local flights, but it is almost unthinkable that all flights could be grounded indefinitely in this day and age. Imagine the tantrums thrown by high-powered executives and celebrity socialites in airports up and down the land. With hindsight, it probably did us all good to remember our insignificance in the grand scheme of a universe we think we own but will never control.

Not that I was thinking that at the time. Oh no. My thoughts then were more along the lines of 'Shite! WTF? I'm on air tomorrow night in London and I'm watching this on the news today in Belfast, the wrong side of the Irish Sea!'

So I had to drive. From Belfast to London. And then present a live sports programme until after midnight for eight days in a row. It was not an attractive prospect, but the silver lining was that if I had to bring my car I could also bring my bike, hallelujah! So I spent the next week either driving, anchored in a TV studio or cycling frenetically on consecutive laps of Richmond Park. It was a schedule that would come back to almost literally bite me in the arse a week later.

Most days I didn't have to be in Sky until around 5pm, so although I hated working late, especially on the shift that was supposed to finish at midnight but was always 'flexible' if news broke after 11pm and that hour had to be repeated for the overnight recording, the possibility of getting a full day's sunshine and training in beforehand was the bonus.

I was staying with Slippy in Putney, and on Sunday when he was off we decided to go down to the renowned Box Hill in Surrey, probably the most famous cycling climb in largely flat south-east England. In the land of the blind the one-eyed man is king, so Box Hill, though hardly ver-tiginous, at weekends attracts swarms of cyclists anxious to go up for even a short while rather than round and round for hours, as in Richmond Park.

Having one of my oldest and best friends living in London made my constant shuffling between there and Belfast so much easier. Since the trauma of the Welsh 1000m Peaks Race I hadn't been able to tempt him into any more fell running but having finally given up rugby he was now really into cycling, which was perfect timing for me. With characteristic charm he'd managed to develop a work role at a big corporation in which he was largely responsible for his own time, which meant he was often about during the day before I went to Sky for my present-ing shifts. So we spent plenty of time together laughing, cycling, drinking coffee, and I actually saw more of him than I did many of our mates that lived in Belfast. Staying with him and other friends and relations, bed and sofa hop-ping around London wasn't ideal, but it meant I avoided what I called the Alan Partridge situation, staying in a hotel near Heathrow, which would have driven me demented.

Slip and I have been pals forever. We were born in the same hospital within a week of each other and have ticked off most of life's major milestones at around the same time ever since. We got married within months of each other, have kids the same age, have usually picked up and later dropped the same hobbies at the same time, and know each other inside out. We have the kind of relationship in which nothing is sacred. When I nearly died in a car crash aged 18, he phoned me from holidays in America and started laughing down the phone. It was just what I needed. He is as proud of me as I am of him, we are loyal friends, but there is nothing either of us enjoys more than seeing the other make a balls of things. Unfortunate incidents that date back 20 years or more are routinely revisited for healthy humiliation, and an evening or weekend's reunion always makes my stomach ache from laughing.

One of the things we share is naïve optimism. Another is a chronic lack of attention to detail. It's not that we're big-picture thinkers, just that we're easily bored. So predictably, despite being armed with a printed map and my Garmin, we were soon lost on the way to Box Hill. But we wagered that joining the back of a passing peloton would probably get us there, and so it proved. Anxious to avoid a repeat of the embarrassing 'No Map Mountain Race' fiasco, we got chatting early to our fellow riders and came clean about being navigationally challenged. A couple of friendly riders, Mike and Julian, promised to not only show us the way, but escort us home as well.

I anti-socially charged ahead of them when we reached the bottom of Box Hill, it's not the toughest cycling challenge by any means but I wanted at least to go as hard as I could to the top. Later, when we were all enjoying ice-creams in the sun at the 'summit' café, I felt the need to explain myself and faux-modestly dropped in that I was training for the Étape du Tour in a few weeks' time.

'That'll be rough,' said Mike through a mouthful of Magnum choc ice. 'Too many hills for me – had enough of them just cycling through Cornwall.'

'I'm more of a swimmer,' grinned Julian. 'Too heavy for this sport!'

'Ah you'll soon get there with a few more miles,' I offered, basking in the glory of what I wrongly assumed to be the 'top cyclist' tag among the four of us.

On the way home it was Mike's turn to blast off the front, powering away on flat sections and down hills. He didn't exactly look like an athlete but he was clearly very strong on the bike. Only after further conversation did we learn that this was Mike Carter, author of a brilliant book charting his adventures cycling right around the perimeter of Britain, a 3,000-mile unsupported coastal epic. Then on the way home something called the 'Arch to Arc' was mentioned, a challenge Julian had taken on a few years ago. Never having heard of it, Slip and I looked it up when we got home. I was genuinely staggered.

The Arch to Arc is an incredible feat of endurance, a magnificent testament to true all-round athletic endeavour. It is a monstrous triathlon challenge involving a run from Marble Arch to Dover, a swim of the Channel, and a cycle from Calais to the Arc de Triomphe. Julian Crabtree was only the third person ever to achieve the feat, which took him 87 hours and 37 minutes. I had just been cycling with true endurance warrior royalty. I blushed at the notion that either of these two would have been impressed by someone taking on a mere stage of the Tour de France.

I finally made it through to the last shift of the Sky Sports eight-night marathon, and was hoping to be out of the studio by quarter past midnight and on the road again up to Stranraer in Scotland for the ferry back to Belfast. Unfortunately for me (and for him, I suppose) David Beckham broke a bone in his foot late in a match in Italy – seismic news in the Sky Sports world – so we had to stay on and regurgitate limited information for an extra hour.

Having finally got on the road after 1am, I headed north and slept in the car park of a massive motorway services, pulling the car up beside all the trucks in which the drivers had the luxury of pull-out beds and curtains in their cabs. I made do with a partially reclined seat, beach towels for covers and a cap pulled over my eyes, and dozed for a couple of hours.

I was pretty stiff when I eventually got home next day and took over the night-shift duties from Claire. This involved putting Christian's dummy back in his mouth every hour or so when he woke and realised it had fallen out. The routine was infuriating, but the only way to break the cycle was cold-turkey dummy removal, a fraught, week-long battle like Ewan McGregor's bedroom lock-up scene in *Trainspotting*.

So sleep was at a premium and stretching was non-existent. Some time in the middle of the night I rolled out half asleep to once again find and replace the wretched dummy, but when I tried to stand up I felt as if someone was stabbing me in the lower back. Pain arrowed down my leg and I collapsed in agony as Christian screamed the place down.

'Alright alright! I'm coming, I'm coming,' I hissed, but I couldn't stand. Crawling over in real pain, looking for the dummy under the cot, pinned down by the twin tyrannies of a teething toddler and personal injury, I felt as if I had suddenly aged 20 years. It sounds strange to recall, but in that moment, amid the stress of a back spasm, a screeching child and a dark room, I was somehow acutely aware of how my life had changed. Despite my unsettling, peripatetic work life, I was no longer really a freewheeling adventurer, but a proper grown-up adult, stressed and constrained by responsibility and a very below par core muscle system.

Everybody bangs on about the work–life balance, but this simple ratio merely compares the amount of time spent at work and the amount of time spent not at work, as if one equals stress and the other equals non-stress. I'm sure I'm not the first to point this out, but the reality is, especially when you have kids, not all non-work time is stress free. Quite the opposite sometimes. Depending on your job, you can occasionally zone out at work. This is not an option with young children. It's a failure of evolution that humans can crawl or walk before they have even the vaguest bit of good sense or notion of danger. The constant vigilance required to look after a child from about six months on is exhausting. And then when they're asleep you have frantically to get on with all the tasks you put off while they were awake.

But the parenting paradox is that almost as soon as the child is asleep or you get some time away, you miss them terribly. Many a morning I spent in giddy anticipation, waiting for Christian to wake up and smile and gurgle and laugh and say 'dada'. Although his presence was the biggest change either Claire or I had ever known, quality time spent with him was the biggest *joy* we'd ever known too.

It's a two-person job, undoubtedly, and I have huge respect for those who do it on their own. Both Claire and I working meant a constant juggling act, and various things had to give. We didn't go to the cinema; we went out on the town only very occasionally but usually separately, and with less drink taken; we didn't visit as many people or places as we used to. But we remained determined not to give up our previous lives completely, and I was still adamant that I needed some adventure in my life. I devised a 'hassle to happiness ratio' that we used to make decisions about our free time. Basically if an experience or trip involved a load of hassle and wasn't going to deliver a more than greater measure of happiness, we didn't bother.

Under any rational, pragmatic analysis, and even under my own system of assessments, taking on any kind of 'Man Test' failed on the hassle to happiness ratio. But on the other hand they weren't about mere happiness, so I took the executive decision to make them exempt from the ratio. They were like a charity getting a tax exemption, I decided; the usual rules didn't apply because they were supposed to be adding something to the greater good. I couldn't quite define what that contribution was exactly, but I knew that it was tied up somehow with feelings of self-worth and general mental wellbeing.

The problem was, my mental wellbeing was tied very firmly to my physical wellbeing, and in the morning, after feeling that back spasm while searching for a baby's dummy, I could hardly get out of bed. I felt like I was made of wood and my body parts were pinned together with rusty hinges. It took me a full ten minutes to shuffle down the stairs. If I stood too long a jet of pain shot down my leg, burning my toes and making me feel nauseous. I recognised this as acute sciatica; I'd got it a few years earlier after putting my back out building a ridiculously elaborate backyard chicken run for my three hens.

With a sinking heart I remembered that back then I'd endured it for months, and only a long, long course of physio and stretching had brought relief. I was booked to do the Dragon Ride in Wales the following weekend, a 100-mile plus 'sportive' through the Brecon Beacons that I'd planned as a vital part of my Tour de France preparation. No way that was happening. Even the Étape itself was in jeopardy, just six weeks away. For the umpteenth time in my sporting life I wished I had paid more attention to my flexibility and core.

Stretching and core work is an absolutely vital component of any endurance training plan, helping the body recover and cope with the stresses of intense movement and improving performance. But it's crushingly boring. And when time is tight, half an hour can always be much better spent somewhere other than a yoga mat. And there's another problem. I like intense training precisely because it's so hard I can't think about everything else when I'm doing it, but when I'm stretching I do nothing but think about everything else. For me, rather than providing a distraction from everyday anxieties like other forms of exercise, stretching and yoga actually give them a focus.

I like either full-bore training or full-bore relaxing, and stretching and yoga seem to exist somewhere in between those two extremes. So the consequence is that without the regular maintenance, I occasionally break down and need a full reconstructive service. It was spectacularly bad timing for this to happen six weeks out from the toughest endurance challenge of my life.

I found a place called Belfast Back Care, just half a mile from my house, and threw myself on the mercy of the owner, John Magee, a sports fan who was treating my mate, Commonwealth Heavyweight Boxing Champion Marty Rogan. If he could manipulate those enormous muscles, I reasoned he could work wonders on my own punier prime movers.

Like big Marty, John pulled no punches on my first consultation.

'I think you have the worst posture I have ever seen in someone of your age,' said John, who must have seen the upper bodies of thousands of patients by then – but also slept through the 'Managing Patient Emotions' seminar of his physiotherapy course.

'You have a bit of scoliosis, a bit of kyphosis …'

'Hopefully no halitosis?' I interrupted.

'I'm not getting close enough to find out,' continued John. 'You also have over-pronation here, over-development there, the full works basically. But the most immediate problem is you also have a bulging disc now, caused by all the stress the imbalances and inflexibility have placed on your lower back.'

'Bit of a mess then?' I paraphrased. I was grinning, and for reasons I cannot begin to explain, I was quite proud of myself. Actually, I *can* begin to explain, but it sounds ridiculous. I was thinking, 'Wow, I've trained myself to physical problems! Endured more than my frame can take. And imagine what I'd achieve if my skeleton and muscular structure were better. It's a real shame that for all these years I've been let down by my components.'

This bizarre sense of detachment from one's own body is a phenomenon I remembered learning about in Sports Sociology classes at Loughborough. It is a symptom of what the sociologists call 'over-conforming to the sports ethic' or, even more intriguing, 'positive deviance'.

What it means is that athletes or sports people get so caught up in their sport that they disregard the impact on their own bodies, and if a part of their body protests, like a hamstring strain or something, they regard that body part as having let them down and sometimes even continue to 'punish' it by ignoring the clear signs that something is wrong, and training on through the pain.

I still feel the same now when I get a cold or a bit run-down. I think, 'Ah, you're not going to hold me back! I'm

Not good times. Slippy and I five hours into our first Man Test and feeling like a couple of grannies. With a run up Snowdon still to come.

Tough Guy's 'Killing Fields'. A health and safety exclusion zone created from the febrile dreams of visionary English eccentric, Mr Mouse.

The Man v Horse Marathon – proof that at least *some* mad ideas generated in a pub actually go somewhere.

© HUW EVANS PICTURE AGENCY

Minja and me at the summit of Kilimanjaro. Spending my honeymoon with a mountain guide rather than my new wife.

Victory! Four quasi-zombies celebrate surviving for three days without sleep and winning the epic Race Around Ireland.

Easy rider. Feeling great (going downhill) on the Étape du Tour, well before the agony of the Tourmalet.

Me as a human fox fleeing a pack of bloodhounds. Surely the most unique Marathon des Sables training method yet invented.

Apart from this one. Finishing the Marathon du Médoc with Slippy. Fancy dress is mandatory, as is drinking the wine supplied at the feed stations on the way round.

Adam ploughs across the
Broad Lough as we race
for the Erne Relay record.

A rare moment of haste
in one of my Ironman
transitions.

A tight squeeze. Pummeling a week's provisions into a day sack is one of the biggest challenges of the Marathon des Sables.

The residents of tent number 84. Six men and one woman naively looking forward to seven days of desert torture.

Forming an orderly queue. Enduring the logistics of the world's toughest footrace is an achievement in itself. Note the paper boiler suits – desert evening wear.

Finishing stage five in some sort of strange transcendental high-energy trance.

Love is blind. (And in Claire's case, deaf, forgiving and superhumanly patient.) Family time with Christian and Reuben after the madness.

going to go out and run myself sick to get rid of you!' The sort of confusion that allows someone mentally to detach a part of their own body from their own overall health is a sure sign that their sport has driven them mad. I was getting clear messages that the cycling and lifestyle load were not making a positive contribution to my wellbeing, but rather than make any adjustments, I chose to blame my component parts and take delight in the pressure I'd put them under and what I'd achieved despite them. Bizarre when you think about it, but very common I'm sure among Man Testers, for whom some sort of self-induced physical problem serves as a campaign medal.

Gradually, with twice-weekly visits to John and a course of stretching and rest, I felt as if someone was oiling the rusty joints and smoothing the wooden ends of my body. I could actually walk without being doubled over and stand for longer than a minute without feeling like my foot was on fire. Eventually I made it back onto a bike, but after six weeks of no training and the usual unsettled, itinerant work schedule, I wasn't giving myself much of a chance in the Étape.

After the mayhem of the Hellespont Swim travel arrangements, it was great to arrive at Toulouse Airport and pass myself gently into the safe embrace of the events company looking after all the Sky riders. I was able to do my best Japanese tourist impression and follow someone with a raised sign on a stick who would put me on a bus, show me my hotel, deliver my bike, give me a timetable, etc. It's what the pros get every day, after all.

Sadly the service didn't include rebuilding the bike, which had been stripped down to travel in the box. Straight after checking in at the hotel I nervously set to work on that, bicycle mechanics not being my forte, in the big conference room where all the bikes were housed in various states of construction. There was a bit of a squabble going on in one corner, a classic clash of pro and amateur.

'Why did you touch my bike?' shouted a MAMIL (Middle Aged Man In Lycra), inexplicably wearing one of those peaked cycling caps indoors. 'It's *my* bike, it has nothing to do with you, thanks very much.'

He was addressing another guy across the room whose muscular, tanned legs and gaunt face marked him out as someone altogether more comfortable in a cycling environment.

'Calm down, mate,' he laughed. 'I just went round taking off the dust caps on all the bike wheels. You don't need 'em! It's stupid having them on! They're only for delivery, they don't do nothin'.'

When he spoke, I realised I knew him from covering the National Champs in Pendle the previous month – he was a proper professional rider from Yorkshire. What was he doing on an amateur event like the Étape? Looking around, I could see the little screw caps from the tops of tyre valves littering the floor.

'You wouldn't leave all the labels on your clothes while you wear 'em, would you?!' he continued. 'I'm only trying to help, mate. You think the amount of times them wheels go round, what's the point of carrying that little bit extra up and down the mountains? It all adds up you know!'

'Well, it is not up to you to decide what we do or don't have on our own bikes. Please don't touch it again,' retorted the MAMIL, petulantly screwing the dust caps back onto his own wheels.

I recognised the pre-event tetchiness immediately, but kept my head firmly in my own bike box while also surreptitiously stretching down to unscrew the caps off my own wheels.

Every day is a school day.

All of these big cycling and triathlon events have an Expo-type gathering the day or morning before the big race, ostensibly to get all the bikes checked and competitors registered, but in reality it's to get better value for the event sponsors. I don't usually hang around at these; there is just too much information, distraction and testosterone around, too much hype about the scale of the challenge to come. Anxious competitors turn up perfectly ready to start their event, but then get exhausted walking miles round all the stalls and turn into nervous wrecks, stressing about their preparation, kit and other competitors, and then panic-buying a load of stuff they don't need or shouldn't eat.

On this occasion I *had* to hang around because I was meeting Simon, and God only knew when he'd turn up. Despite peddling himself into a near coma, after the Race Around Ireland his hunger for cycling remained undiminished. In fact, it had sharpened, and had now reached utterly obsessive, evangelical levels. But some things hadn't changed; he was probably the only person in Pau who traditionally sorted logistics less effectively than me. He had finally secured his Étape entry a mere two weeks earlier and was determined not to spend more than the absolute minimum on accommodation or travel, so was driving from Oxford and sleeping in the car with a semi-pro cycling mate from his club. He was even planning to ride a bike he had built himself. I wasn't sure I needed his special blend of chaos when everything finally appeared to be running uncharacteristically smoothly.

Because of their late entry, Simon and Tom's race numbers were in the high 8,000s, out of a total of 9,000 competitors. This meant that they started at the back. Right at the back. Not only would they go off up to an hour after the first wave of riders, but they'd also have to fight their way past the thousands of people in front of them who'd be meandering at their own pace along and across the narrow roads. Simon's ambition was to finish in six and a half hours, which would place him among the very elite and land him a Gold participant medal. But with close to 9,000 riders in front of him at the start, this would be almost impossible.

'Here, do you think anyone would notice if I doctored this eight with some Tipp-Ex to make it look like a two?' he asked with a serious face.

'Yes,' I said. 'An eight looks nothing like a two.'

'But it'll be dark and the number two might look a bit different in France.'

'I'm pretty certain that French figures look exactly the same as English figures, Si.'

Then I noticed he was staring quizzically at the gears on my bike. It always made me feel self-conscious, as if I was half-naked or had a spot on my face.

'Let me see your chain set,' he said suddenly.

'Why, what's wrong with it? You have seen my bike before.'

'You haven't changed the gearing?'

'Of course not, why would I?'

'Er, because you're going to be cycling up and down the Pyrenees?! You'll probably need at least a 28 on the back.'

'A 28 what?'

He and Tom burst out laughing. 'A 28 as the rear sprocket,' said Tom, as if that cleared it up.

'Right,' I said, nodding wisely.

They were adamant I needed a bigger gear ring at the back, with more teeth, to allow me to spin it more easily when the going got tough up the hills. One of my key event rules was never to make late adjustments to kit, nutrition, technique, etc. but if there was a chance to make things easier, I didn't want to miss it.

It wasn't as simple as just slotting in a new ring, of course. Tom and Simon were discussing compatibility issues with words like 'cassettes', 'derailleurs' and all sorts of other shite I didn't understand in English never mind French, which would of course be required in a random Pau cycle shop, if I even found one at this late stage.

'Excusez-moi, avez-vous le sprocket vingt-huit?'

After six months of preparation, the whole idea of charging round an unfamiliar city to change something as fundamental as the gearing on my bike the night before the start of the event was giving me palpitations. I needed a second opinion, and ignoring my own rules about the interaction between amateur and professional, I asked the Yorkshire Cap Remover back at the hotel.

'Ah, you could cycle up a wall with that gearing, no problem. You'll be fine with that,' he said with a hint of a smirk. I relayed this to Tom.

'Well, maybe *he* could,' said Tom. 'I seriously think you need a bigger gear.'

'There is no point in getting here having done all the training, had the injuries, and then not give yourself the best chance because you are missing a gear, is there?' added Simon in a rare moment of sense.

'Alright, let's do it,' I said suddenly. Not finishing the stage after all that training and hassle was unthinkable. 'So where do we get one at this stage?!'

'There'll be loads of bike shops in Pau. I'll ask around,' said Tom. 'Shouldn't be a problem.'

But of course it was a problem. Perhaps everyone else had received the same advice or felt the same last-minute panic, because for some reason the cassette system we were looking for just wasn't available. By half past five that evening the search had proved fruitless, a double blow since I was now both unsettled after the frantic search and also, since we didn't get it sorted, concerned that I was stuck with a set-up that would make the whole thing much harder than it needed to be. Starting an extremely difficult challenge with a pre-packaged excuse was never good.

We had a Sky briefing over a pasta dinner in the hotel, which I had to attend, so while I sat and stressed with some of my work colleagues, Simon and Tom – to their eternal credit – continued the search. Having raced in France for a few years, and given that he actually knew how a bike worked, Tom was the man to sort this out.

I sat beside Martin Corry, the former England rugby captain, who had kind of fallen into cycling after retiring from rugby a few years previous. I found it interesting that Martin, having survived the prolonged physical assault and the intense daily challenges of a professional rugby career, should still want to put himself through a day's sports torture when he wasn't going to be paid for it. I had always considered this environment to be the preserve of unfulfilled pen-pushing sports part-timers like me.

He laid the blame at the enormous feet of his fellow Martin and fellow ex-England rugby captain, Martin Johnson.

'I used to absolutely love the strength and conditioning training in rugby,' he said. 'And I did most of it with Johnno. We used to always do this mindless rowing session.

A minute on, a minute off. We'd do 20 of those and the first 10 we had to always get above 330m in each minute. And that became our fitness gauge. It doesn't sound tough but by the end you're properly knackered.

'A year after he retired, Johnno went down to the club gym when we were all away, to see where he was fitness-wise. He started but then he gave up halfway through. He told me he just thought, "What's the point in me doing it?" And *I* thought, shit, Johnno's never given up on anything. I don't want to ever be in that place.'

So when he faced his own retirement a few years later, *continuing* intense training was the most obvious way for Martin to make sure he didn't stay away long enough to lose the desire or capacity to complete that test. But I couldn't understand why he felt he had to still try and hit a target of extreme fitness that obviously would be much more of a challenge when he wasn't able to train full-time. Why couldn't he just keep ticking over and keep reasonably fit for life, rather than killing himself trying to maintain a level of fitness he only needed when he was an international rugby player?

'I can't socially train. Going to the gym and just ticking over doesn't interest me. I always need to have something to aim at. I'm all or nothing. And if I have got that in me, I'd much rather be all than nothing. Because nothing is … well, where's the sense of pride in that? Blimey, it's almost cathartic talking to you like this because I have never fully thought about it!'

'Sorry,' I said. 'This probably isn't the time or place to make you question it all! Do you think you'll always be like this? All or nothing?'

'No, I don't, because I know there is a lazy man in me. And I don't want to see this lazy man, because absolutely I think I could just let him out and suddenly be 20 stone and eating doughnuts for breakfast and I don't want to see him.'

'But that would be more normal for an ex-rugby international, surely,' I replied. 'What's surprising is the fact that rather than sitting back and taking pride in once being captain of your country and being at the very pinnacle of your sport, you continue beasting yourself in training, for no money, with nobody watching, in other sports and not at the same standard.'

'Well, what I really loved about rugby was the measured part – where are you with your weights and all of that.'

I nodded enthusiastically. I recognised that in myself during my own rugby days, although I never had anything like the same process of measuring that Martin had as a professional.

'You can say, "Right, what's the strongest I have been, where am I at now compared to that?" You'd always have a gauge, and I got a kick out of that. So when I realised I couldn't play any more, I was thinking, how do I get the other kicks? And the training side gave it to me, and still does.'

He was invited to do one of the Sky charity cycle events as he was working as a rugby pundit for the channel, and from there, less than a year later, had ended up agreeing to do the Étape. He's a big guy, Martin, and looking at him I was thinking the weight that was probably handy on an indoor rowing machine would not be so appreciated halfway up one of the Pyrenees. But I knew he'd make it, he clearly had the right mindset, the right mix of pig-headed stubbornness, single-minded determination bordering on mania, and pride. I wished him well and went off to see where the hell Tom and Simon were.

I met them crossing the lobby, triumphantly carrying new gearing and a chain found in a tiny shop in a suburb outside the city. Simon had been visibly embarrassed by the dirt and repair of my old chain at the Expo earlier. They got to work on my bike. More organised people, on their way to an early night with bikes all prepped that morning, passed us in the corridor, smiling down sympathetically at the bits strewn all over the floor.

I was going through all the usual self-loathing for having left things this late, watching the clock tick towards tomorrow's early start (4.30am, to be at the start line in our groups at 5.30, before pedalling off around seven).

'But sure you always need a bit of adrenaline to get you going before these things,' grinned Simon, picking up on my stress. 'We wouldn't want to be too organised, it's not what we're used to!'

He was nibbling at a block of coconut cream while he and Tom worked on the bike, insisting that this was the latest scientifically proven wonder-food for endurance support. It tasted foul. Finally, with the coconut block half-eaten and melting over the chain oil covering his hands, Simon looked up wild-eyed and triumphant from the floor of the hotel lobby and said with an air of pomp, 'Now you're ready.'

'Fantastic, lads, thank you so much.' I was genuinely moved by their efforts on my behalf, and spun the back wheel in an attempt to look as if I spotted the difference they'd made. 'Perfect.'

'You'll have a much better chance now,' said Tom. 'Should get you up any hill.'

'Just mine to sort now,' laughed Simon with a hint of hysterics.

It was nearly 11 o'clock. I looked over at Tom.

'His bike is in bits in the back of the car,' Tom confirmed with a grim smile.

Simon laughed again. 'I told Tom already, this is always how we do it! Total chaos! Anyone want to finish this coconut?'

I slept fitfully as usual before a big event and an early start, but within a minute of the alarm going off was wide awake, adrenaline coursing through my veins. I stared into the mirror, reminded myself what I'd gone through to even be at the start, and vowed not to go home without having completed the stage. Just the usual self-motivational bullshit you're no doubt accustomed to delivering into a mirror while wearing lycra at 4.30am.

Breakfast was odd, a lot of nervous people trying to force food down their throats in the middle of the night despite not being hungry, and openly discussing bowel movements and piss stops and other biological considerations ahead of a long, competitive day on thin saddles.

If breakfast was strange, arriving at the start area in Place de Verdun in the centre of Pau was downright weird. We'd been told to get there for 5.30am, so it was still dark, and 9,500 inappropriately dressed people were corralled like sheep into different pens according to their start number. We would be going off in waves of 500, with those fortunate to have the lowest registration numbers leaving at seven, while the rest of us had to sit on the road and wait our turn, shivering with either cold or nerves or both.

Having been warned of the long, early morning wait by previous entrants, I had brought an old fleece that I was going to chuck away when we finally got going. I was very glad to be able to sit quietly and not have to hop about to keep warm like most of the others, whose various dances were burning up potentially vital stores of energy.

All the Sky contingent were numbered in the upper 4,000s, so our wait was only half as bad as some of the rest. I hadn't spotted Simon, so had no idea whether he had risked the Tipp-Ex corrections to get nearer the front, or was stranded, stewing, shivering and plotting, somewhere in the back pen. If it was the latter, I knew an uncontrollable fury would be unleashed on the road by the time he got let loose, well over an hour after me. Hopefully he had plenty of that God-awful cream coconut to get him through the wait.

Gradually the day got brighter and our group slid ever closer to our start. If ever there was a time for last-minute bike tinkerers, this was it. I could see them everywhere, twitching, twisting, spinning and polishing. I joined in, of course. I lifted the back wheel off the ground and turned the pedals by hand. My heart sank. Something was going 'click, click, click'.

'Ah, Jesus Christ, what is that?!' I shouted out loud.

Typically, at that very moment, in the classic 'hurry up and wait' mode of these things, the prolonged sit on the road was suddenly interrupted by a flash panic all around as it was announced in French and English that our group would cross the line in the next few minutes. I was spinning the wheel frantically, checking the bike over and over, trying to find the source of the clicking, while all around me tension ratcheted and faces were set to grim.

One of my fellow Sky Sports News presenters, Jeremy Langdon, in an overt display of typical pre-event stress, was harrumphing in the queue behind me, rattled that my clicking problem might stall him and cost him a valuable few seconds over the course of the mega-long day that lay ahead. I tried to move out of his way but there was nowhere to go, we were all penned in and the ten-second countdown began. With a final resigned curse I climbed on the saddle, properly rattled.

Each real stage of the Tour de France begins with a ceremonial lap of the host town or a casual 'neutralised' spin for a few kilometres while the riders relax into the stress of the day ahead. It's one of the great paradoxes of the amateur version that similar mannerly procedures are not observed when the stakes are much, much smaller and the riding groups much, much bigger. The start of each wave of riders at the Étape instead signals the unleashing of a moving mass of chaos as technically challenged cyclists charge off, swerving into each other while trying to click into their pedals and set their GPS devices, shouting at colleagues to stay together, hurtling like herds of buffalo through narrow gaps, swerving to avoid drains and other suburban road furniture, squeezing through bottlenecks at corners, burning through nervous energy before the first kilometre is passed.

As this great moving mass bobbed tensely down the road, the clicking of my bike was getting worse and I knew I'd have to stop and sort it. I was furious. How could this happen just as I was about to finally get going after six months' preparation?! Ignoring the 'tuts' of everyone else – not much of Mr Mouse's solidarity on show at this stage of the stage – I negotiated my way to the side of the road and hopped off. My hands were shaking. I told myself to get a grip, to be rational. This was probably just a simple issue that would hold me up for a minute or two.

It was. The new gears had changed the angle of my back wheel slightly and every time it spun round it was catching on the arm of the cadence sensor placed on the frame. This was a little plastic wireless device placed close to the wheel, counting the turns and telling me on the Garmin how many revolutions I was doing per minute. It's useful, because you need to remember to spin the pedals at a high cadence when you're climbing mountains to make sure you don't put too much of a load on the leg muscles and burn them out too early. I was aiming to push the pedals round at about 90rpm the whole day, and having the figures to focus on was one of my plans for making it through.

I tried twisting the arm away from the wheel a bit, but then the revolutions weren't picked up on the Garmin. Moving it back started the clicking again, and there was no way I could face the idea of each wheel turn for 185 kilometres being impeded, no matter how small the impediment. Each grind of the pedals would be hard enough as it was. I had trained using the cadence counter and enjoyed the rhythm and comfort of sticking to the numbers, but what is it the best generals say? 'Make a plan and be prepared to rip it up', or something like that – or rip it off, in this instance. I put the cadence sensor in my back pocket and got back on the road.

Everyone I knew was well gone by this stage, and with such a mass of people on the road I didn't hold out much hope of finding them again. I felt strangely lonely, and a bit unsettled. I cheered up at the sight of so many others pulled over too, some with punctures, some having crashed, all irrationally irate at what we'd normally dismiss as minor inconveniences. All this in the first five kilometres. I reasoned that everything would settle down once we all got warmed up and more spread out, and I tried to relax.

It was still a bit chilly, quite a dull morning, and I was glad of my arm warmers as we coasted through little valleys and villages only half awake despite the invasion. I'd dumped the old fleece at the start as planned, so was actually looking forward to pedalling my way to some body heat when the roads began to turn upwards.

Hmm. Be careful what you wish for. Out of another little village and through a pine forest I suddenly had a long sight of the road ahead for the first time. And it seemed to climb for quite a distance. The gradient kicked up and the people ahead of me were going backwards. This continued for a good few minutes and I began seriously to wonder if we were starting the Marie Blanque climb already. I knew we couldn't be, but the route had been foolishly simplified in my head to just three climbs, so this one was a bit of a shock.

And so it continued, a steady procession of hills that would have been more than significant on any ride in England and Ireland but had barely registered in the analysis of this one, where the epic climbs in the Pyrenees had understandably focused all the attention. I had this strange sense of being conned or cheated, that this softening up was unfair and uncalled for. From the cursing and whingeing all around it was clear that I wasn't the only one caught out by these unexpected pre-fight body punches.

I still hadn't seen any of my Sky friends and was starting to stress again about how much time I'd lost fixing the clicking, when I gradually became aware that the road had become sticky. The pedals were churning rather than spinning, something seemed wrong. This is when technology is useful to override the senses. I checked the Garmin and saw that the gradient had risen to 6 per cent, even though the road looked fairly flat.

I was relieved. Not noticing a gradient like that for a few minutes must mean I was in decent shape and the new gearing system was very effective. Ahead, cyclists were bobbing up and down, and some were out of the saddle, a sure sign of a slope rising beyond the comfort levels. The road seemed more densely packed than before as the teeth of the climb began to bite and evened the pace throughout. We had arrived, I decided, at the Col de Marie Blanque.

Paradoxically, my heart lifted. This was what it was all about. Finally, we get stuck in. Back problems, bike problems, logistics, unplanned hills behind me, now it was straightforward. Man versus mountain. Just pedal and suffer, pedal and suffer, and get the job done. A few minutes into the climb I was going well. The slope varied quite a bit – there were manageable sections of 4 or 5 per cent, then shocks of 12 per cent and steeper, then gentler bits again, so it was hard to settle into a rhythm and the heavier gradients and narrowing road were causing big bunches of riders to form. Space was at a premium, and losing focus meant ploughing into someone barely moving, or ending up in the ditch.

We hit 15 per cent at one point according to my Garmin, and there were people really struggling, some even off the bikes and pushing. It was going to be a long day for them, I thought. Or a short day more than likely, as the 'broom wagon' comes along soon after the last group sets off, 'sweeping up' those who aren't moving fast enough, so that they can re-open the roads to cars along some of the route.

Half an hour in, the constant uphill grind was starting to really bite and I was hugely glad of my new gear set-up. I owed Simon and Tom a few rounds for that and started to fantasise about the evening ahead once we all made it back to Pau, which was more than a bit premature.

I guessed the *average* gradient of the climb so far had been about 8 per cent, the same as the steepest sections of Box Hill, which only last for around 30 seconds. I felt sorry for the majority of our Sky group, whose training and previous cycling experience would largely have been confined to Greater London and Surrey.

Spinning away, I passed more and more people grinding tortuously slowly up the climb, and finally spotted someone I knew – big Martin Corry. Fair play, I thought, he's all of 16 stone, and ahead of me. I got a charge of good feeling and some sense of comradeship at last when I caught up with him – it had been a pretty lonely ride up until then – and found the energy to give him a good roar on the way past.

'Keep it lit, big Corry! Come on ye boy ye, this ain't Twickenham!'

He grinned through a face of contorted effort and managed to spit some good-natured obscenities back, followed by an accusation that I wasn't trying hard enough if I could still shout like that. I laughed and spun off, pretending it was easy. It wasn't, but I did feel strong and comparatively comfortable.

This was supposed to be the shortest climb of the three, at just less than nine and a half kilometres, but it didn't feel like it. In the final third, just when everyone was burning out, it bit harder, with the steepest slopes of the whole climb and big straight sections extending the horizon to let you know exactly how much longer this torture would go on. The tree covering kept the summit hidden from view, so there was no clear target; and each distant corner brought the promise of the end but then a kick in the balls when it revealed only another, even steeper straight.

Finally, a corner revealed a plateau and a flurry of activity ahead, just a few hundred metres away. The summit! Out of the last few trees and into the open I could see the promise of great views down the other side and got up out of the saddle to get out of the recurring nightmare of spinning up and up a slope. At last the road flattened and all was flat. I felt a lump in my thigh, a weird pulsation that felt awfully like cramp but which I soon forgot as I climbed off to fill my water bottles and grab a few cut oranges. What bliss as the sweet juice filled my mouth. Ah ... one down, two to go!

My legs felt a little bit shaky but my back was totally fine, not a murmur of discontent as I stretched hurriedly, took another long slug of water and swung back on the bike. I crossed the plateau and took in the fabulous views down the other side, over the foothills of the Pyrenees and what seemed like hundreds of miles beyond.

I felt great, energised, comfortable, actually enjoying myself. And the descent was amazing, not too many sharp corners, really smooth roads, steady, and fast, very fast, but no sense of being out of control. These were 'free miles', I decided, the overall distance being eaten up without any effort, and as I flew past those more cautious, I decided all the hassle was definitely worth it for these precious, serene and supreme moments when I felt super strong, in the zone, at peace, and at 40mph.

Occasionally a loud shout of 'à droit!' would interrupt the serenity as lunatics descending at potentially fatal speeds announced their racing lines and flew past my right shoulder. I remembered the old saying about the two types of drivers – idiots who drive slower than me and maniacs who drive faster – and found my own balance.

Down I glided, feeling at one with the bike and at peace with the world, down into the valley and along the flat roads towards the second big battle of the day, the Col du Soulor. I was getting focused on that when I spotted another swelling in the road up ahead, another unadvertised climb, and a bloody long one by the looks of it. I could see it shimmering off into the distance – it was beginning to get quite hot – and again I felt an irrational burst of indignation, as if somehow I'd been conned.

About halfway along this annoying speed bump, I again felt the pulsing in my right thigh, and this time it lasted longer and was bloody sore. It was undeniably cramp. I didn't want to believe it, I'd only been cycling two and a half hours and I'd never cramped up on a bike before, not even during the non-stop Race Around Ireland. I stood up in the pedals, took my foot out of the clip and shook my leg a bit, and tried to forget it. Cramping this early was a potential disaster and I couldn't understand it. It must have been the long injury lay-off. I hadn't had the chance to cycle more than two hours at a time since I'd had the bulging disc, and maybe my muscles had forgotten that this was what they were supposed to do. I was seriously worried, but told myself I'd soon shake it off and I'd be OK when I took on more food.

There was supposed to be 40-odd fairly flat kilometres after that, and my plan was to get into a big group to share the wind breaking. Unfortunately I hadn't seen any of my Sky colleagues, even though we were all wearing the same replica kit, and I had no idea whether Tom and Simon had even started, so I latched on to a group of French cyclists from the same club.

There are all sorts of unwritten cycling rules pertaining to riding in groups, covering everything from correct attire to the position of your wheels in relation to whoever is alongside you. (Being slightly in front is called 'half-wheeling' and is punishable by an extended stay in the Tower.) It's a sport that I love but it's hard to deny there's a certain collective smugness about many of the aficionados, and although many who prefer a bike to a car regard themselves as free-spirited individualists, there is a paradoxically cliquey group-think that I have always found a bit uncomfortable.

So as I joined the back of the French group I was ready to do more than my fair share of the wind work at the front to justify my place and ensure acceptance. But there was the issue of my Team Sky replica kit. I knew from working in professional cycling that, in their short existence, Team Sky had quickly become the outfit everyone else loved to hate, and it would be entirely in keeping with cycling prejudice to pass this on to me.

So it proved. A couple of riders glanced back when I joined, didn't return my jaunty 'Bonjour', and began muttering up the line. I went to the front to show I wasn't planning to freeload, and worked hard for a few minutes, giving them all a good tow through the headwind. Pulling off to rejoin the back, as is normal procedure, I got only head-shaking and muttering.

A few minutes later I took another turn at the front, deciding this time to work even harder and for longer to prove my worth. Nobody came up to relieve me, so I stubbornly kept going. When I eventually looked round in frustration to give my best Gallic remonstration, the feckers were about 200 metres down the road, and the lead cyclist waved his arms to shoo me on. *L'entente uncordiale.*

I ploughed on alone, feeding off the injustice. I had planned a quick psychological check at the 100 kilometres point, to give myself a pep talk if I was struggling and a caffeine tablet if I was *really* struggling. Just as three figures clicked through on my Garmin for the first time, enormous mountain peaks appeared up ahead. The Soulor and Tourmalet passes were among the, huge, malignant masses enveloping the horizon, giving my pep talk a real edge.

The Soulour was one long constant slope, unlike the variance on the Marie Blanque, and it just drained me. I didn't have the first-time ferocity I'd had on the Marie Blanque and couldn't let it all hang out the way I planned to on the Tourmalet, where it would all end. It was something in between, both literally and figuratively, and I knew it was slowly sapping my legs. The constant grind – gradients of between 6 and 9 per cent for 13 kilometres non-stop – was interrupted a couple of times by arrows of pain and contraction in my thighs as they erupted in cramp. This was becoming a major concern, and I wanted the Soulor out of the way so I could stretch and work out how to cope with it on the Tourmalet. It was a low point mentally, all grind and not enough progress, and with so much still to come I was a bit anxious.

Once we passed through the densely wooded lower slopes there were majestic views over mountain pastures, with gorgeous scenes down one side and with the silence broken only by the sound of bikes creaking, pedals spinning and bodies panting, there were more peaceful moments as we all struggled, together on the road but alone in our thoughts.

The Sky support people were on the plateau at the summit, handing over the individual food bags we'd packed the night before for a very welcome boost. They had parked the Sky vans in a little car park on the side of the mountain, and behind them was just the most stunning scene of blue sky, hazy lilac mountains and distant horizons. I had a burst of enormous good feeling, a rush of endorphins, elation and strength as the guys handed out the drinks and advice, taking the chance to give us all a quick once-over as well.

I looked on this point as a restart, gave my thighs what I hoped was an effective self-massage, got rid of everything I didn't need, and set off on the descent knowing that within a few hours I'd be finished.

There was total silence between riders on the descent from the Soulor, and this continued on the approach to the Tourmalet. The most infamous climb in all the Pyrenees cast a mighty shadow, more figuratively than literally as I don't remember being able to see the summit or get a sense of its enormous bulk. Looking at the Garmin boosted me greatly, though – over 160 kilometres done, and surely just getting through the last 25 was achievable whatever the gradient?

Twenty minutes later I was rapidly unravelling and trying not to notice. All of the big Pyrenean and Alpine climbs have road signs with a cyclist marked on them telling you how many kilometres to go until the summit, and what the gradient is going to be for the next kilometre. The first time I saw them, when climbing the Alpe d'Huez a few years ago, they gave me a sense of support and I enjoyed ticking them off on the way past and preparing mentally for the kilometre ahead. But I hated them on the Tourmalet. It was just so unrelenting that each kilometre lasted forever and the road signs served only to give me a reference of how long it was taking to get from one to the other. I grew a beard between kilometres five and six.

My thighs at this point were cramping horrendously every few minutes, so badly that I feared they would lock up permanently at some point and I would be forced off the bike, legs rigid like a bionic man. My quads, not the most impressive slabs of meat ever seen on a cyclist, were literally rippling with each wave of cramp, jumping and pulsing as if something was alive inside and trying to burst out. Every time I tried to stand to relieve the strain on my back and shift muscle position, a lightning stab of protest from my thighs sat me back down again. It was going to be a seriously long final climb if I couldn't move position after over six hours in the saddle. I was so frustrated by the cramping and really concerned about the next stages in the progression. Do muscles go from cramping to bursting?! I had no idea, but there was nothing I could do except ride on and find out.

The heat was stifling by now; I was soaked in sweat and really boiling in the direct sunlight, with no prospect of shade and no breeze. Every so often someone on the side of the road would offer a plastic cup of water, which I would pour over my head for some blissful cooling – and then fret about the extra soggy weight. The support was incredible. Even though the proper Tour de France stage was four days away, the fans were already in position with campervans lining the high slopes, and they gave us nearly as much frenzied encouragement as they would give the professionals later in the week, even though our efforts must have looked pathetic by comparison.

I started to think of those men who do this for a living, pitying those who have to suffer like this day after day in the full glare of both the sun and the watching world. Professional cyclists not only have to get to the top of each mountain, but get to the top before everyone else. It was bad enough having to get up in your own time, but to have to get up quicker than everyone else's time would be a crippling added pressure.

Stories of suffering on the Tourmalet are part of the very fabric of the Tour de France. It was the scene of some of the most infamous moments in the race's cruel and unusual history, including the legendary exchange between 1910 winner Octave Lapize and the race organisers at the summit.

'Vous êtes des assassins!' Lapize yelled furiously at the officials when he finally reached the top. 'Oui, des assassins!' That day, the stage was over 300 kilometres long with seven horrible climbs up rough tracks rather than roads, and the bikes had only one gear. Sometimes bikes even had to be carried. Those early warriors of competitive cycling were a different breed.

With all the modern advantages, my own Tourmalet experience should have been a breeze by comparison. But I was really struggling. My head was banging, I felt nauseous and dizzy, a little delirious, and I thought I heard someone shout 'Come on, Little!' in a French accent. When I heard it for a second and then a third time I knew it was real, but totally perplexing. Who knew me up here?! How weird. About halfway up I passed another Sky rider, veering wildly over the road and in more trouble even than I was, but like the climbers on Everest I had to ignore him and save myself. But I noticed that a surname was written on the side of his top, under the arm. I checked my own. 'LITTLE'. Aha! I smiled for the first time in hours.

The Tourmalet road is 19 kilometres long. Why on earth anyone thought a road that climbed to 2,115 metres up a mountain was ever required is beyond me. Why not just drive round the fecker? When the early Tour organisers were compiling their race routes they ranked each mountain climb from Category 4 (quite easy) up to Category 1 (very hard). When they found a mountain road that was too steep and challenging for them to get up and measure, they simply classed it as 'Hors Catégorie' (beyond categorisation), and then sent the cyclists over it anyway. Assassins indeed. I need hardly add that the Tourmalet is Hors Catégorie.

There was a ski resort called Barèges halfway up and a feed stop on a big bend in the road shortly after. It was dusty and roasting, and with riders arriving in various states of distress, it resembled an army field medical position in some distant outpost of the old Empire. I wanted to lie down, but I wasn't sure I could get up again. My right thigh locked as I tried to swing my leg off the bike and I almost fell to the ground. I was wobbly; walking felt alien. A medic came over.

'Ça va?'

'Non,' I smiled in what I hoped conveyed suitable irony.

He smiled back, satisfied, and walked away. I gave my thighs another vigorous but probably pointless rubbing. They were actually sore now to touch. I assumed the pulsing of the muscles wasn't good for them, and I did have serious concerns about the full leg lock that would spell the end happening before the summit. Like a driver running out of petrol, I was stuck between the need to get to the destination as soon as possible and the requirement to travel conservatively and preserve what little fuel was left.

Five kilometres from the top someone with an unmistakably Northern Irish voice shouted, 'Come on, Graham, you're going really well!' I smiled weakly in the general direction and shook my head ruefully. Four days later, back on Sky Sports News, I found out live on air that it was my colleague Orla Chennaoui who had spotted me. She was reporting on the Tour, and as we were previewing the Tourmalet stage she told the world that she'd seen me struggling up the same mountain the previous weekend.

Five kilometres from the end I got my first proper sight of the summit. Up until then I had almost been afraid to look up from the road passing beneath me. Now the top, and the end of the day, still seemed impossibly, infuriatingly far away. Long zigzags carved into the side of the mountain marked the path I still had to take. It was deflating and counter-productive to look up again until I was finished, I decided. I was fed up now, bored, sore and hating it.

At some point in those last few desperate miles, Tom arrived alongside me. He seemed annoyingly fresh, as if he'd just been on a casual training ride.

'Here you are at last!' he announced breezily. 'I thought I'd get you before now. How's it going?'

I could barely speak. 'Struggling,' I slurred. 'Simon?'

'God only knows. We got split up after about half an hour, it was just chaos trying to get through everyone in front of us, he was going mad. There was a big traffic jam on the Marie Blanque.'

I churned on in grim silence. Two kilometres to go. Tom was still breezy. I tried to convey my utter desperation through one-word answers and groans.

'I'm going to do this, right?' I panted, almost pleadingly, to Tom.

'What?'

'I'm going to finish this …'

'Yes, of course you are,' he replied, bemused. 'The top is just up there. Try to stand up a bit, bounce on the pedals, nice and light.'

'Aaargh! Cramp!'

'OK. Sorry.'

The pain was excruciating and the pulsing cramps were now coming with frightening regularity. I felt helpless and just desperately hoped my legs would somehow hold together to the end. Not being able to finish at this point would be absolutely heart-breaking, I would never get over it.

'It's just the six weeks you were off the bike, don't worry about it, your muscles forgot how to do this for hours and hours. You'll be OK next time,' said Tom. I couldn't even smile. There would be no next time.

I reached the last kilometre marker and was nearly sick.

'Aargh!' I roared again, when I saw the gradient.

'Moyenne de la pente: 10%'

I honestly felt aggrieved, as if someone was deliberately making me suffer, making this pointlessly harder. Why would the final kilometre out of 185 be suddenly steeper? Why?! Who did this?! Who could I blame? The anger spurred me on. I still couldn't stand without my legs locking, so I just sat there grinding the pedals, quietly seething, roasted, nauseous, spent, inching my way to the finish.

Round a narrow corner there it was. The finish arch. The end of the torture. It had taken me nearly two hours to get up the Tourmalet.

'Vous êtes des assassins!' I shouted at a grey-haired official standing to one side with a clipboard. He laughed. Other officials were lined up on either side, probably ready to catch people who collapsed over the line or fell when finally getting off the bike and returning to life on two legs. Tom and I were shepherded further down the road and off to a bit of waste ground on the left. Despite the turmoil I somehow remembered to stop the timer on the Garmin. I had been cycling for 8 hours and 38 minutes. A week later, Andy Schleck won that stage during the pro race. It took him 5 hours and 3 minutes. The bastard.

Dizzy and exhausted, I dropped the bike on its side and lay down on the ground. I was utterly wrecked. Sky had a videographer on site and he arrived for some reaction. My heart was still thumping, my head was spinning, but between pants I told him what I'd thought on the early stages of the Tourmalet.

'The worst job in the world … has to be … professional cyclist. Just … awful … doing that … every day … for three weeks … madness … madness …'

Tom found me a couple of bottles of lovely chilled water. I gulped one and threw the other all over me. It was so good to drink something that didn't taste of sweetened energy drink. I felt better almost instantly and moved on a bit, over to the side of the mountain for a bit of quiet reflection. Another epic struggle, another perfectly pointless torture that my grandfathers' generation would not have understood. My strength returned, and so too the flood of good feeling, the great 'runner's high' that makes it all appear to mean something. I felt fortunate to have been born at a time and into circumstances that provided such opportunity for adventure and self-exploration. As usual, just ten minutes after questioning everything and detesting the task at hand, it all seemed worth it and I was ready again to preach the Man Test Message.

There was still no sign of Simon, which was odd. I didn't remember him coming past me and Tom was adamant he was behind him. We waited for ages, getting stiffer by the minute, but there was no sign of him. Sickeningly, Tom was fresh enough to cycle back down the mountain a little bit to try and find him so they could ride the last bit together. I headed on down to the first Sky meeting point about a kilometre from the summit, and waited. And waited.

Simon's plan for getting back to Pau was 'just cycle back or maybe hitch a lift or something', so I knew I'd have to wait and try to sort him out. But it really wasn't like him to be hours behind everyone else in a cycle race, even if he started from the back.

Finally, I saw him coming down the road side by side with Tom, gesticulating wildly and scratching at his arm, which was bandaged quite significantly at the elbow.

'Yo!' he shouted as I stepped into the road to meet them. He hung one foot and dragged his shoe on the ground. 'What …' I began.

'Back brake snapped. Well done! Eight and a half hours?'

'Yip. What happened to you?'

Simon shook his head ruefully, looked at Tom and blew a raspberry.

'What didn't happen?' he said laughing, before launching into a high-speed recap. 'Couldn't get out of back group, couldn't get past anyone, had a load of mechanicals, got them fixed, went mental down Marie Blanque trying to make up time so my back tyre exploded from the heat of the brakes. Had to wait half an hour for the race mechanic guys! Half an hour! Then I just went more mental trying to catch up again. Didn't drink or eat anything other than these caffeine gels, those magic French ones … pretty much just sugar and caffeine … I think I had all of them and I brought ten. So then I passed out at the end.'

I stared, dumbfounded. Passed out? Before he continued the story, we tried to work out how much caffeine he'd had. The caffeine gels he'd found delivered about 150mg of caffeine each. So he'd had roughly 1,500mg of caffeine in about eight hours, which is the equivalent of about 15 cups of very strong coffee, without water or any food to wash it down or mop it up, while cycling up and down mountains in the heat of the French summer. It wasn't quite a cocktail of Tom Simpson proportions, but it was – and remember, Simon is a doctor – at the very least grossly irresponsible. Of course, I also found it a wee bit admirable.

In his excellent book on the life and death of the great Simpson, William Fotheringham wrote that there are very few people with the ability actually to destroy themselves in pursuit of an athletic goal, but sometimes that's what it takes. The champions are those who are prepared to sacrifice everything to achieve the goal, push their bodies way beyond the safe limits, whatever the cost. Sadly for Tom Simpson, this ability or willingness cost him his life. He pushed himself to death on his bike, on the ascent of Mont Ventoux in the 1967 Tour de France.

Simon was one of those with the ability to push into the abyss, and I found it all too easy to imagine the scene at the top of the Tourmalet when he collapsed over the line. He had come round in the medical tent, being laid down on the bed with his whole body in spasm. A hastily prepared drip was being hoisted above him and needles were poised. Struggling to balance his GCSE French with his own medical training, he realised he was about to be given a huge dose of glucose, which was the worst thing possible after his earlier sugar overdose. Simon was adamant that it could have killed him.

He blathered on about calcium and sodium and stuff I wouldn't have understood even if he hadn't been speaking faster than an auctioneer on speed. I gathered he'd eventually got what he needed in the drip from the medics, been patched up from the fall, and sent on his way after an enforced lie down. Tom eventually found him attempting to get back on his bike. He had crossed the line and been carried into the medical tent while the two of us were relaxing and reflecting.

In some respects his recovery just a few hours later was remarkable, but if the effects of the ride appeared to have worn off, the effects of the caffeine and sugar certainly hadn't. Aside from that elephant dose of caffeine, he was also surfing a powerful wave of post-exercise endorphins, some sort of survivor's euphoria, having come back almost literally from the dead – and of course we have no real idea of everything that was in the drip.

The machine-gun verbosity was accompanied by eyes as wide as espresso cups and the fidgety movements of an Ecstasy-addled raver. I phoned the Sky support people, told them the story, and they agreed both he and Tom could come back to Pau with us. We still had to cycle off the mountain and down to the town at the bottom where the bus was parked. The prospect of hurtling down the Tourmalet with a man who had been in some sort of coma just minutes before, appeared to be as high as a kite and was riding a home-made bike with no back brakes, was not appealing. I let Simon and Tom go in front. Way in front.

It was nearly 11 o'clock by the time we eventually made it back to the hotel. Dinner was long done but I'd texted ahead and a friend kept us some cold meats and some kind of coagulated gravy stuff. Not quite what I was looking for after such an epic day. Simon had of course come right into our hotel looking for free food and whatever else he could pick up before sleeping in the car and then starting the ridiculous drive home. He was really quite warped at this stage, and I am sure I saw genuine fear in the eyes of the other Sky people sat beside us in the dining room.

After a rowdy but exhilarating half-hour, we said good-bye. Simon clip-clopped across the hotel lobby in his cycling shoes, and he and Tom headed out to try and find where they had abandoned the car in the dark that morning.

I met Martin Corry again the next day as I was waiting in the lobby for the airport bus. He'd finished in nine and a half hours, and the story of his day seemed quite similar to mine. The Tourmalet had broken him completely, taking him two and a half hours. And when he finally finished, he didn't exactly find it all rewarding.

'I got to the top and I was like, right, what do I do now, just descend 20K to meet up with everybody else? I just sat on the side of the road for a little bit and it was the most surreal feeling, watching people just finishing what was absolutely brutal, and then just dandering down the other side. It put me in such a weird place. "OK, you've finished it, well done. Now, go down."'

I felt that this was where the big difference between professional and amateur sport probably hit home for Martin. There was no fanfare, no trophy lift, just a small medal and then get back on your bike to cycle to the bus back to the hotel, fly home and then go back to work. It wasn't what he was used to, but it was the way more and more of us did our sport, spent our weekends, found fulfilment. It worked for me, but he was right, it was bloody weird to empty yourself completely targeting something that was ultimately transitory.

Eight
FROM LIDO TO LOUGH

It was because of the low-key way these adventures often seemed to end that I always liked having the next one lined up. I was hardly home before I got another email from Robster, relaying all the information he'd gleaned from poring over the Marathon des Sables event forums. There were a couple of these forums, online spaces where veterans and prospective runners would meet. Some of the veterans had done the race as much as five years ago and yet were still engaged with the forums, which I actually found a bit sad, as if nothing had happened in their lives since.

I felt guilty that I hadn't up until now been giving either the MDS or Robster proper attention, but now that I'd got the Byron swim and the Étape out of the way I could concentrate on it a bit more. I was concerned that Robster was doing a bit too much too soon however, both in terms of logistics and training. One evening we were chatting and he was telling me about a session he had done that afternoon on a treadmill in the gym.

'You know those socks that don't quite come up over your trainers? Secret socks, I call them.'

'Yes, little anklet socks,' I replied.

'Well, I was doing an hour on the treadmill and wearing a pair of them but they didn't cover my heels properly, so my trainers started rubbing really badly. It was getting quite sore, but I thought it would be good training for the MDS to keep going and toughen myself up.'

'OK ... so ...'

'So I just ran on and on, and it got pretty bad, they started bleeding, the tips of my socks were bright red and the backs of my trainers were covered in blood, but they did go numb after a while so maybe it worked.'

There is blood, and there is bloody-mindedness. This was the summer before we were due to take part, so the event was still a good nine months away. A few days later, I was sitting on the grass in the evening sun watching Christian toddle about. Claire came out of the house and sat down a bit sheepishly beside me. The instinctive spousal trouble radar kicked in.

'Sweetpea ...'

'Yes?' I tried to sound breezy but I knew there was a big request, a big admission or a big bollocking about to be delivered.

'I think I might be a bit pregnant again ...'

'Oh.'

Wasn't expecting that.

'That would mean the baby being born in April next year.'

'That's the Marathon des Sables time,' I said quietly, my voice trailing off. It was awkward. Of course we were talking about a potential new life here, a massive blessing, so obviously I was delighted, but I also had this immediate, instinctive sinking feeling. I knew that if the MDS was ruled out I'd really be letting Robster down, and something that had been slowly building momentum would come to a sudden, unfulfilled halt.

'I know, I'm sorry, I miscalculated.'

I laughed at the twenty-first-century idea of such a natural, primeval process being 'miscalculated'.

'Well, how sure are you?'

'I have done two tests now ... and I have been feeling a bit funny. I'm pretty sure.'

We went inside and started checking calendars, and 'cycles'. Mid-April looked like being the time. The Marathon des Sables started on the fifteenth.

'I better ring Robster ...'

'Oh, Sweetpea, I feel so bad, I don't know how I messed that up! It's ...' Claire tailed off with tears in her eyes. 'Maybe you can just go anyway, it's only a week, isn't it? And it's such early days ...'

I didn't know what to say. It was fantastic news that we might have another member of the family joining us, and we had made a conscious decision to double our kids, but we *were* aiming for later in the year. The idea that I would be halfway across the Sahara when Claire was in labour was so ridiculous that not even *I* would have suggested it. There was no option but to pull out of the race. But it was so early in the pregnancy, anything could happen and we wouldn't be telling anyone for months yet. I didn't know how to continue chatting MDS with Robster while knowing that with each passing week it was more and more likely I wouldn't actually be going with him.

A couple of months later Claire was still pregnant and it was confirmed that I wouldn't be running. I put it off day after day, but when I finally got round to calling Robster, who had thankfully gone a bit quiet recently, he was very understanding and adamant that he would push on and do it himself. But he didn't. A few months later he was forced to pull out as well. Regular five-hour road runs carrying a rucksack loaded with weights brought on the recurrence of an old rugby neck injury, which a series of specialist doctors told him could lead to permanent damage if he continued with that volume of training. It was a big decision for him, he'd set his heart on running the Sahara and thought about little else for a year, but when one of the specialists told him that he risked not being able to pick up his kids if he exacerbated the problem, he had no option but to forget about the whole thing for good. So, having made such a fuss about the waiting list, neither of us even made it to the confirmed *starting* list, never mind to Morocco.

Sheepishly, I called Sarah from the official UK Marathon des Sables agency to explain why neither of us was going to join her in Morocco after all.

'Do you want to transfer to the following year?' she asked immediately.

'Yes,' I responded, even quicker, surprised that was even an option. I never even thought about the fact I'd be going alone or that I'd be going without Robster, whose idea it was in the first place. Just like the Hellespont Swim, this was just something that was now in my head that I knew wouldn't leave until I finished it, so I had to get there as soon as possible. Going alone wasn't ideal, but if that's the way it was, then so be it.

It was back to being two years away again, but this time I was definitely going, surprise pregnancies notwithstanding.

Two years was of course much too far away for just training, so I needed something else to do in the meantime, preferably something in Ireland so there'd be less logistics to sort with a new baby arriving in April. There *was* a big itch that needed scratching and it did at least fit the requirement of being in Ireland, but it was a bit of a monster.

Years before, I was working at UTV as a sports reporter when I heard about a team that was attempting to become the first ever to swim the whole 48 miles of Lough Erne, in my native County Fermanagh. The Erne stretches right across the county, the most westerly in the UK, draining the boggy farmland on all sides into its Upper or Lower Loughs, which are connected by a river running round the island town of Enniskillen. I'm biased, of course, but it's a unique, beautiful and peaceful part of the world, and I was only too keen to go down and report on the swim.

The attempt had been set up by Dr Julie Bradshaw, a part-time lecturer at Loughborough who had actually taken me for a few swim classes when I was there. She'd amassed an astonishing haul of world records, including swimming the Channel when she was only 15, and then swimming it butterfly a few years later. Butterfly is the most exhausting, pointless swimming stroke of the four, and the fact that she'd kept that up for 14 hours was incredible.

She'd pulled together a team of six women who took turns of one hour in a series of relays, and was confident of setting a time that would be a marker for future attempts. Each attempt would have to be facilitated by Fermanagh District Council and officiated by the Irish Long Distance

Swimming Association (ILDSA). Julie's team swam the 48 miles in 22 hours and 12 minutes, much quicker than they'd originally thought they would, and I was hugely impressed by their organisation, commitment and speed.

Years later, after I'd started open water swimming in triathlons and then swum the Hellespont, I went down to report on another attempt being made by an Irish male team. They were nowhere near as organised or as disciplined as Julie's team, but seemed very confident of breaking their record nonetheless. They didn't, missing it by more than three hours.

Watching those guys, I felt they'd made a number of fundamental errors, and began to think of the ways I'd do things differently. They were probably better swimmers than me, but I felt sure I could find others as good as them to make up a team and, by being better organised, could possibly get closer to the mark set by Julie's team, if not beat it. It was just an idle thought at the time of course, but then came the Race Around Ireland. Ever since then I had been of the opinion that a team could achieve anything with the right mind-set, even if they were brought together at the last minute by a calamitous nitwit. It had worked then, why couldn't it work again?

Any rational analysis of the year ahead – a new baby coming, an existing baby just a year old, a mammoth Sahara run on the horizon and work still chaotic for both husband and wife – would probably have led to the conclusion that things were pressurised enough as it was. But in a carbon copy of the delusional thinking that led me to book a team place on the Race Around Ireland two months after Christian was born, I decided to pull a team together for a crack at the swim record two months after our *second* child would be born. Yes, I'm a slow learner, but the rationale was that swim training didn't take as long as cycling, that it could be done indoors through the winter, and that when the time came I wouldn't have to travel anywhere further than an hour and a half down the road. The irrational part of the rationale was that I couldn't get the swim out of my head and I desperately wanted to hold a record in my own county.

If getting four cyclists prepared to race non-stop around Ireland was hard, it was nothing compared to finding six swimmers prepared to swim sections of a 48-mile course in cold murky water wearing only swimming trunks. Long Distance Swimming rules expressly forbid wetsuits, which was the first thing I'd have to get used to. A lot of triathlons expressly forbid competing *without* them, so I hadn't done a lot of proper swimming in either lake or sea wearing only my trunks.

Other stipulations specific to the Lough Erne record were that teams *had* to consist of six members, the relay *had* to consist of hourly shifts, and once the order of swimmers was set, this could not be changed. After securing the Council's backing, I contacted the ILDSA, who also eventually gave the go-ahead, although I sensed some disapproval on their part. I wondered if, just like Colm hesitating to back me forming a team for the Race Around Ireland, they had been put off by my curious Internet sporting footprint. It was fair enough. I wouldn't have believed me either.

I started the search for team-mates almost immediately, but after two months only had one confirmed swimmer other than me. Colin Hill was the Channel swimmer who had won the Europe to Asia swim. He didn't remember me from there, of course, but knew of Lough Erne and Julie's record, and was more than happy to give it a go. I wanted everyone else to be from Ireland if possible; one ringer was enough if we were to call this an Irish attempt. I would also have liked the team to have more people actually from Fermanagh, but strangely for a county dominated by the lake, there weren't too many people keen to get in it.

I had just finished training in my local leisure centre one afternoon when I bumped into Tony, an old triathlon friend of mine. A former Irish champion boxer ubiquitously known as 'wee Tony' in Belfast sporting circles, he asked me what I was up to. I told him all about the swim and he said he loved the open water and would gladly help out any way he could. I think he initially meant as crew, but I went upstairs to the café while he swam so I could surreptitiously time him from the viewing platform.

I'd spent ages calculating the average speeds of Julie's record. I estimated we needed to swim 3.5k in every hour to have a chance. An average speed of 3.5kph would be close; 4kph would smash it. So, breaking it down, that was swimming at about 1 minute 45 seconds per 100 metres pace, for an hour. I wasn't there yet, but I reckoned if I could get five other swimmers who *were* at that level to compensate, we'd be fine. I checked Tony's splits on my watch. He'd said he was just going in for a recovery swim so I was amazed to see him steadily clock 1:42 or 1:43 per 100. I was delighted, and phoned him later that evening. He was in.

So I was halfway to having my team. Another Fermanagh candidate finally bobbed to the surface in the shape of Paul, a former swimming club star who hadn't swum competitively for years but loved being in the lake. He was young and almost impossible to track down, but I persisted and he half-committed. He didn't inspire me with confidence by not returning any calls, but I had very few other options so gave him one last chance weeks later.

I'd told everyone else we needed to get close to 4kph to break the record, just to make sure they'd be in the best possible shape, but in my desperation to fill the team slots, I decided that if Paul could do 3, he was in. When he said he'd managed 'the 4' in the pool the previous week, I nearly jumped for joy.

So that was four swimmers in total, and each one better than me. Meanwhile, work was getting busier and busier. I had set up a new Northern Ireland office for a big English sports production company called Century TV after helping them win the contract to produce the BBC's Moto GP coverage for three years. We would be running most of the production from Belfast and needed a new editor.

By an outrageous quirk of fortune the job went to someone who turned out to have finished an Ironman the year before. Even more outrageously, Adam claimed that the swimming leg was his strongest of the three. After he'd heard me on the phone telling a journalist from the local paper about my Lough Erne ambitions, he sent me an email – which I found a little odd given that he was in the room next door – asking if I was still looking for swimmers, and if so would I consider him.

It seemed too good to be true, and after he repeated a few times that he hadn't been training much lately I was reluctant to commit. But then a few mornings in a row he arrived in the office smelling of chlorine. He'd been leaving the house at six, was probably training harder than I was – and was also, I suspected, a better swimmer. He even produced one of his old Ironman training plans. We were five.

One to go, and then I hit the jackpot. I'd put the onus on Paul to find me another Fermanagh person so we could at least claim half the team was from our county. I jokingly asked him one afternoon if Northern Ireland international swimmer Chelsey Wilson would be available. She wasn't long home from competing in the backstroke at the Commonwealth Games. Matter of factly he replied that he didn't see why not, and said he'd ask her at the club that evening. I laughed and we agreed to catch up the next day.

He texted me the following morning with her number. She was interested. I couldn't quite believe it but phoned her immediately. She'd been swimming competitively almost all her life, had lived in Enniskillen for even longer, but had never, ever put so much as a toe in the lake. The very idea of it, she said, was a bit creepy. I asked her how she'd handle the cold water. Her reply that sometimes she found the pool water so cold she had to bounce for a whole length before summoning the courage to duck her head, did not inspire me with confidence. On the other hand, 4k an hour for Chelsey facing forwards or backwards would be a breeze. She was worth the gamble. We were six.

There was a whole myriad of logistical issues to be sorted too, of course, including a team of canoeists to escort us down the lake and a cruiser big enough for six swimmers, two ILDSA officials, Adam's girlfriend Ellie who was going to double up as cook and masseuse, and a driver. But my most pressing concern was my own swimming, and how to get in the required amount of open water practice.

*

Our second son, Reuben, was born at the end of April – another monster, this time just one ounce off ten pounds. That is one big baby, and the natural delivery was traumatic for Claire. He basically wrecked the place and she was in and out of hospital a few times in the following weeks. She did incredibly well to cope with that as well as Christian, who was still only 20 months, being back to work almost immediately, and me.

Reuben was to be baptised in a church in her hometown of Magherafelt, which conveniently for me was on the far side of Lough Neagh, the biggest expanse of fresh water in the UK. I couldn't help myself, I had to seize the opportunity. It was windy, wintry and choppy and perfect as a means of toughening myself up. But not as a means of settling Claire's nerves before a big family day out. I can scarcely believe now that I put her through it – feeding a six-week-old baby in the car while also entertaining a wriggly toddler, and standing by to get the coastguard on speed dial if I didn't come back.

I was still spending a fair amount of time in London, so I scoured maps for bits of lakes, rivers – any water at all that wasn't an indoor swimming pool. I swam in Hyde Park at lunchtimes, nearly choking on pondweed, and then discovered Tooting Bec Lido, a man-made 1930s outdoor pool and a true gem of English sporting heritage. It's an enormous 90 metres in length and not heated, which made it pretty much the perfect training base for me. It was bloody freezing in fact, and I would get out and shiver for at least ten minutes after each swim. That was an improvement, however, on the shivering times after my swims in lakes and seas in Ireland.

The ratio was about 1:1 swim time to shiver time. So if I swam for 20 minutes, I'd shiver for 20 minutes. I began craving my wetsuit but had to persist without it, hoping I'd adapt somehow as the water warmed up later in the year. It was still only late May and the water temperature in the lakes was about 12°C. My plan was just to get in as often as possible, even if only for short swims, and hope I'd acclimatise eventually.

At last I felt I could cope reasonably well with the cold, and two weeks before the Lough Erne attempt I felt ready for a big test. The lake was likely to be about 15 or 16°C by then, at least three degrees warmer than the sea, so I felt if I could survive an hour in the sea I would be more than able to cope with each hour of the relay in the Erne. I'd been travelling to the North Antrim coast on day trips and holidays since I was a boy, and had always wondered about the possibility of swimming between coastal towns Portrush and Portstewart. It was only three or four miles by car, I reasoned, and would probably be less by sea.

Yes, 'probably'. I recruited Rachel, a strong and experienced open water swimmer I'd been training with, and Garth, one of Claire's friends who was up on holiday, had done a few triathlons, and happened to have his wetsuit with him. Claire and Garth's wife Gillian would look after the kids while also keeping an eye on us from the road. Foolproof.

We did the proper research and planning, of course ... The morning we decided to try it we asked someone who was out walking their dog on the headland which direction would be best to swim in, to take advantage of the prevailing current.

'Oh, I think you'd swim from Portstewart to Portrush for sure, rather than the other way round,' he said. 'That would be the direction of the current.'

Forgive me going all Lynne Truss for a minute, but it's a curious thing, the Northern Ireland use of the word 'would'. Elsewhere in the English-speaking world it is used for something that *will* happen should a certain set of circumstances be met. But not here. We use it to introduce things that have *already* happened, or that are already established facts, the most common being identifying people by their relations. 'He would be a cousin of Brian's,' for example, or 'She would be a sister of your mother's.' English friends of mine find this exasperating. 'He would be a cousin of Brian's if what?!' they screech. 'What would make him a cousin of Brian's? Is he a cousin of Brian's or not?!'

I think it's because, despite the volatile reputation created by our politicians and terrorists over the years, most people of Northern Ireland are actually gentle and non-confrontational, so the use of the word 'would' turns a direct, barking fact into a more pitched, softer supposition.

So 'that would be the direction of the current' in this instance needed no further examination. The dog walker was gently informing us that the current without a doubt flows from Portstewart to Portrush, and we accepted it. Except it doesn't. Being from England, this was the one time Rachel should have stepped in to query the employment of the 'Northern Ireland Would', but she didn't. Big mistake.

Off we went to Portstewart, with the wives following in cars laden with babies to see us off and take my keys once we stripped in the car park. Because he wasn't training for a crazy cold-water challenge, Garth had the luxury of a wetsuit. Portstewart has an old deep-water rock pool called the Herring Pond, filled by the high tide each morning and used by countless previous generations for summer swims before we all got a bit soft. We leaped in there, and I ploughed straight out to sea to get moving as fast as possible and pretend I was warming up.

I swam flat out for a couple of minutes, telling myself the great lie that I had generated enough body heat now to be warm, while knowing full well that actually I'd just become numb, and then stopped and floated a bit to look for Rachel and Garth. It was quite choppy actually. Not wildly rough or anything, just with a fair bit of swell rolling us around in the water. Back on land I could just make out the wives' cars, but could much more clearly sense the disapproval.

Rachel was heading towards me and briefly looked up. I waved, she waved back, and I could see Garth coming behind her. I pointed vaguely up the coast and took off again. After a few minutes I was quite enjoying it, swept along by the thrill and occasional terror of being in the open water, especially a monstrous sea that would next embrace land on the Hebrides and, beyond that, the Faroe Islands.

But it was choppy; there was no doubt about that. Each time I stopped to check on the others it took me longer and longer to spot them in the waves, until eventually I couldn't find Garth at all. But he had a wetsuit, so he'd be OK, I reasoned. It was a bit of a quandary, floating about looking for them; on the one hand it was much, much safer to swim as a group, and that was what Rachel and I had always done in training and always promised each other; but on the other hand, the longer I floated about waiting and searching, the colder I was going to get.

I dropped the pace a bit but swam on, hoping that Rachel and Garth would catch up and I could keep moving and warm. After 50 minutes I couldn't see either of them any time I stopped, and had a decision to make. To float about waiting for them wasn't an option any more, so that left just going on alone, which would at least get me closer to Portrush. Like the irresponsible optimist I am, I decided to swim on a bit and think about it as I went.

Shortly after, I realised I couldn't make any decisions because my mind was going a bit fuzzy. And I was warm. I knew enough to know these are both bad signs in cold water. Confusion and poor judgement are two of the principal symptoms of hypothermia, and swimming alone in the Irish Sea is not somewhere you want to be confused or making bad decisions. Heat is lost much quicker in water than in air, and it's reckoned that being in water temperature of 10°C for an hour or so is enough to kill some of us. Everyone is different, of course, some can cope with colder water for longer, but I knew from the previous few months that I wasn't one of those. I had to get out, and fast. I looked back to land. In the swell, it was hard to get a fix on any one point, and although it all looked so straightforward when we were driving earlier that morning, I now felt a bit disoriented. Again, a bad sign.

Further up the coast I could see only tall cliffs of black rock on a headland jutting out before the West Strand of Portrush, which I guessed was still at least a good 20 minutes' swim away. And it would be 20 minutes on my own, as I had no idea what had happened to Garth and Rachel. I could see a house and a rough path alongside me on the shore. This was the last chance to get out before the headland, so it was either get out here and climb into this random garden, or attempt the swim to the beach where Gillian and Claire would be anxiously waiting.

Getting out early would arm them with enough 'I told you so' to last a lifetime, but carrying on and potentially not getting out at all was (just about) even worse. I also reasoned that if I got out at least I could hopefully see the others, about whom I was getting very worried.

I swam to shore, where the waves did their best to smash me into the rocks, not prepared to let another idiot go without a final demonstration of their power and dominance over all. I had to pick the moment and the spot but finally managed to haul myself out on hands and knees, staying low to keep some grip as the waves washed in over me. Eventually I made it out of the grasping pull of the sea and clambered over the sharp rocky points to a little beach of stones and shell.

I was suddenly aware of how violently I was shaking, how poor was my co-ordination, and how befuddled was my thinking. These are all classic symptoms of hypothermia. I was also suddenly aware that I was standing at the bottom of someone's garden. What an arresting site that would have been for them at breakfast, a vibrating creature suddenly coming alone out of the sea and walking up their garden. Terrifying.

Befuddled as I was, I knew I had to get warm pretty quickly, and that meant getting to Portrush. I found a steep path up the hill to the right and pranced up it, gingerly picking out steps with my shoeless feet but trying to keep moving quickly to get body heat generated again. It was not a battle I was winning. I was shivering wildly and uncontrollably. There was a red car pulled in on a flattish area of grass on the headland, the driver was reading a newspaper in the sun with the window down.

I ran over. 'H-h-h-h have you a t-t-t-towel or sp-sp-sp-spare t-t-t-T-shirt or anything p-p-p-please?' Alarmed, he mumbled, 'No, I have nothing like that,' and wound up the window! I stumbled on and soon reached the main road, where I hadn't the faintest idea what to do next. Run down the main road to Portrush in my tight budgie-smugglers and lilac swimming cap? The good Presbyterians of the north coast, on their way to church, would have a fit.

A Good Samaritan couple out for a walk stopped beside me to help. The lady even took off her coat, but before I could gratefully put it on, the wives arrived. They had watched everything from the cliffside and Claire was furious. I did my very best to stop shivering and assume an air of nonchalance, but she wasn't having any of it and let me have both barrels for being 'stupid', 'irresponsible', 'ridiculous' and all sorts of other adjectives that would have hurt had they not also been true.

She took an old picnic blanket out of the boot of the car and ordered me to wrap up in that and get in the front seat. Garth was sitting in the back, sheepish and green. He'd turned back to Portstewart after feeling really sick in the choppy conditions. Rachel, meanwhile, walked up another path to join us, bemused as to what all the fuss was about. She isn't married. She'd got out about the same time as me, but at a proper beach path, and not through someone's garden. Whereas Garth and I were downplaying the dangerous reality of our own helplessness, Rachel – unfamiliar with disapproving wives – was positively delighting in the misadventure and rabbiting on about how quickly we lost each other and how mad it was out in the sea. I tried a few times to interrupt her as we drove the short distance down to Portrush but was stammering so much through my shivers that I couldn't talk properly. The heat of Claire's anger soon warmed me up.

On the plus side, I'd swum for an hour without any real bother, apart from the cold, which I reassured myself was exacerbated by having to keep stopping and waiting for the others. If I'd been able to just swim at my own pace I would have comfortably made it round to Portrush, I decided ... of course. On the minus side, Claire's patience had finally snapped, and the rest of the swim preparations would have to be made in semi-secret.

Time and again I asked myself why I hadn't learned a lesson at the Race Around Ireland. Why had I again taken on a challenge in which by far the most significant difficulty was likely to be getting everything in place, and for which I was likely to turn up already exhausted from the effort? Going on a solo challenge like the Étape du Tour I had to worry about one person. In this one, I had to organise 15 people and 2 boats.

The plan was that two Council reps, both of whom I'd known for years, would drive 50 metres in front of us, following the course on a GPS unit. The three kayakers would take it in turns to follow the Council boat's course, and the swimmer would stay beside the kayak. Then the rest of the swim team plus two ILDSA officials and Ellie would follow them in a big six-berth cruiser I'd borrowed from a friend. One of the criticisms I heard of the team that had failed to beat Julie Bradshaw's record was that they meandered all over the place, adding quite a bit of extra distance to an already hefty swim. Their kayakers basically acted as safety escorts, drifting with each swimmer, whereas I wanted ours to act as navigators.

I managed to get in touch with the same trio that had escorted Julie's team, and asked them to guide us. Their main advice was about following the right line. We agreed that they'd set the course and not move from the correct line. So the swimmers would have to keep to one side, and if they began veering off, the kayaker could nudge them with either kayak or paddle to straighten them up again. We made a note of which swimmers breathed on which side so that the kayak could always stay in vision.

I felt a great sense of relief when I picked up the boat on Friday afternoon and was motoring down to the start at Crom Castle, one of the most southerly points of County Fermanagh. With the hateful logistics element hopefully now completed, surely the rest would be easy?

Chief joiner-inner Chris from the Race Around Ireland had signed up for another adventure without hesitation, and he was driving the boat. The conditions were forecast to be perfect – overcast and without a breath of wind – and since there'd been a fair bit of rain that summer, the lough was full, which meant an extra bit of flow pushing us on. Just like on the Race Around Ireland, all the pre-challenge effort seemed to be paying off, and as I gave a quick briefing to all the team and crew in the Crom holiday cottages that night, I was confident we would at least give the record a good rattle.

I slept fitfully in the cabin of the boat. We'd agreed to set off just before first light, which meant a 5am alarm call, with Paul being the first brave soul to crash into the cold water in the eerie pre-dawn gloom. One of the ILDSA officials started him off with a blast of an air horn, which echoed round the quiet estate, and the other started the clock. We were off.

Unlike in the Race Around Ireland, the changeover times couldn't be varied. But deciding the *order* of the swimmers could still make a big difference to our record bid. If we were to get inside Julie's 22-hour record, four of the group would have to swim four times, and two of us would get away with only three swims. It therefore made sense for the two slowest – Tony and me by quite a margin – to go last, and also for us to try and put the two fastest – Colin and Chelsea – in positions three and four so that if we were getting close to the record near the end they could really hammer along and bring us home.

The first cycle of our relay went really well, everyone swam as if their life depended on it, and we were well ahead of the marks set by Julie's team. I felt real pressure, since I knew I was one of the weaker swimmers and was also the last of the six to go, but I thrashed hard for the hour and when I hauled myself back into the boat, Chris said he reckoned I'd covered well over the 3.5k needed in each hour to break the record. I heated some pasta on the little stove in the cabin and warmed up.

The only spectators were swans and the occasional cow squelching down to the water's edge in curiosity, and the whole county seemed quiet and peaceful. The ILDSA observers were mightily impressed, especially with Colin and Chelsey. She was an absolute revelation, a girl that had been in the lake just once with me on a test session, now slicing through the cold, dark waters as if she was parading up and down the pool.

We reached Enniskillen, roughly the halfway point, about an hour and a half ahead of schedule, but I knew from talking to the Council guys about previous years that halfway down the Lower Lough was when the real challenge started. This was a much wider, deeper body of water than the narrow, winding Upper Lough, the flow was nowhere near as strong, and if the wind blew and the water got choppy, it would seriously slow us down. It was here that the men from the previous attempt had seen their ambitions blown apart, whereas Julie Bradshaw's women had actually lifted their pace when the going got tough and finished the Lower Lough quicker than the Upper Lough, which was quite some achievement.

I leaped in again when it was time for my second shift and immediately felt more of a shudder than I had the first time. The Lower Lough felt significantly colder somehow. And darker, and more foreboding. Tony was swimming before me, and I had to tread water to let him past before overtaking him again so the ILDSA could verify the changeover.

I felt strong again at first. I'd done well in my first hour, nowhere near as quick as the human fish at the start of our order, but good enough. But as the second swim went on, and time moved much, much slower than on my first shift, I started to become aware of tightness in my hips and groin when I kicked in the last 20 minutes.

Instantly I knew what was up. Ever since the bulging disc episode before the Étape I'd made sure to always make time for a proper core strength and stretching routine. But in the three months after Reuben was born I had no more time to make, and no more energy to give. I was doing well just to be in the pool or in open water. Also I'd completely changed my swim stroke with the help of a coach and the only way to make sure it worked was to add at least 15 minutes of drills to every pool session. So the core work and stretching had been pushed aside again. And again, I would learn the same lesson the hard way.

My core was weak, and now, being asked to perform the same kicking motion over and over again and without a wetsuit to add to the buoyancy, it was protesting through a great strain in my hip flexors. This developed from a dull pain and general stiffness to periodic pulses of cramp that I could do nothing about. My hips would seize and my only option was to trail my legs behind me for a while without kicking and hope the cramp would subside, which it usually did seconds later.

But as one of the officials sounded the air horn that let us know there was 15 minutes to go, I was dealing with the issue more and more frequently. It was frustrating because my arms and shoulders felt fine and I wasn't struggling with breathing or the pace, it was just hip cramp and the threat of hip cramp holding me back. I changed up a gear anyway for the last quarter of an hour, hoping that a break in rhythm might help, but it didn't really and that last 15 minutes was a bit of a trial.

Finally I heard Paul hit the water beside me, I drew up alongside him, he grinned and was gone in a flash with enormous churns of his arms through the water. I hauled myself up the steps at the back of the cruiser, received everyone's congratulations, but I knew this hadn't been a particularly impressive swim. I got inside and warm as soon as possible and began stretching. I had five hours to recover, which I reasoned was loads of time, and a recovery shake would hopefully restore everything I needed. I didn't ask for an estimate of the distance, but I was pretty sure I'd done enough to keep us ahead of the record at least.

Tony provided one of the comedy moments of the day during his third hour. I'd warned everyone about any shallow water sections as we tried to take the most direct route, and reminded them that under no circumstances were they to walk forward or even stand up, in case the

ILDSA were forced to rule that we hadn't swum the whole way. If any sections got too shallow, we were all to keep flat in the water and swim or crawl to deeper water. We were watching Tony as the dusk gathered, and strangely it appeared that he had stopped moving. His arms were still windmilling, his feet were still kicking, but he wasn't going anywhere. Turned out he had swum onto a flat rock, and remembering my advice and scared shitless of costing us a time penalty or even disqualification, he had manfully just kept up his swimming stroke while beached, until a wave gently eased him off again. God bless him!

I was getting ready for the third and final time. It was almost completely dark by now, so I had to fix little glow sticks to the back of my goggle strap and swimming trunks. Kayaker Gary had a head-torch on, and every so often Chris would sweep across the lake with the spotlight from the cruiser. We were on course to smash the record by about three hours, had crossed the worst of the infamous Broad Lough, the deepest and choppiest part of the Erne, and all we had to do now was keep things on an even keel all the way to Belleek.

Everyone was pretty pumped up by now and desperate that each swimmer would go the extra mile, if only to make sure they themselves didn't have to get back in for a fourth time. Paul mentioned that I might make it all the way to Belleek to the finish point if I swam hard enough, but this was very wishful thinking on his part, since he was coming after me.

It was ten o'clock at night when I leaped in for the final time. The water was noticeably colder again, I'd guess about 13 or 14°C, maybe just a degree or so warmer than the sea in Portrush that near fatal day, and I swam about a bit to try and get warm as I waited for Tony. The average swimming pool is maintained at about 28 to 30°C, and of course you can see the bottom and it is well lit. Being in the lake in this half-light, where already hills and trees on the shore were nothing more than spooky dark silhouettes, was completely alien and more than a bit daunting. Normally I liked taking stock of unusual or extreme situations, the 'mindfulness' was one of the key parts of each crusade, but in this instance I dared not dwell on the eeriness of it all. The cold and the dark were best ignored as much as possible, and I just needed to turn off the brain and get through it.

Tony was struggling a bit by now, this had been a slow leg from him and we'd worried at one point if he was going to get the hour done. The ILDSA officials keep a count of everyone's stroke rate, and his had dropped dramatically. So as soon as he got level with me I was determined to inject a bit of pace into our effort and kicked off towards the dark horizon.

It was my only sober experience of swimming at night and certainly the first time I'd done it alone. It was one of the eeriest experiences of my life. Every sense was alive and slamming, and although I was churning through the water with all the grace of a moose, at the same time all around me was quiet and weirdly still. The only sound I could hear was the rhythmic splash of my arms hitting the water, and the odd paddle stroke from Gary in the kayak beside me.

I tried to blank everything out for a while, knowing this leg would be a real struggle, hoping the peace of the darkness and the water would have some hypnotic effect. It worked for about 15 minutes, and then I felt the same nagging in my hip flexors. Shit. This was early. Within minutes this had progressed to the dull ache I'd endured in the final quarter of my last swim, and shortly after that came the pulsing pain of muscle cramp.

For 40 minutes I put up with that. Gritting my teeth and trailing my legs like dead weights behind me, I swam on in pain, just letting the cramp get deeper and deeper with each spasm. It was one of the longest and darkest 40 minutes of my life, both metaphorically and literally. To my left every time I breathed on that side I could see the lights of the interior of the cruiser winking at me over the rise and fall of the waves. I was almost deliriously dreaming of the moment when I'd get back in there.

I was still cold and not getting any warmer, the reduced kicking ability depriving me of the full body workout that would help generate body heat. Feeling cheated by this handicap, I tried to get angry. I picked on the lake, and with every arm stroke dragging my body and trailing legs behind me I repeated, 'I'm going to beat you, I'm going to beat you, I'm going to beat you, you bastard.'

I kept imagining I'd heard the air horn, and then, when I did, it crushed my spirit to realise I still had a quarter of the hour to go. I could vaguely make out shouting from the boat, and it was clear my team-mates had realised I was struggling and were trying to lift me for the final stretch. I did my best to kick at different angles but it was no good, my hips were stuck in one painful solid cramp and I had only my upper body to drag me through.

I was hating this, and that was the next repeat. 'I hate this, hate this, hate this. I hate this, hate this, hate this.' Then I remembered that Winston Churchill had said, 'If you're going through hell, keep going,' and repeated that for a while. I tried counting next, reasoning that every time I got to a hundred I was probably a minute and a half closer to finishing. Then the agony and exhaustion got so great I couldn't think any more. And then finally, finally, I heard Paul's splash and a shout. A few more last, desperate strokes, the spotlight caught us in its beam, it reflected off Paul's pale body, he was beside me, and he was gone.

I nearly sank as I didn't even have the energy left to tread water. My body was wracked in pain. The cruiser was too far away, 20 metres or so. I didn't think I could swim another stroke. I tried to breaststroke but my hip flexors rejected that even more violently, spasming my legs wider apart with a huge pulse of pain. I cried out and turned onto my back, hoping to float over with a few useless arm pulls. I made it eventually and had to be helped up the ladder. With each step my hips spasmed in cramp again and I was shivering so violently I could hardly stand. Someone gave me a towel and I went straight inside, my teeth chattering so drastically I couldn't begin to speak.

I rinsed my face and body as best I could with the warm water in the tiny toilet in the cabin; then, in between shiver convulsions, I struggled into as many clothes as possible and pulled a duvet over me. Ellie came in like an angel with some hot chocolate and left it beside me.

I was in another world, a dark world of discomfort, pain and near panic. I actually thought I was in trouble – that my body had gone to a point of no return and that I'd finally pushed too far. I didn't recognise these feelings at all; this wasn't like the numb fatigue after the Welsh 1000m Peaks Race or the painful exhaustion of the Man v Horse or the nausea of Kilimanjaro; this was something else entirely. I felt strangely irresponsible, not for the first time obviously, but with a bit more clarity. I had never, ever been this cold and it was surely dangerous.

I lay without moving, hoping the shivers and convulsions would subside and I would return to normal eventually. I should have been up celebrating the end of my part of the challenge; instead I was lying curled up in the foetal position, shaking and confused, like a sailor with some ancient tropical disease.

This must have gone on for at least 45 minutes before I decided that getting some movement into my limbs would probably help. I stood up shakily and could hear the muffled sounds of everyone else talking up on deck. I felt a bit better standing up, rubbed my arms and legs vigorously and went to join them.

Adam was getting changed again, which meant Paul's fourth hour was nearly up. A *fourth* hour? I could not have done that. I felt weak again at the thought. I sat down in the seat beside Chris, who had been driving the entire time without a break. He looked tired, but happy.

'Alright, captain?' he asked, with a mock doff of his cap.

'Just wondering how I get you into these situations,' I replied, still stammering slightly. I rubbed my jaw and face, trying to encourage warm blood to flow so that normal talking could resume.

'I don't know why you sign up,' I said, 'but I'm very glad you do. Thanks very much, mate.'

'I enjoy it!' he replied emphatically. 'Just look at this,' he said, gesturing out to the dark shapes all round us. 'It's an adventure, isn't it? What else would I be doing at midnight on a Saturday?'

'I can think of quite a few other options,' I laughed, suddenly wondering what time the pubs closed in Belleek.

It's a little village at the very tip of the Erne, from where the great lough becomes a thin river flowing to the sea a few miles away. A mostly disused old marina was the finish point. We could see the lights of the town up ahead now, a faint orange glow low in the sky, and soon more and more definitive shapes as we came nearer. Poor Paul, having done a full hour more than everyone else, wasn't going to be the person actually to finish the swim. That looked like being Adam's honour.

He was swinging his arms and getting mentally ready for one last leap into the cold and the dark. I really didn't envy him but he wouldn't be in there too long. I hugged my clothes tighter as he threw off a towel and jumped in. One last changeover, lit by the spotlight, approved by the officials, and he was off. Paul climbed out with a huge smile. He was shivering just slightly but in great spirits and nowhere near as wrecked after a fourth shift as I was after three. What a warrior.

I apologised to him for not swimming further in my final hour, which would have put us further up the lake and allowed him to be the one finishing the challenge, only fair since he swam about 4k further than anyone else. But when Adam touched the jetty in the marina to set our record at 19 hours 6 minutes, more than three hours inside the time set by Julie and her team, there was a certain poignancy in him being the one to do it.

The reason he had come back from England to work for us in Northern Ireland was that his mother was dying of cancer and he wanted to spend more time with her. She had died just a couple of months earlier, and we were raising money for one of the cancer charities in her memory. I couldn't think of a more fitting ending to the swim. I was very proud of him for managing that grief with a stressful job and a stressful so-called recreation, and it was very emotional when he got back in the boat after bringing us home. A bottle of champagne was produced from somewhere, and as a half moon cast a silvery light back up the dark lake, we toasted each other and every last inch of that ancient water.

It had been another challenge that completely swamped me at times but once again ultimately delivered moments of triumph, tension, elation, clarity of purpose and joy. We still hold the Lough Erne record, and every single time I go back to Enniskillen I privately look out at that huge malevolent mass of dark water and I nod. You nearly killed me, but I beat you, you bastard.

Nine

THREE WEIRD WAYS TO TRAIN FOR THE MARATHON DES SABLES

The Marathon des Sables had been bubbling away in the background with regular email bulletins from the organisers about kit, training ideas, discussion forums and logistics timetables, but the only real demands to be met up until then had been financial. I had paid the £500 deposit shortly after the conversation with Sarah that secured my place, and then shoved the whole thing way down my list of priorities until the Erne swim was done and things were easier at home.

Having two kids under two years of age was a mammoth challenge in itself. Much like a Man Test, it was about endurance, keeping going through exhaustion, trying to find humour in the toughest of circumstances, and maintaining a long focus. I joked with Claire that the big difference was that there was no end in sight for this one. This was no training session that finished at a set point or time, there was no event on the horizon getting closer with each passing day. In fact there was no horizon at all; this was literally now the challenge of a lifetime; parenthood was a state of permanence.

The scatological implications alone were considerable. Two boys in nappies with efficient digestive systems meant a daily tsunami of shit to be wiped and disposed of. And as Reuben moved from milk to semi-solids, we now had two little hand grenades spraying food in all directions at each mealtime.

I knew full well I was adding to the pressure by combining the epic and relentless new 'adventure' of parenting with the selfish quest for some sort of other fulfilment, but I defended myself when asked by repeating that I didn't play golf, rarely got out to the pub or anywhere else, and didn't watch football unless I was getting paid for it. In other words, I was merely replacing the escapes of other fathers with something arguably more beneficial. For Claire, putting up with the slight strain of the extra commitments was the lesser of two evils. Tolerating fitness sessions being squeezed into a packed schedule was preferable to having me 'moping about the house like a caged bear' as she put it. I often heard her explain pragmatically to her friends that she knew full well what I was like before marrying me.

Although the physical demands of the Marathon des Sables would be monstrous, knowing that I only had myself to sort out felt like a blessed relief after the Erne swim. And with no target other than just to finish the course, I wasn't really worried about what was – in theory – the biggest test of my sporting life. Yes, it would be hugely difficult, but in the late summer after the swim, when I first started thinking properly about the MDS training, I felt a sort of freedom, or simplicity.

There would be no drills like in swimming, I didn't need to go to a pool or find a lake, I wasn't going to risk my life in cold seas – all I had to do was lots of running. Running is fabulously simple and can be fitted in anywhere and around anything. I didn't want to follow a big plan, I was convinced Robster had over-trained massively, which contributed to his neck problems, so I decided to just do what felt right, gradually building up the length of time on my feet again before trying it all with a rucksack on my back. I wasn't nervous, I was excited by the whole prospect of it and confident that I had come through enough up to this point to know how to get the approach right.

I have always been a decent runner, but having done nothing but swimming for the previous six months, on the first day back running I felt like I'd never run a step in my life. I had no rhythm, my legs were sore and stiff, and everything felt generally uncomfortable. I wasn't even slightly out of breath, having the big bank of swim training under my belt, but my legs didn't want to know and after 20 minutes or so I limped home.

The next morning, I felt like I'd just finished the actual Marathon des Sables. My hamstrings were tight and aching, my back was stiff. And that after a mere 20-minute jog! It was going to be interesting to see how long it took to progress from pedestrian shuffler to ultra-endurance candidate. I had loads of time – the race was ten months away – and knew that one of the biggest threats to being on the start line in optimal shape would have been to over-do it either physically or psychologically.

I remembered years earlier I had presented a local news report about a guy heading out to the MDS. He had talked through the race and the insane amount of training he was doing and I'd thought him utterly barmy for even wanting to try it. It was weird to find the running shoe on the other foot now and I resolved to do better than he had done, which was quit a few days into the race. I was pretty sure that his over-the-top training programme was to blame, and that memory, coupled with Robster's experience and Sarah's insistence that almost everyone on the waiting list finds a place when others drop out, had me convinced that over-training would be far more detrimental than under-training.

That was lucky, because the boys had somehow developed a rota system whereby they would each wake in turn but never together, ensuring that Claire and I were up multiple times at intervals each night. Finding the extra motivation required to get out and pound the roads without regular, unbroken sleep, and when most non-work hours were spent in constant vigilance at home, is tough.

There was one event I thought would be perfect to break me back into long-distance running. It was advertised, in fact, as the longest marathon in the world. That was debatable, but it was certainly one of the most unusual. The reason it claims to be the longest in the world was that the average finish times are greater than for any other marathon race. And that was because most of the participants are drunk.

The Marathon du Médoc takes place every year around some of the most fabulous vineyards of Bordeaux and has grown to such an extent that 8,500 runners now mass on the start line every year. It is a proper marathon in distance only. Fancy dress is not only encouraged, but obligatory, as is sampling wine at each of the feed stations situated in vineyards roughly 5k apart. I was struggling trying to think of a connection with the MDS to sell the idea to Claire, and then I just gave up and said I was going anyway. Even worse, Slippy was coming with me.

The trip had all the logistical planning of a Caribbean hurricane. Slippy had followed the ruptured Achilles that nearly ruined his wedding with a knee ligament injury, sustained playing full contact rugby on the paving stones of the Piazza del Popolo in Rome after a Six Nations match. He'd come through an operation to mend that issue less than two months previously, and had last run over ten miles in a row back in 1999. But as soon as he heard the words fancy dress and red wine combined in one sentence he agreed to come.

What he hadn't agreed to was the hours spent with me in a rental car, lost in the narrow streets of Bordeaux, or on a completely unnecessary 60-mile round trip out of the city due to my confusion over our registration. But he should have known the craic by then ...

I didn't feel that a rental car was compatible with the outrageous consumption of vin rouge, so next day we hitched a lift to the race start with a pair of American sisters dressed as chickens. The fancy-dress theme was 'Superheroes'. I don't remember a Super Chicken, but since they were doing us a favour we didn't quibble, and certainly not when we started covering their hire car in green body paint.

Slip is a fit guy but he does sweat like Silvio Berlusconi at a Miss Italy pageant when he's doing exercise, so we'd needed an outfit that would allow the body to breathe and not impede the liberal consumption of red wine. I decided ripped clothes and green body paint would make us instantly recognisable as the Incredible Hulks. Except for the muscles.

The American chickens loved the idea until they saw the green handprints all over their hire car. With the race about to start we ran off into the crowd and hid until the gun went off.

The first wine stop took ages to get to as (ironically enough) there were bottlenecks along the route, which unfortunately meant that when the runners at the back (including Les Incroyables Hulks) arrived, they were feeling a little short-changed in the wine consumption and necked three glasses each. Silly boys.

The course meandered gently through country roads and vineyard tracks, and as the wine kicked in, runners were soon meandering too. There were beautifully manicured lawns, rows and rows of neat vines, regal châteaux, and then thousands of escapees from Marvel comics charging through the middle. It would have been weird even without drink taken.

The entire Simpson family was there, several versions of them in fact. Obelix overtook us at one point, carrying a huge rock on his back. We were also passed by a tram carried by ten conductors and a man on a bike towing a dog in a small trailer. In a running race. Unless somebody put something in the wine, I am not making any of this up.

The wine stops became more frequent as the race progressed, which was fatal for the chances of Les Incroyables Hulks finishing in any sort of respectable time. By the halfway stage the combination of sweat, wine and water diluting our body paint meant we now looked more 'lemon and lime' than green. We could have been the products of an illicit liaison between the Hulk and Marge Simpson.

Each château put on quite a show, with live music, fruit, cheese and huge vats of wine greeting us every few kilometres, which was especially generous given how the runners were busy desecrating the vines along the route. I'm no sommelier, but I assumed that year's Médoc vintage would taste a little ... over-fertilised.

It's a terrific event, a surreal sporting experience the like of which could only ever succeed in France, but by mile 20 the novelty of novelty characters, running while tipsy and even fine French wine had well and truly worn off. Slippy's knee was aching, my legs were heavy, and I was starting to get a hangover. The last six miles weren't much craic. The parties continued in the last vineyard before the finish, a heavy metal band playing what sounded like a great set as we stumbled through, but our *joie de vivre* had jogged on.

Les Hulks stumbled over the line in six hours and seven minutes and were presented with a medal and a carved wooden box containing a souvenir bottle of red wine. At that stage I would have swapped it for a gift-wrapped grenade. Slippy was totally wrecked, with both knees hurting by the end as he was clearly over-loading one to compensate for the weakness in the other.

'How far is the Marathon des Sables again?' he panted as we fell down in the shade of a tree.

'Six marathons in seven days,' I replied forlornly. 'In temperatures about twice as hot as this.'

It was the first time he'd smiled in over an hour.

*

It was hard to argue the case for the wine marathon being effective preparation for the Sahara marathon, but I did so anyway. I told everyone that running 26.5 miles in the heat of a French summer while deliberately dehydrating yourself and training your guts to cope with unusual food had turned out to be near perfect in terms of mimicking the MDS. I almost believed it.

It did at least get some miles in my legs, and when I got back I gradually stepped up my training but stuck to the plan of not taking on more than one long road run of two hours or more every fortnight. I supplemented that with mountain running, shorter interval sessions, core work and, of course, being chased by bloodhounds.

I'd been thinking about ways to make the MDS training a bit more sociable, and to get out of the city more regularly. Running cross-country alongside a hunt club was one of my vague ideas. But I wasn't sure how some of the traditional hunt clubs would react to that bizarre request, and I *was* sure I didn't want to be there in the fields if they ever caught anything. Then I remembered hearing about a club somewhere in Northern Ireland that instead of going after wildlife, used bloodhounds to chase a human runner. In the Sky Sports studio I set about trying to find the club online between live bulletins. If ever there was an incongruous moment in my life, this was it. Sitting elegantly in the most slick and professional TV studio in the UK, researching how to get chased through muddy Irish fields by a pack of bloodhounds.

Eventually, my own online hunt found a quarry. The Holestone Farmers Bloodhounds Hunt Club seemed far from your typical horsey set. I'd never heard of a hunt club identifying themselves as farmers. I had also never previously heard of a club that ran a bloodhound pack rather than a foxhound pack, and could only hope that it was because they liked foxes rather than that they hated humans. There was only one way to find out.

I sent an email to a generic club address and didn't really expect the farmers to answer. But next day in the Sky canteen before my shift I got a phone call from a lady at the club saying she had received my email and would be passing it on to the committee. She knew they were keen to have a few more runners but I would have to be approved by the club, which might take some weeks. I assured her I had the necessary skills to be hunted, having both strong legs and strong scent, and was available for selection.

When I finished my shift at midnight, I picked up an answerphone message from one of the club who said they were meeting the following lunchtime at a country pub in the middle of County Antrim and I was very welcome to come and meet them. That was a strange departure from the previous conversation about the committee vetting procedure, but sounded hopeful. As luck would have it, I was flying home first thing in the morning anyway, and rang the number when I landed back in Belfast. I asked if I should bring my running gear to the pub. 'Yes, of course!' was the enthusiastic response. So within one 12-hour period I went from greeting the nation's sports fans in the Sky studios to meeting a slavering pack of bloodhounds in a pub car park. Such is life.

I couldn't quite believe I was going to be chased that very day, having only made contact with the club for the first time a few days before. I hadn't a clue what it really entailed. The hounds were corralled in a trailer while the huntsmen either got tanked up in the pub or prepared their horses. I loved the whole scene – the smells of horses, dank old pub, brandy breath, and the stench of bloodhound. It was deeply ironic that nothing they would ever sniff out could smell as bad as they did themselves. I felt pretty certain that if the tables were turned I could easily track them down.

I was presented with a shot of neat brandy and then invited to meet my tormentors. I made the mistake of calling them dogs, and the club secretary hissed: 'Hounds! We call them hounds … not dogs.' I was told to put my arms in through the slats of the trailer so they could get the scent. They were big, very big, howling (or 'baying') already, and looked hungry.

'They won't hurt you, don't worry,' said the secretary, spotting my hesitation. 'Not yet, anyway,' he laughed. I resolved to run like the fecking wind.

Suddenly all was commotion. There was no brandy left, the riders were ready, the hunt was about to start. I was ordered into the back of a pick-up truck and driven at mad speed for a mile or so up a small road. The hounds would be released shortly and I had to now hare off over a hurriedly explained course through some fields and up and across rough lanes.

'Will the hounds be able to follow my scent up the road?' I asked.

'Oh, they'll catch you, son, don't you worry about that,' sniggered the pick-up driver.

'What happens when they catch me?'

'You'll see!'

I had no intention of being caught. I reckoned the course was only a couple of miles and the hounds hadn't yet been released from the pub car park. I set off. Blue plastic bags tied in a knot to the hedgerows at irregular intervals marked my course, and there were jumps built along the route for the horses following the hounds.

It was heavy going. The fields were flooded in places and I was soon sodden and splattered in thick mud, which more than doubled the weight of my trail shoes and socks. After a few wrong turns I lost time going back and re-finding the course, and suddenly I could hear the war cry of the bloodhounds. It was an eerie noise, at once both exhilarating and frightening, reminiscent of the thunder of hooves at the Man v Horse but scarier because these animals were actually bred to hunt me down and had much sharper teeth.

It filled the air, and suddenly I saw them appear over a hill a few fields back. Flooded with adrenaline I upped my pace. There was a gate at the top corner of a field with some jeeps and the pick-up truck parked on the other side. That was the end point of the first stage, where the hounds would be gathered again and held back until I got away for the next run and the huntsmen had more brandy.

My heart was slamming as the hill kicked up and I churned through the muck and long grass. My God, this was exhilarating. I looked round again and the hounds had closed to within a few hundred yards and the horses were also now close behind them. I could hear their panting now as well as the baying and the echoing ba da bum ba da bum ba da bum of the horse's hooves, and I sprinted like a man possessed.

People were leaning over the fence and the hedges, watching. I felt like a fox or a hare that had unwittingly stumbled into a country sport fair. I made it to the corner just in front of the hounds and leaped up onto the gate. Everyone burst out laughing and I felt like a total prat. The hounds looked up inquisitively, panting and wagging their tails excitedly. 'What did you do that for?'

they seemed to be saying. 'Come on, let's run again, that was fun.'

And so began a fantastic afternoon of human and hounds, a wonderful gallop and chase across rivers and fields, up farm lanes and through bogs and woods. I ran away from and alongside the hounds, now my firm friends and not at all frightening. They were quite timid actually, one crack of the hunstman's whip dropping their bellies to the ground and herding them all together for safety. We must have covered 12 miles or more, and at the end I was utterly knackered.

Darkness was falling as we arrived back at the pub again and the horses and hounds were led for a wash in the river. I was clapped on the back and given a bowl of steaming hot stew and some homemade wheaten bread. My legs were heavy and aching, but my joints weren't sore at all, in contrast with the sharp protests I was used to after a road run.

Quite unexpectedly I reckoned I'd stumbled on the most perfect preparation for running an ultra-marathon on sand. The sodden fields and sticky bogs of County Antrim might not seem to have anything in common with the dry Sahara, but the heavy going and shifting surfaces perfectly replicated some of the demands of all off-road running, and the extra cushioning would certainly be better for my joints. I was fairly sure I'd be the only one trying it, but for many of the next eight weekends I would be a human fox on farmland all over Antrim.

Yes, the training and preparation methods were a little unorthodox, but I could never have followed a proper road-running plan for the same length of time as everyone else. I would have been bored stupid. I also felt I was doing more than enough. Despite the scale of the challenge – 150 miles across the Sahara Desert in what was widely referred to as the 'toughest footrace on earth' – I wasn't really worried about it. I knew I had the mental fortitude to get through it, and my body was getting used to big mileage now as well. I was getting skinnier all the time; people kept asking me about whether I'd lost weight and made it clear they didn't approve. I found this a bit irritating, because they wouldn't have dreamed of making similar comments if I'd got fat.

As the weeks passed I also needed to get used to running with a rucksack on my back, as carrying all one's own essentials was a pretty significant part of the MDS challenge. I hated this at first. I felt weighted down, heavy legged and clumsy, and that was with the pack fairly light. I did get more used to it and gradually added more weight, filling the pack with disc weights wrapped up in towels and adding clothes to fill it out, but running with all that extra burden didn't feel very athletic.

One evening, en route to a dinner party at my parents' house, and trying as ever to fit the training in around normal family commitments, I decided to get out on the main road what I thought was 14 miles from Enniskillen and run in from there, with the heavy pack jumping about as usual on my shoulders. Unfortunately the distance was actually more like 17 miles, took me much longer than I thought, and had dangerous sections with no footpath. By the time it was fully dark I still had five miles to run on one of the busiest roads in the county.

As a long line of cars heading out of town whizzed by just inches from my side it became increasingly clear that

running this road was a monumentally stupid and dangerous thing to do in the gloom of a north-west Ireland winter.
I took my phone out and held it in front of me, hitting the
keypad every ten seconds to light up the screen. Judging by
the exaggerated swerving of the oncoming traffic, it worked,
and soon I was at the town limits and onto a footpath.

I arrived well over an hour after the other dinner
guests, who were more than a little surprised to see me fall
through the door in white lycra, carrying a rucksack full of
weights. They all looked sympathetically at Claire.

A more conventional – but in retrospect still slightly unusual – training opportunity was offered in Qatar at the
end of February. Robster's initial offering of a place on
the race alongside him had been made considerably more
attractive by the fact that he had found a way to pay for it.
Another of our former Loughborough rugby team-mates,
Westy, had moved to the Middle East and set up a successful property company with the slogan 'Keep Moving'.
In Robster's head, this was providential for us all, and
Westy's new company should sponsor us. Amazingly,
Westy agreed, on condition that I came out to Qatar to
do some training in the desert and to get a few PR pics
and interviews with local journalists.

It was a strange party that left the sanctuary of shiny
Doha and set out for the vast Arabian sands in a Land
Cruiser with deflated tyres. It consisted of: one expert
dune driver and guide; one lycra-clad runner proudly
emblazoned head to toe with 'LS: Keep Moving' logos;
one budding property mogul and his bichon frise, Casper;
one other university friend, Dan, coming along for the
craic; and one bemused Qatari photo-journalist.

After a good hour of bumping across gradually diminishing tracks, during which I fielded inane questions from the journalist with contorted efforts to mention 'LS: Keep Moving' in every answer, we were deep in the desert, surrounded by enormous dunes in every direction. It was quite daunting actually, and we had no plan other than for me to be turfed out of the jeep and start running in any direction. The jeep would then follow and move ahead at intervals for the journalist to get action photos of this strange, modern-day Wilfred Thesiger.

The whole thing was ridiculous, and I felt like a total plonker, heading off across the dunes with a rucksack full of useful survival essentials like disc weights and rolls of towels while a Land Cruiser followed behind. After an hour of this I was thoroughly bored, but not as bored as those in the jeep behind who had been jolting about at seven miles an hour for all that time. They pulled up alongside at one point and Westy told me they were motoring ahead to get some wider pics. They roared off over the sand hills and I put my head down and decided to focus on the big benefits of a proper desert dry run.

In an alarmingly short space of time I was completely alone. There wasn't a sound except for my panting and the occasional squeak of rubber soles on compressed sand. I ran on and on, trying not to think about the fact that there hadn't been any sight of the jeep for ages and that there were no visible landmarks in this billowing sea of huge orange sand humps.

The ground shifting beneath my feet was adding a serious challenge, and my trainers had long since filled with sand, so my toes were grinding on gritty deposits and rubbing nice blisters. In the style of Robster and the bleeding ankles, I kept going without addressing it, hoping that his theory of pain thresholds and calluses had some merit. I was afraid to stop in any case, lest the potential seriousness of being lost in the desert with only a load of disc weights and some towels to help me survive should hit home.

After another 20 minutes alone, even an incurable optimist like me was starting to consider an awful truth. In this environment of undulating sand hills, no landmarks and hundreds of miles of desert wilderness, getting lost was all too easy, could happen suddenly, and could be permanent. I stopped at the top of the next big dune I could find and scanned the horizon.

Nothing. And then, Allahu-Akbar! A faint line of dust between two sand hills was getting thicker. Could it be a Land Cruiser with an eclectic mix of passengers? It was! God is great indeed. A full ten minutes after that first sighting of the dust line they pulled up alongside me. The relief was palpable, though Westy tried hard to be breezy.

'GL, sorry, man, we didn't mean to be away that long but we had a slight issue …'

'More than a slight issue, thank you!' roared Dan, stepping out of the jeep with no top on. Carsick Casper had thrown up all over him and, side-tracked by this drama, they'd forgotten to check on me. Probably the only person not happy with the reunion was the journalist, who I'm sure had been beginning the outline of a cracking story of extreme western foolishness, complete with the last known pictures of the deceased.

The warm waters of the Persian Gulf were just a few miles away, so I decided the run could finish there, where my reward would be a leap into the sea. It was three hours in total, and my feet had definitely suffered. They stung when I walked into the salt water, and I made a mental note to properly research the gaiters that everyone had recommended to keep the sand out.

On the way back to Doha, Westy and Dan were giggling together like schoolboys.

'GL, we have to tell you something,' Westy began. 'Earlier on, I'm so sorry, we actually really lost you! For quite a while ... couldn't see you anywhere. You were somewhere in the middle of the dunes but we didn't know where, and then we started to shit ourselves that you'd cross the Saudi border. It's quite close. We couldn't find you for ages.'

I grinned. 'That would have been hilarious. I can see the headline: "Suicide runner makes Saudi incursion armed with water bottles and weighted rucksack".'

'Well, actually that wasn't the only problem. There's a pretty important Qatari military base called As Salwa around here too, and they would have shot you!'

So, all things considered, I got off pretty lightly from my first desert training run, blisters being the only issue, and actually I was pleased to see them since I now knew which areas of my feet needed most attention with surgical spirit. I'd read somewhere that toughening your skin in advance was a good idea, and surgical spirit is used in hospitals to protect against bedsores since it toughens the skin without cracking it. So after a good inspection post-Qatar, I began a nightly ritual of smearing this over my feet before I got into bed. Claire never complained about the idea of going to sleep in a room that smelt like a hospital ward. She had long been disgusted by the dreadful state of my reptilian feet and toes, and I think she reasoned that any treatment at all was bound to improve things.

*

A head inspection would have been a sensible idea too, but the only medical tests the MDS insist on are physical. Each prospective competitor has to have sign-off from a doctor, who has to perform a number of readings and tick a load of boxes. This was the second sporting contest I had entered that required medical clearance. The first one was the World Sauna Championships in Finland, a sporting contest of wonderful simplicity in which the winner is the person who can sit in a furnace-like sauna for the longest, with the temperature increasing every 30 seconds. I'd entered that a few years previous, but their clearance required a doctor simply to attest that sauna sitters were 'of sound mind and body'. My doctor at the time, an old rugby mate, pointed out the obvious paradox – nobody of 'sound mind' would ever dream of entering – but he signed the form anyway.

The MDS check-up and forms were a little more stringent than the sauna declaration. These forms required a series of actual results, including an ECG to check for potential heart issues. I was confident of having a heart like a horse after years of endurance activity, so was a little taken aback when the doctor checked the graph and frowned.

'There's just … something … not quite … right … with this,' she said slowly and hesitatingly, the way people do when they're trying to work things out, as if they'll come up with the answer before finishing the sentence if they extend it a bit.

'What do you mean?' I answered, a little sharply. I had been unimpressed by this doctor's attitude from the start of the consultation. She had not only remained unmoved by the enormity of the challenge I was bravely taking on, but actually seemed vaguely irritated, as if the whole thing was pointlessly hazardous and a complete waste of everyone's time. Which of course it was, but I didn't need her to remind me of that, and I certainly didn't need to be on the receiving end of the tone I assumed she normally reserved for people with drink-related injuries, smoker's lung or other self-inflicted problems.

She continued to study the graph from different angles, ignoring me. Any minute now I expected the 'builder's suck', the sharp intake of breath that precedes bad or expensive news.

'This heartbeat seems irregular. I'm not sure about it. How hot did you say it would be?'

'Well, I feel totally fine, honestly. I have been running hours and hours with absolutely no problem,' I breezed.

'How hot?'

'Well it's the desert, so you'd have to expect ... erm, they reckon about 40.'

'I think this needs a second opinion. Sorry.'

She was smiling beneath that frown, I knew it.

'Are you sure? It's just I need to send this form off soon and the event is quite close now, I have booked the flights and stuff and ...'

She was scribbling heavily on the graph, then piled all the forms into a file and told me to give them to the receptionist on my way out. Case dismissed.

I was raging. I was as fit if not fitter than I'd ever been, I didn't need some stupid chart to tell me otherwise, and I certainly didn't need some party-pooping doctor who seemed to have an issue with adventure putting yet another obstacle in the way of me getting to the start line of this bastard race. What a torture! I sat in the car and could have cried with frustration. Once again I reminded myself that the most difficult part of a major challenge was actually getting to the start line. So many times I had thought that over the past few years, but this one was beyond the pale.

A week later I was called up and asked if I wanted to see (and pay for) a specialist at a private clinic. Goddamn right, I thought, let's throw money at this event ... again. I had no option. If I couldn't convince a doctor to release and sign my form, I wasn't going.

I liked the specialist immediately. This was a much more considered individual, I decided. He had the calm assurance of someone who had seen it all before, and just smiled benignly when I told him what the Marathon des Sables entailed. He seemed to recognise the sense in it. He studied the heart-rate chart carefully, held the stethoscope to my chest for what seemed like ten minutes, and then put all his instruments away slowly and methodically before telling me he was satisfied that I had nothing more than the enlarged heart muscle he had seen before in other endurance athletes.

'It's a condition known as athlete's heart,' he said. 'Exercise-induced cardiomegaly. The heart is enlarged as a by-product of an active lifestyle or heavy training. The training makes it stronger and bigger, nothing to worry about. Usually accompanied by a slow resting heart rate, which you also have, it's about 40 beats per minute.'

I felt like my athlete's heart was going to burst with pride. At last, some recognition. I am an extraordinary physical specimen, like one of the X-Men or something! Superathlete, beyond normal, how fantastic ... A more rational analysis would have queried how advisable it was to have produced abnormal growth in my heart, and been more cognisant of the fact that exactly half of the medical opinion sought was concerned about this. But I was focused solely on the doctor signing the form and me and my athlete's heart taking another big leap towards the Sahara.

Another feature of the training was that I'd had enough of it. I was pretty fed up by now, and there were still six weeks to go. It wasn't just the volume of training, but also the fear of getting injured at this point and wasting all the time, money and effort that had gone in up until now. I'd come to recognise the point at which I got a bit sickened by training for an event as the point at which I was physically ready. It was a sign that the challenge no longer held any fear and that my body knew it was able to cope with what I was about to ask of it.

It was hard to keep motivated in those final few training weeks, especially as unlike the swim, I wasn't racing against or for anyone. All I wanted to do was finish the MDS, a matter of personal pride, and it didn't really matter how quickly I did it. When I groaned about how tough the training was or how mad the event would be, Claire, trying to be supportive, would say something like, 'You'll do it easily, all you have to do is keep going, anyone could do it, maybe not in a good time, but anyone could go slowly and finish it.'

My irritable reaction to this suggestion was a symptom of the fact that I knew she was right. I'd seen some news footage of the race and enough pics to recognise that not everybody out there was going to be a great athlete. I also knew that it didn't really matter if I didn't push that extra mile or find that extra ounce of effort now in training; I was easily fit enough to cope and doing it in a certain time or finishing in a certain position was a bit irrelevant if all I wanted to achieve was to be able to say I had done it. As usual, Claire had unwittingly given voice to my conscience. She has an irritating knack for it.

That said, I had one more big training day I wanted to do in the Mourne Mountains to finally sign off on the more extreme side of the preparation before tapering for the event. I went down alone to run with the full pack weight of 11 kilos on my back. This was the last big blast. A friend of mine who has been preparing professional sportsmen for years always says there is no point 'training like Tarzan and competing like Jane', and I knew that one of the key factors in a race of such enormous distances as the MDS would be how we all coped with accumulative damage. I didn't see the point of arriving half-damaged already; being under-cooked was better than over-cooked, especially when the race lasted a week.

I had planned to follow a certain loop through the mountains that would include lots of steep summit climbs but also long stretches of plateaus and downhills where I could run. The key thing was for the rucksack to stay on for the duration, and I was aiming for about five hours non-stop.

It was a big day. I put on my headphones halfway through and picked some epic film tracks as the soundtrack of my own last big push. The theme from *Last of the Mohicans* was playing as I came off the last mountain and hit the rough path back to the car park. I ran harder and harder, and as I drove myself on, tears suddenly filled my eyes, there was a lump in my throat and my heart seemed to fill my chest.

I'd done it. Three weeks out and I knew I was ready. A huge wave of emotion swept over me. The music and the fatigue contributed but mostly this was a great rush of strength and confidence, an affirmation of my own ability now to get through whatever the MDS had in store, and a heart-swelling pride at having soaked everything up for seven months to arrive at a point where I was ready for the start line.

Well, physically I was ready to be there, but logistically I was miles away. I was still nowhere near organised enough. The travel, for once, was relatively straightforward since I was part of one massive group from the UK and Ireland and just had to get my arse to Gatwick one Tuesday morning in mid-April. But what to pack? There is a book in that alone ...

If you were to cut and paste every word ever written about kit and preparation for the Marathon des Sables you'd be one sad bastard, but you would also have amassed enough text to make *War and Peace* look like a sonnet. Like looking at every exhibit in the Natural History Museum, reading every word of the Great MDS Kit Debate on various forums would age you by four or five decades. There are even regular seminars about it for Christ's sake!

The forums sagged under the weight of so much opinion. I decided to start with the non-negotiables, those items set out clearly in the rules, and without which one would not be allowed to start. A venom pump? What on earth is a venom pump, why would I need one and where would I find one of them on Belfast's high street? A pocket mirror?! A week without running water and I had to bring a pocket mirror? I wasn't sure I'd want to look. Then the food. The rules stated 2,000 calories per day minimum, with each day's nourishment contained in an individual bag with total calories to be calculated and presented ready for inspection. (Please show workings …)

This all prompted another frenzied round of research and online shopping. The obsession with numbers, calories and energy values brought me as close as I'll ever get to Weight Watchers. It offended me to reduce something as marvellous as food to a series of weights and measures, and for taste to be a minor factor in the selection criteria. There was one brand of freeze-dried 'expedition foods' that seemed to deliver the most bang for the buck, so I settled for one of those per night, porridge for breakfast, and then a load of snacks like nuts, coconut and cereal bars, and one Peperami per day. I spent ages carefully adding these up to 2,000 calories and making myself little lunch packs with date labels. This was fitness-challenge preparation on an all new hyper-geek scale, and was totally alien to me.

The fun didn't stop there. As I knew from the Qatar adventure, gaiters were another essential, and after much more trawling of the forums I opted for getting a pair made from parachute silk stitched into my trainers by a firm in Scotland. The material was light and strong as advertised but I wasn't happy with the stitching, so brought them down to an old cobbler in Belfast to get them redone. Commendably, he took on the job without the slightest murmur or hesitation, despite the fact that it must surely have been the most unusual request of his career.

Aside from the entry fee of almost £4,000, the Marathon des Sables also does well from its own official online shop. I'm being uncharitable calling it a shop. They insist that it's a 'boutique'. How charming!

I ordered the list of stuff they insisted on, and of course added a few other bits that looked half decent and half useful, including foldable flip-flops, a mini-stove and a wide-brimmed cap with long neck flap like a mullet for extra sun protection. A large box arrived a week later and I unpacked it excitedly.

It was like getting coal in my stocking at Christmas. The hat barely covered my hairline let alone the rest of my neck, the stove was about the size of a matchbox and hopelessly flimsy, and the flip-flops ... well ... they were the biggest joke of all. I suspected they'd been made by a child drawing round their own foot on a sheet of paper, cutting round the shape and connecting the two sides with a length of elastic. They were actually hilarious, each one literally only paper thin, covering only a central strip of each foot and leaving the heels completely exposed. Not for the last time, I began to wonder about the commercialisation of the 'world's toughest footrace'.

The Marathon des Sables was born in 1984 when a French concert promoter called Patrick Bauer set out alone on foot to cross the Sahara Desert. He walked over 200 miles, and somewhere along the journey had the idea of setting a similar challenge as a race. Two years later he was back to organise it and his event has continued every year since, growing to become the best-known ultra-endurance race on the planet. It has a slightly varied route each year but always roughly the same total distance of 150 miles, split over six stages.

It was now more than three years since Robster had first mentioned the MDS, and although I had distracted myself with other challenges, including helping to bring two little boys into the world, three years was a long time to have had this looming over me. In the last few months it had increasingly taken centre stage in everything. The training had peaked, but an enormous amount of effort had been expended both physically and mentally before we'd moved an inch over the course. Just getting all the kit and food sorted took weeks. Specialist sleeping bag from Poland, gaiters from Scotland, stove and fuel tablets from France, food from camping shops and a range of supermarkets, survival and running gear from all over the place. It was too much.

I laid everything out on the floor and stared, appalled, at the amount of stuff. It almost completely covered the bedroom floor. A mosaic of food, first aid and general accoutrements. I put the rucksack down beside it all. There was just no way that was all squeezing in there. I felt I'd been very economical with my kit selection, this was the absolute bare minimum required for the week, so there was nothing that could be taken away. I would also have to find room for a 'Distress Flare' we'd be given in Morocco at the kit check-in. After ten minutes of despair and head scratching, I just grabbed a shoehorn and started to shove.

Ten

THE MAN IN WHITE

Lying on a bed in the Premier Inn at Gatwick the night before our flight to Ouarzazate, I felt a strange sense of accomplishment. Not the usual pre-event nerves or tension. I felt as if I'd somehow passed the test already, having come through the training and the admin and put myself in a position now to at least have a crack at it. This behemoth of a Man Test had been part of my life for ages up to this point, so strangely I felt closer now to the end, although I still hadn't even reached Morocco.

It wasn't hard to find the MDS group next morning. Everyone looked the same. Mostly thirty-something men with new haircuts, new rucksacks and visible cheekbones gathered in small pods comparing trainers, accessories, the weight of each other's rucksacks, and stories of frustrating equipment hunts and minimalist packing. My pack weighed about 12 kilos in the end, which was certainly at the upper end of the scale. I stopped listening.

At the check-in for our charter flight I wasn't allowed to take my hand luggage on board with me – it was too heavy apparently. I'm not the first person to rant about the arbitrary nature of airport security and I won't be the last, but allow me this moment. If weight were the issue, how on earth would moving a bag from under my seat into the hold make a difference? It was still going in the damn plane, just into a different part.

One tip I noted among the avalanche of pre-event advice was to bring your trainers and other essentials in your hand luggage in case the main bag went missing. And now I had to hand the whole thing over. The only other carry-on option I had was a paper Café Nero bag currently containing a muffin and apple juice. Soon it was also holding a book, a newspaper, an iPod, a wallet – and half holding a pair of trainers with parachute silk stitched round the bottom.

After my daily checks of the online weather reports for the past few weeks, Ouarzazate didn't disappoint. It was probably only mid-twenties when we landed in the early afternoon, and there was a refreshing breeze. The stories of deadly heat seemed greatly exaggerated. We were only a few hours' drive from the middle of the Sahara, where the race would begin in a few days' time, and surely there couldn't be a doubling in the temperature over such a short distance and time? What a difference mild weather would make.

We had one last evening of modern comfort, staying in a hotel in town and eating enormous piles of carbohydrates. I'd been carb loading for days now in my usual fashion, but from the next day would be reduced to eating only what I could carry, so at dinner I hit the buffet really hard, going through several courses but studiously avoiding anything with even the remotest food-poisoning potential. The possibility of picking up a stomach bug at this stage didn't bear thinking about.

That dinner was also where the groups of tent partners were sorted out. This was where I missed Robster. I felt sorry for him missing out, but also sorry for myself not to be doing it with him. All 900 competitors would be sleeping in big tents each night in the desert and had to arrive there neatly divided into groups of eight per tent. The 150-mile course was split into six different stages with a campsite being built each day at the end of each stage. Although I was really looking forward to looking after myself and being gloriously selfish for a week, I knew that having the right tent partners would help make it all a bit more bearable. Or, more accurately, having the *wrong* tent partners could make it *un*bearable.

I had met two other lads from Northern Ireland, Rob and Norman, before leaving for Morocco, and between us we added others we'd met on the flight out to form a group of eight. Given that we'd be sleeping and suffering beside each other in extreme conditions for the next week it was pretty important we all got along, though of course it was impossible to know for sure until the stress started.

Rob's sporting background was more mountain-based; he liked hiking, rock climbing and the great out-doors, but this was going to be far more demanding than anything he'd taken on before. He identified himself as a determined plodder, and like me he just wanted to finish. Norman couldn't even remember why he'd signed up. He was from County Armagh, had spent time in the army, and gave off an air of gentle country-boy 'hardness' that was unthreatening but tangible. He struck me as the kind of man who would turn up in leather shoes and jeans and still get through it, who might not have thought too much about the undertaking but would stick it out.

I'd sat beside Piers from Birmingham on the flight from Gatwick; he was going on his own and amazingly had only signed up six months ago. Sarah had been right about the dropout rate then. For some reason this year it had been higher than ever, and when Piers had casually phoned up to enquire about when the next entry call was, he was told he could actually go on the next race if he wanted. I envied him, six months' build-up was much better than three and a half years, and he appeared fit and confident. I liked his breezy, optimistic outlook and we invited him to join our tent.

Rob had met a Scottish couple called Derek and Yvonne who had done some serious long-distance trekking before, which made six, and we had also met another lone traveller, David, in the passport queue at Ouarzazate Airport. He was 60, introduced himself as a male nurse, and then added quickly with a smile, 'But don't worry, I don't get the wrong bus, if you know what I mean …' He seemed a gentle soul, a little more nervous than the rest of us perhaps, at least outwardly. We didn't bother trying to find an eighth person because if we could get away with only seven we'd have an extra bit of room in the tent.

I got a fairly early night, reasoning that since it was my last time in a proper bed for a while, I might as well make the most of it. I'd brought the surgical spirit with me, but I wouldn't be carrying it through the desert so gave the feet one last lavish application. I was very pleased with how they felt. Tough as old boots but with a bit of give. If the skin cracked I can only imagine the discomfort, but they felt good, like stretched leather. I laughed at how important taut skin had become to me and then slept soundly.

Next day was Good Friday. It was too easy to crack tasteless jokes about crucifixion and suffering, but we cracked them anyway as we were bussed through suitably dusty, biblical roads. Five hours we travelled, deep into the desert, just stopping once for a packed lunch in a field of rocks. It was certainly hotter than yesterday, and there was noticeably more glare, but it wasn't yet oppressive, or frightening.

Turned out the five-hour bus journey was just to soften us up ahead of the second leg of the journey – half an hour in the back of a cattle truck standing on piles of our own luggage. It was a long day, but another giant step closer to the start line.

I wasn't sure what to expect from a week in the desert, but it certainly wasn't to be standing in a series of the longest queues I have ever seen. I felt like I was living through this horrible recurring dream I get, in which I'm trying to pack or prepare for some approaching deadline, but constant little barriers and interruptions hold me back. There were queues for breakfast, queues for water, queues for handing in forms, queues for equipment. The whole scene reminded me of some unfortunate refugee camp – anxious, inappropriately dressed groups of people carrying all their belongings in a bag waiting to see a doctor in a tent in the middle of a desert.

The equipment queue was the worst. It doubled back several times across the large area between the admin tents. Every ten minutes or so we got to take a stride forward. It was tortuous and hardly the man versus the elements wilderness week for which I had been preparing. It felt weirdly corporate in fact. Even more weird was the fact that hundreds of people were walking round in white paper boiler suits, like the government scientists in *ET* or the inept henchmen of a Bond villain. I think these garments had been advertised in the MDS 'boutique' as light and handy evening wear. I couldn't believe anyone had actually bought one.

My meticulously labelled food bags weren't even looked at in the admin checks, which made me feel all the calorie counting and food selection had been a total waste of my time. I also saw loads of people with rucksacks about a third the size of mine in which there was absolutely no way they could have fitted the required amount of food plus kit. I was getting a bit pissed off with everything and found myself wishing the time away, if I'm honest. I was fantasising about the return trip out of the desert before we'd even spent a single night.

I think this was probably just some manifestation of pre-event tension, but also the scale of the whole organisation was getting on top of me a bit. I've never been much of a queuer, and I have already explained about my hassle to happiness ratio. Previous Man Tests had been made exempt from the ratio, but the Marathon des Sables was so impossibly high now on the hassle spectrum that I felt it was over the limit before I'd run a single step. That was sad, given the amount of time and money that I'd spent getting here, and I tried to snap out of the mood.

That evening we queued (again) like condemned men for the last meal we'd have for a week that wasn't freeze-dried and carried on our backs. Once it got dark it was absolutely freezing. I clutched a North Face gilet tighter round my neck. I had been planning to send it back in the civvies bag, but if this was the nightly temperature I didn't see how that would work; it was easily in the low single figures. Many of the paper boiler-suit people were wearing woolly hats.

And so to bed. The roll mat carefully researched and donated by Robster provided all the cushioning of an empty bag of crisps. I had expected the sandy Sahara Desert to be a bit more … well, sandy. I'd fondly imagined feeling like I was lying on the beach, with warm soft sand moulding itself round the contours of my body. But this was basically just sheet rock ribbed with rogue stones. I folded the North Face gilet beneath me for extra cushioning – and tried to pretend its goose down would create a featherbed effect.

Lying beside me, Northern Ireland Rob had the luxury of a blow-up lilo-style bed, and every time he rolled over, farted or merely twitched, it would squeak the way a taut balloon does when you rub it with a finger. I was hoping it woke him as often as it woke me. Well, I say 'woke', but to be woken I would have needed to be asleep first. And I'm not sure that happened at all that night. The temperature had plummeted again and the Polish speciality sleeping bag wasn't quite cutting it. The North Face gilet was staying with me.

The next morning we were all up shortly after six. It was still cold and judging by the groans and curses, nobody else had slept much either. The first stage was 34 kilometres and, like them all, it would start at half eight. It would have been a long enough wait, but there was plenty to be done. We started the first cooking of the week, each of us experimenting with preparing hot water for various breakfasts on an assortment of tiny little stoves that had come recommended on the forums.

How I would have loved a shower after rolling out of the sleeping bag. I always think I can get through almost anything with the reviving properties of hot running water. I was genuinely concerned about how I would deal with not having a shower for a week, not being able to cleanse the sand and sweat from myself after each day running through the desert. And then getting into a confined sleeping bag stinking and sticky? Horrible. Little comforts make big impacts on our general wellbeing and I'd have to try and do what I could to replace the full effect of a post-exercise shower. I also had a bit of a talk to myself. I'd thought nothing but negative thoughts since arriving in Morocco and it was time to shut up and get on with things. I reminded myself this was all just pre-event tension, and that getting started would restore my normal good humour.

The porridge was gloopy and bland without any milk, like eating wallpaper paste, but I thought of each mouthful as a little energy deposit and forced it down. Teams of locals in blue overcoats arrived to dismantle the tent while we were all still trying to get organised. We re-grouped on the sand and everyone began their own laborious preparations. I knew that establishing the right pre-stage routine would be absolutely critical, a series of checks and re-checks to make sure everything was sorted before the suffering and irrational behaviour began. The sun came out and warmed my back and I finally felt a little frisson of excitement. This was more like me.

The preparation I took most care over was the Vaseline. There had been a lot of online debate on the forums about lubricant in the crotch area, with no trace of irony. There were pro-lubes and anti-lubes, and the anti-lube lobby was loudest, citing the potentially agonising dangers of Vaseline or any other grease catching and holding sand and grit wherever it was applied, especially round the privates.

The prospect of having sand stuck in grease rubbing on the most sensitive areas of my body for five hours a day was terrifying, but for years now I had lubed before running or cycling and I wasn't about to ditch the practice before taking on the most epic challenge of my life. Suffering with jock rot for a week was unthinkable, and so I decided that if I took the utmost care with freshly rinsed fingers before application it would probably be safe enough.

The problem of course was there was no running water and the Saharan winds constantly blew sand and dust around everything. In between gusts I decided the priorities were feet and crotch. These areas were critical and must be sand and dust free, and also properly lubricated. I would become fixated with this aspect of the challenge, but it paid off.

I'd picked bright white as the only colour to wear in the desert. It seemed an obvious way of combating the heat. But my white lycra shorts, top and hat combo had caused some mirth everywhere it had been paraded at home, and did so even here among the MDS fraternity. It was as if nobody else had thought of the idea of reflecting rather than absorbing the sun's rays.

'The man in white!' roared Rob. 'Can't wait to see the colour of it in a few days' time.'

I just smiled and retorted that my wisdom would shine through in the end, when I was shivering while everyone else collapsed with heat exhaustion. With little groups of people going through their own preparations, evenly spaced out over acres of sand, a battalion of 4 x 4 jeeps being packed and mobilised, first aid tents and big marquees being packed away, it all had the feel of an army preparing for battle.

In time I knew we would all develop our own rituals, but this first morning – like the pre-event Expo at any big endurance challenge – was a time for sharing information and panic, for over-analysing, for taking as gospel someone else's guess, for re-assessing big decisions about kit that had already been made and remade countless times in the previous few months.

There was another pressure that first morning: we were about to lose our lifeline to the normal world as our suitcases would return to Ouarzazate and we would for the next week be stuck with just what we could carry on our backs. So this was the point of no return for some items, and for me that included the North Face gilet. I wrestled with that decision for fully an hour, the already bulging and heavy rucksack saying 'no gilet', the memory of that freezing night and lack of sleep saying 'yes please gilet'. I sought advice.

Every tent was assigned a member of the 400-strong support crew to act as monitor. If there was a problem, he or she would try and solve it. Ours had been on the race for several years now and knew all the tricks. He covertly suggested that I take the gilet for the first day and, if I decided it was too much hassle, casually drop it near the tents in the hope it would be picked up by the daily lost property collections and I could retrieve it from there at the end of the week. It was hardly in keeping with the self-sufficiency spirit of the MDS but was worth a shot. I left the gilet on top of my rucksack, padlocked the suitcase in a show of finality from which there would be no turning back, and joined the inevitable queue for luggage deposit. I gave the suitcase a little pat when it was finally my turn to drop off, and felt a weird pang of emotion at the thought that the next time we touched, it would be all over and I could return to normal. I had to stop this ridiculous wishing the time away; it was pointless building up to this for years and then hoping it passed as quickly as possible. I knew I'd be OK once I got going, but this negativity was starting to weigh heavily.

I gave myself another talking to as the Tannoy crackled into life, reminding us that we had to gather at the start line for 8am. Each announcement was made in both French and English and blared out with distortion across the sand. The race start time was 8.30, so I didn't see why we had to be at the line a full half-hour before. I would rather have spent time stretching and warming up on my own, getting my head in the right place as opposed to where it was at that moment. I just needed more than ever to get going at last.

Having promised myself there would be no last-minute kit changes, inevitably I suddenly decided to copy Rob, who was ringing the sides of his trainers with thick black tape to protect the base of his gaiters from getting ripped on the rocks. The parachute silk felt so flimsy I decided this was a late change worth risking. I taped right round the perimeter, and then strapped on the little Velcro ankle transponder we'd been given the previous day. This would record our times through each checkpoint along the stage and across the finish line.

Finally, there was the rucksack. Remembering my Duke of Edinburgh Award training at school, I had been conscientiously packing the pointy, hard things at the front and the softer things at the back for greater comfort, but it was clear that with far too many things to go in, now also including the gilet, a less rigorous system of 'shove it all in and strap it down as firmly as possible' would have to be applied.

The weight was shocking. It felt much heavier and bulkier than when I'd packed in everything at home, and certainly heavier than the training weight. Of course it was too late to worry about it now, but as everyone gathered at the start there was widespread weighing and comparing of each other's packs, which only served to increase the general tension.

I looked enviously round at the packs of those runners who had taken their positions at the front. There was no way they were following the same rules I was. Tiny backpacks that might just about have held my swimming gear? No chance they contained distress flares, sleeping bag and 2,000 calories of food per day.

A man and a woman climbed up on the flat top of one of the Land Cruisers and a murmur went round the runners. This was the celebrated Mr Bauer, founder and organiser of the MDS. He spoke at length in French about the history of the race, which we'd already read about; his affection for Morocco, which we'd already read about; the race etiquette, which we'd already read about; the rules, which we'd already read about; the course, which we'd already read about; and the routines over the next week, which we'd already read about. It was then all translated into halting English by his assistant.

Half eight came and went and still Patrick droned on. When he'd finished going through the series of rules and guidelines he turned his attention to birthdays. Anyone whose birthday fell that day got a cheer and a round of 'happy birthday' songs in French and English. I was getting very pissed off, and I wasn't the only one. It was getting hotter by the minute, and still he wouldn't let us go. When he introduced a local dignitary to make a speech there was an audible protest. Finally, some music crackled through the Tannoy and Patrick shut up. It was AC/DC's 'Highway to Hell', and he burst into a wide smile. Perhaps he was laughing at the thought of anyone wearing his flip-flops.

'Highway to Hell' led to the countdown, which was chanted in unison. 'Ten, nine …' I turned to Rob and we shook hands. 'Good luck, mate. At last!' My heart was beating hard. I took a long, deep breath, closed my eyes and turned my head to the sky. Here we go. Finally. Three and a half years it had taken me to get here. I gripped my hand into a fist as an air horn signalled the start and we were off.

Most people had declared that they would walk the first five miles or so to adjust. But most people were sprinting within seconds. I was shocked at how quickly the bobbing mass of runners was spread out in a thin line across the desert. From behind me, people galloped past, rucksacks swinging and bouncing. I recognised the early race madness and tried to settle into my own rhythm.

I actually felt elated. At long last this was no longer about preparation. This was getting the job done. After ten minutes, I reckoned we'd gone a mile. Just another 149 to go. But there was a problem. Of course there was. Something was digging into my back. I humped the pack up with one hand and felt in between it and my back. There was a definite spike, a hard edge, and I realised it was the distress flare. I tried to shift it about in the pack, and carried on.

It moved back into position. I jogged on and tried to ignore it. It would soon move. It didn't. I had to stop. I couldn't stop this early into the race. I should stop now and get the problem looked at or else I could do some damage for the rest of the week. I didn't go through years of preparation to stop half an hour after we got started. It won't take long. It'll take too long. Just repack the rucksack. I can't repack the rucksack. It'll get too hot later to stop. It's already too hot to stop.

I saw a tree and a tumbledown wall up ahead. There was a bit of shade and I made for that. I needed to settle down a bit. It was a long, long road ahead and there would be many speed bumps that would need to be overcome sensibly and rationally. But unpacking and repacking the rucksack AGAIN?! I *hated* it already! That bloody gilet. Shouldn't have brought it. Nothing fits in. Calm down.

I wriggled out of the rucksack, dropped it onto the ground and with a deep breath began to delve inside for the flare. This all needed a rethink. I remembered the film of James Cracknell running the race. He was carrying a bag about a third the size of mine. I'd have to ditch more stuff. I thought about dumping things there and then but crammed it all back in for sorting later, taking more care this time to put pointy things at the front and spread the now unfolded gilet down the back. Problem with that, of course, was that the goose down wasn't going to help in the now suffocating desert heat.

Annoyed at having wasted time, I was about to sprint off but told myself to wise up and settle. I picked my steps carefully through the rocks and back onto the rough path, rejoining the hordes and finding a rhythm again.

The first checkpoint finally arrived about an hour later. At the admin checks the previous day we'd each been given a little plastic card on a bungee cord that was to be attached to our rucksacks. This had to be presented at each check-point along the course, where a hole would be punched on the relevant marker, clocking us in. Holes would also be punched to identify who had received their water ration each evening. Checkpoints were sited at roughly ten-kilometre intervals along the route of each stage, and I was dreading another series of queues at each one.

This part was really well organised, however, and with everyone well spread out by this stage there were no hold-ups. Our plastic passports were punched as we passed through a fenced corridor; then someone else thrust two big bottles of water at each runner and pointed to some canopies stretched out from the roof of the Land Cruisers, providing merciful shade. I refilled the water bottles without taking the rucksack off yet again and took my first salt tablets, which had been handed out as compulsory kit when we arrived.

I nearly boked. Salt filled every crevice of my teeth and coated my tongue. I had instinctively crunched them like sweets despite being advised to swallow them whole. Idiot. I gulped down water, swizzelled it about in my mouth and tried desperately to spit the taste out. One of the medics came over.

'Chew a salt tablet?' she asked with a smile.

'Yip.'

'You won't do it again.'

'Nope!'

'But they are important, seriously. You need them. To stop cramp. Just swallow them.'

Something about her earnest manner made me pledge to stick to the two tablet per water bottle formula. There was also the terror of the cramps I'd endured on the Étape and in Lough Erne. A repeat of those on a race of this scale would be impossible to survive. If nothing else, remembering about the tablets was another of the little routines to mark off, the little disciplines that break the whole down into small and more manageable parts.

The heat was really quite extraordinary now. It wasn't that my head or skin was on fire the way you notice when overdoing it on holidays; it was more of an all-encompassing general weight, like being oven cooked rather than grilled. The white lycra was clearly doing its work repelling the direct sun rays, but it could do nothing about the air temperature. We found out later that the first two days of that year's race were among the hottest they'd ever recorded – 40°C on the first day and almost 50 at times on the second! The difference between here and the spring-like Ouarzazate was startling. Surely 24 hours and 100 miles couldn't make that much difference?

It really started to affect me. I didn't notice at first, trying as I was to shuffle along in my own world, concentrating on the regular food and drink intake, not chewing the salt tablets, taking careful steps on the uneven ground, but slowly this great lethargy crept over me, like a warm, nauseous blanket. Eating was a problem. I was trying to chew through a sweet oat bar I'd eaten dozens of times before, but felt repulsed by it, as if I was going to be sick. My mouth was dry and it was difficult to swallow. I reduced my jog to a walk for a while as I drew up alongside a couple of English lads in identical kit.

They were helicopter pilots. Helicopter pilots crossing the Sahara Desert on foot. *Boy's Own Magazine* stuff. We all had our first name emblazoned across a big race number attached to both rucksack and front of chest, and also a little flag and initials identifying nationality, as if we were cars bound for the Continent. So complete strangers, through a mesh of suffering, would offer personalised encouragement to each other as they passed.

The pilots were in jaunty humour and had resolved to speed march the rest of the first day. They were moving pretty fast, so I joined them for a while and the reduction in internal organ bounce from not jogging made me feel a bit better. There was a massive hill up ahead and we could see a line of little people snaking along a cut in the side of it. This is one of the things they don't tell you about the Marathon des Sables and the Sahara Desert. It is hilly. And in the conditions, a slight change in incline proves to be significant.

Ordinarily, this was my kind of territory. I'd done so much of my training up and down Belfast's Cave Hill and in the Mournes that I knew I'd be stronger going up than most people, but this heat was a great leveller. I thought I'd push harder going up, to vary the pace and break the monotony, and then surf the usual post-climb endorphin rush down to the finish a few miles below. That was the plan anyway.

I did lift my pace on the climb, but halfway up I felt dreadful. It was something akin to altitude sickness: banging headache, nausea, weakness, dizziness and shortness of breath. I was back to a fast walk, and really struggling. Chastened, a little disappointed, I walked the rest of the way with a group that certainly didn't appear too athletic, and the thought that this might be my level at the MDS appalled me. I was probably going to finish easily in the top half of the pack, but had got used to better.

I could see the finish line for absolutely ages but it never seemed to be getting any closer. That was one of the longest half-hours of any endurance challenge I have ever done. I'd lost my mojo, and very nearly my motivation. I didn't feel like I'd gone hard enough to be exhausted; it wasn't that I was out of breath, I just felt generally shite. Like trying to do housework when hung over.

I found a modicum of energy to at least jog the last 400 metres and take the bad look off myself, and passed through the checkpoint. The transponder on my ankle bleeped and the first day was done – 21 miles out of a total of 150. I was laden with four bottles of water and slumped down heavily in the shade of a canopy without taking my rucksack off.

I was still feeling nauseous and dizzy but forced myself to prepare a recovery drink with the chocolate powder I'd brought. I hardly had the energy to shake it up, but slowly as it went down I felt a bit better and thought a bit more clearly. So obviously this was just going to be a horrible slog, and didn't need to be run. Just plod. Did I drink enough today? Maybe not. Did I eat enough? Thought so. Am I fit enough? Fitter than all of the people I finished with anyway. So what the hell was the problem? Nothing. One down, five to go, and I'll be stronger tomorrow. End of conversation.

The race organisers create a little map of the tent village with all the nationalities together in rows and each tent numbered, and by the time I'd found ours I was feeling a lot more positive. I dumped the rucksack off my shoulder and lay down with my feet raised on it to get the blood flowing away from my legs to (hopefully) help recovery. The ground was ribbed with rock and the carpet was stinking, thick with dust and sand.

Moving a race of this size every day must be a massive operation. As well as the 900 runners, there were the 400 crew, 270 tents, 100 vehicles, 2 helicopters and a Cessna plane for filming and spotting, 23 buses, 1 incinerator lorry for burning waste, 4 quad bikes, 50 medics, computers, satellite systems, camera and editing kit plus truck, and 120,000 litres of bottled water. There was also all the food for the crew and a huge range of medical supplies. This was like an army battalion going to war. I had a grudging admiration for Patrick; if he could just keep his morning waffle to a minimum from now on, he'd be a hero.

Piers was already back in our tent. He claimed to have quite enjoyed the first day and did look annoyingly fresh, in an eager puppy sort of way. I told him I struggled. But so had a lot of other people evidently. I was comfortably in the first half of finishers but it didn't take long for a queue to develop round the medical tents as everyone arrived back. Some took ages. There is a cut-off point on each stage, but the application is fairly lax and so long as you're moving you'll be allowed to make it round. At least half the competitors never run at all, I'd guess.

After lying down and taking more of my recovery medicine – a Peperami, some dry oat crackers and a full two litres of water – Piers and I tried to sort out the tent. The camel-hair sides were flapping about and sagging on each side, reducing the space considerably. It was already tight for seven people, so we spent some time tightening ropes and securing the ends with boulders, then turned our attention to the carpet. We couldn't lie on rocks and stones, so spent half an hour clearing them, battering the dust and sand from the carpet and re-laying it. This housekeeping became a frustrating daily ritual for Piers and I who were always the first to finish each stage, but it allowed us to pretend we had improved comfort levels and had somewhere we could call home for the rest of the day.

The rest of our tent arrived back at intervals and in various states of health. My fellow Northern Irishmen, Rob and Norman, were both limping. Every few minutes Norman's body would be contorted in a twist and a haunted, agonised look would flash across his face. He had been suffering from cramp for the last half of the stage.

Rob's main concern was his feet. When we'd met in Belfast before the race he said he was opting for sturdy trail shoes a size and a half too big as he'd read that your feet expand in the heat. I couldn't imagine they'd expand by that much and didn't fancy a full week of unforgiving trail shoes, so had instead opted for normal Asics trainers a half-size too big, which proved to be perfect.

Rob made a quick inspection of his hooves and with much shaking of his head and oohs and ahs hobbled off to the medical tents. I'd noticed there was a small group gathered across a dry riverbed outside the tent village, standing around something and chatting excitedly, so I put on the pathetic paper flip-flops, secured them with elastic bands and went off to investigate.

It was a well. How on earth there was a well with actual water in this godforsaken dustbowl I have no idea, but there it was. I half expected Omar Sharif and his camel to arrive out of the shimmering horizon any minute. The lads around it, who I think were French, were taking it in turns to stand on the rim of the well, drop a plastic container on a long rope down into the water, and then pour it all over themselves. Bliss. I hobbled back to get my bar of soap and facecloth.

Twenty minutes later I was a new man. Having struggled to adapt to the idea of a crusty week of sweat, salt, sand and dust, the sheer joy of standing naked on the raised rim of the well and cascading cold water over myself cannot be over-hyped. I had a good scrub, dried in seconds in the warm air and dressed for dinner.

Merino wool boxer shorts, recovery tights, a horrible off-white old vest and a thin red lycra long-sleeve was my post-race fashion statement, with the controversial gilet added when the sun went down. I'd cursed it all day but was very glad of it that night as the temperature went from suffocatingly hot to shiveringly cold in a matter of hours.

Eating was a pleasure, not because the freeze-dried maxi-calorie beef stew was tasty, but because eating through one whole day's rations created more space in the rucksack. There was a strange cross of cool campfire vibe and primeval protein envy about the evening cooking procedures, each of us lighting and protecting small individual stoves and preparing meals for one. There was much discussion and comparison of lighting methods and calorie content, but taste seemed to be sadly irrelevant.

I went for an evening stroll away from camp. The moon was enormous and halfway up the sky. It cast a weird half-light over our little village, the black of the tents contrasting with the darkened navy-grey sky and the last orange glow of the sand. On the perimeters of the camp little groups of local kids gathered like jackals, hoping to feed on anything we discarded. They must have been all too familiar with the over-loaded rucksack routine. Throughout the week we seemed so far from any sort of civilisation that other people were a continual surprise, especially the kids that would pop up randomly from behind dunes and elsewhere. I never saw a village or town so assumed these were mostly semi-nomadic people. Bizarrely, one of the kids was even wearing a Barcelona football top.

It was a striking scene that evening, and gave me a positive sense of the here and now. I had a bit more clarity. This needn't be a week of constant agony. There would be little windows of enjoyment and fantastic experiences that I had to be ready for. Yes, I could close off and suffer when required, but really this was a special, one-off experience and I needed to take it all in. There was inevitably a bit of physical adjustment on the first day, but it would get easier and I would get stronger.

Once it goes dark, there's not much craic at the Marathon des Sables. Generators powered the medical tents and the admin centre, at which there were yet more lengthy queues. I was surprised and faintly disgusted to find these were queues of people who couldn't go more than one day without checking or sending emails, and were waiting in line for a computer. In the desert, in the middle of 'the world's toughest footrace'.

Medical treatment and queuing aside, there wasn't much to do once it got dark other than unpack and repack your rucksack by torchlight. So that's what we did. Every night. My other favourite ritual was washing my feet. I'd brought along a shower cap, and used this as my basin. Water was strictly rationed for both drinking and cooking but I reasoned that healthy feet were worth the sacrifice.

After bathing and carefully drying them out of the wind and away from any blowing sand, I rubbed an anti-fungal cream all over and buried them deep into my sleeping bag. Over seven days of outrageous heat and 150 miles of rough terrain, I had no problems whatsoever with my feet, so as ridiculous as my nightly shower cap basin and pedicure routine looked, I was doing something right.

*

It was another bitterly cold and uncomfortable night. The North Face gilet again doubled up as a very small mattress over the crisp-bag roll mat, but I had already decided that it wasn't coming on the rest of the race. Early the next morning I dropped it self-consciously near the Lost Property pile and hoped I'd see it again at the end. I spotted half a roll mat lying on the ground, one with thick cushioning and an undercarriage made of foam shaped like an upturned egg carton. Someone else who had brought too much gear had halved and dumped it. I pounced.

The kit cull was quite cathartic. Small items admittedly, but anything that made this whole madness even a mite easier was precious. The flip-flops were next to go and good riddance. A copy of Aldous Huxley's *Brave New World* followed. (I was sure I'd be bored so had brought the thinnest book with the smallest text in my collection, the ratio of word to weight being vital.) A coffee cup and plunger combo was next. I had insisted that small luxuries would make a big difference late in the race, but someone else had filter paper, so the cup was gone. Having to sacrifice my own possessions but keep such bulky and almost certainly unused things as a venom pump and a distress flare irritated me immensely.

Eating breakfast lost another bit of luggage from the rucksack, and even with the addition of the egg carton roll mat it was a bit easier to cram everything in. I made sure to completely drain the water bottles and start on the salt tables early, and felt ready to run again. We delayed our arrival for as long as possible, hoping to miss Patrick's self-indulgence on the microphone, but alas he insisted on waiting for absolutely everyone to get to the start before beginning, so yet again the sun and the temperature rose higher and higher while we all stood and waited.

A couple of English girls in front of me were talking about hygiene and etiquette.

'There was a well out beyond the camp but by the time we found it there was just mud.'

'Yeah, I heard that. There were blokes actually washing in it. Lucky bastards. Didn't leave any for anyone else either.'

I kept my arms lowered for fear that the waft of Imperial Leather would unmask me as one of the lucky bastards.

'Highway to Hell' kicked in again and we were off. There wasn't quite the same mad flurry as the first day. Maybe people had learned the hard way, or maybe it was because the course map revealed a massive feckin mountain about three miles in. It was steep, really steep. There was a rough course marked up one side, and at times it was more like rock climbing. I was concerned about the sharp stone edges ripping the parachute silk and was glad of the thick tape, which was starting to look frayed.

The Mourne Mountains training gave me the perfect base for tests like this and I was happy to tap out the steps and stay bouncy on each hoist to keep the strain off my hips. Suddenly something scurried beside my foot. Jesus Christ, a scorpion! Waaow. I'd thought several times about dumping the venom pump and taking a chance on avoiding the kit spot checks; carrying this little plastic vacuum was nonsensical tokenist health and safety box-ticking, but there was no point tempting fate …

I recoiled a bit and warned the people behind me. It was just the injection of adrenaline I needed, a bit of wild to relieve the tedium of lifting one leg after another, tap-tapping up the mountain.

The view at the top was sensational. Miles upon miles of desert and scrub, the heat shimmering off the surface and up and around enormous dunes, collected like lumps in a vast unmade bed. If I hadn't already been out of breath from the mountain climb this would have taken it away anyway. Piled below us, a huge heap of glorious, glorious soft dark orange sand for us to slide down. The way up was rock, the way down shifting sand blown against the cliff for millennia. I let loose, charging down with great leaps, enjoying the cushioning of the joints and freedom at last from the monotony of carefully tapping out measured steps of effort and positioning. It was exhilarating.

A few hours later, I thought I was going to die. Past the mountains and dunes, there was a vast ancient floodplain to cross. The bottom of a massive saucer without a breath of breeze, and the sun was at its peak. Everything shimmered, and the six miles between the final checkpoint and that night's camp were the longest of my life. The temperature apparently peaked that day at a scarcely believable 52°C – another MDS record.

Like the previous day, I wasn't conscious of direct sunlight as much as a general, heavy, all-consuming heat, as if my organs were being slow-cooked but my skin wasn't. Like the perfect Sunday roast, I presumed. I felt sick again, dreadfully weak, and quite alone. I hadn't the energy or the inclination to talk to anyone. This was suffering, and best done in solitary. The featureless nature of the floodplain and distant horizon was cruel and psychologically wounding. Every step felt insignificant, almost pointless in the face of such impossible distance and in such outrageous conditions.

I shuffled past a number of other runners all suffering in solitude and silence, and we exchanged nothing more than grunts. The jauntiness of the previous day and early morning had evaporated in the furnace. I wondered how many would quit that day. Stopping there and then was no option – no shade, no water, no hope – but I reckoned that crossing this eerie hell on earth would destroy a lot of people psychologically. I turned my brain off, tried to go into auto-pilot, tried to remove all awareness of the dark, dark place I was in, and repeated that Churchill quote over and over in my head, 'When you're going through hell, keep going.'

Finally I wobbled over the finish line, stood shakily while an official punched my plastic card and loaded me with water bottles, then slumped in the shade of a canopy. My head was slamming. This was not fun and it couldn't end quickly enough. I felt weak, impotent. I poured some of the cool water over my head and down my neck, and sipped. I was too nauseous to guzzle it properly.

Bizarrely, 20 minutes later, I felt great. This mad swinging from desperation to exaltation was like life in microcosm. Great ups and great downs, daily existence stripped down to struggle and recovery, survival being the only focus. Lying in the tent, out of the demonic intensity of the sun, I felt liberated, mindful, confident, and high as a kite. Piers arrived back shortly after and we chatted elatedly. Sometimes the most painful experiences to endure are the most enjoyable to recall.

I went to walk off the stiffness and stretch, and bumped into another Northern Irish competitor we'd met at the airport. He had appeared to be the ultimate endurance athlete – an experienced Ironman with a teak-tough physique and an aura of manic determination. He was sitting now in the full glare of the sun on a pile of rocks beside the centre of the camp.

'How's it going?' I asked him. He looked suspiciously fresh.

'Ach, I have just quit. Had enough.'

'What?' I thought he was joking.

'Too much for me, this heat. Don't fancy it,' he confirmed, jauntily. He just shrugged his shoulders and stretched his arms in the sun, as if he was saying he'd decided not to bother going to the beach for the afternoon. He was so matter of fact about it all that I was shocked. No wailing, no soul searching, just simple resignation. It properly put it all in perspective, I supposed. He wasn't enjoying it, so he just stopped.

I thought about that quite a lot. Paradoxically, it showed great sense of character to just stop. None of us was being forced to do this. Why shouldn't he try it, decide he didn't like it, pull out and just enjoy a few days in the sun? Why shouldn't I? Why didn't I? I couldn't. There was far too much invested by now. Money, time, emotion, effort. And I didn't need to quit. Physically I was grand, mentally I was still tight. And tomorrow was a couple of miles shorter than today's 23.

I went for a wash. Since the joyful discovery of the well in the desert on day one most people hadn't washed at all, but I always felt better after getting the old smell reservoirs freshened up. I was happy to sacrifice a little bit of water for the armpits and undercarriage, since any saddle sores, blistering or infections would mean no race, and also just because it felt more human.

There is no privacy at the MDS, but I found I could create the illusion of it by walking alone out of camp a bit, as if distance made me invisible. Others felt the same, and most evenings you'd see white arses glinting in the sliding sun as people bent over and washed as best they could.

I was starting to recognise and almost enjoy the routines of the day. I always found establishing some kind of routine – even if it was just a breathing pattern – really helped me survive big challenges. Finding something controllable in the face of chaos felt positive. So I was in an altogether better frame of mind that second evening. Unfortunately the same could not be said for poor Norman.

He had arrived at the tent in an even worse state than he was the first day. His body spasms were more intense, violent even, and he seemed to lose control of his limbs and facial features every few minutes as if he was being electrocuted. It was some of the worst cramping I'd ever seen, and made my jumping thighs on the Étape look merely ticklish by comparison. He would be curled up in the foetal position between spasms, then writhing in pain.

He announced he'd had enough, something was wrong, and he couldn't continue. He was for quitting immediately, but his cramping legs wouldn't even let him walk to the admin tent.

He lay down and I fixed him one of the chocolate drinks.

'Have you been taking the salt tablets?'

'Sort of, well, I took the odd one … aaaaooowww!!'

I tried stretching his hamstrings for him but it didn't help much.

'Have you got any good recovery drinks?'

'No, no, I didn't want to take anything I wasn't used to. I had some gels, though.'

'But nothing for after?'

'No.'

'Right, you're drinking this, and take these salt tablets too. Don't chew them.'

'Aaaooooww, sheesh! Goodness me.'

It made me laugh that even in this extreme discomfort Norman wasn't going to swear. Fair play to him.

'I'm not used to taking anything like this,' he began, before another spasm shut him up.

'It's only chocolate and some proteins and things. Trust me, you'll be totally fine, and if you don't take something you won't recover. Just drink this, take the salt tablets and see how you feel in the morning.'

'I'll not be far behind you, Norman, to tell you the truth,' said Rob, ruefully. 'My feet are a disaster. I'm not sure I can take any more of this.'

He was slowly peeling off the swathes of bandages and didn't like what he saw, shaking his head and wincing. This was a serious turn of events. There had already been one Northern Irishman pulling out that day; we couldn't lose another two, people would start to think we'd all gone soft since the ceasefires.

Everybody was in better humour on the morning of day three. Judging by the deep resonance of his epic snoring, which woke me several times, Norman had slept soundly, and the cramps had gone. Rob was still limping and looking pensive, but he was determinedly re-dressing his feet, which was a good sign. I offered him a lend of my shower cap footbath if he made it round that evening.

The morning post arrived at just the right time to give us all an extra lift. There was a central email address through which people at home could send messages to each competitor, and these were then collated on sheets and delivered by the tent moderators each morning. I hadn't bothered telling anyone at home about the service before I left, and now regretted it because there was a fabulous First

World War 'news from home' feel about the whole process, as everyone sat reading their mail around their stoves.

To my surprise, there *were* actually a couple of messages for me. Slippy had found the message-leaving facility via the website and been in touch to say he thought I'd 'absolutely nailed day 1'. I realised then that the results of each stage must be published daily. He also told me his son Jamie had woken the previous night at 11pm, 2am, 3am and then 5am, which made me laugh out loud. 'I would much rather be in a tent in the middle of the desert,' he added. I was touched. My mum had also found out about it somehow and was in touch with some news from home; they'd been looking after the boys for the afternoon and having a few adventures. I truly did feel like a soldier on a six-month tour at this stage, and I'd only been away from home for five days!

Rob had a couple of emails from home too, and the messages arrived at the right time. Freshly determined not to let anyone down, he had a renewed grim determination to walk on broken glass to get the race finished. But first he had to get through another of Patrick's morning sermons, which were really beginning to take a toll now and had caused considerable dissension in the ranks. Delaying one's appearance at the start line did not mean missing his waffling, it just pushed the start time later and the temperature hotter as he refused to speak until *everyone* was present. It didn't matter how long we had to stand waiting under the rising sun, he was going to deliver the full unabbreviated briefing in two languages for half an hour every day and we'd better get used to it.

It was especially annoying because, other than the tyranny of this pointless nonsense, I was beginning to really value the strange freedom offered by having nothing to do all day except put one foot in front of the other as fast as possible for as long as possible. No work issues, no social challenges, no big decisions, no changing nappies, no entertaining the kids. Just disengage brain, run and suffer. Simple and cathartic.

With 6,000 calories of the food now gone, the rucksack was lighter, less bulky and seemed to fit better. I'd been strapping my shoulders and upper back with kinesiology tape since the previous morning, trying to alleviate what felt like pulled muscles, and it seemed to help because about half an hour in to my usual slowish start I realised I was going pretty well. Almost as an experiment I upped the pace a bit and by the last half of the stage was really pushing on. I didn't notice the heat as much, it certainly wasn't the outrageous 50°C of stage two, and I was comfortable.

There was a camera live streaming to the MDS website on the finish line, and I ran right up to it, grinning from ear to ear and giving the thumbs up. I'd got my mojo back. That was particularly good timing, since the next day's course was over 50 miles in one hit.

I'd tried not to think too much about that day before we came out. It was almost unfathomable. How could anyone run for 50-odd miles in one go? It didn't make sense. But people had done it every year on the MDS, and if they could, I could. I repeated Anthony Hopkins's line to Alec Baldwin in the film *The Edge*, over and over.

'What one man can do, another can do.'

I'd always used this as a motivational quote as I liked the message. Even better, I fancied I could do a great

Hopkins impression and this was a more useful line than 'Have the lambs stopped crying, Clarice?'

There was a noticeably different atmosphere at the start of the fourth day. Yes, we were moving into the final three stages, which was a good way to look at it, but the magnitude of the challenge on this one alone seemed to hang over everyone. But it was the strongest I'd felt yet and I was weirdly confident and almost excited – intrigued about how I'd cope and what would happen, as if I'd be nothing more than a dispassionate observer of the proceedings.

A local dignitary had arrived to officially start the race, which of course meant an extra speech plus translation, and even longer standing in the sun. As if we wouldn't be out for long enough that day ... The growing dissension finally spilled into revolution. Having shifted angrily from one foot to the other for a good half-hour, the serious runners at the front had a consultation and decided to take back some element of control. Ignoring Patrick's choreography, after 'Highway to Hell' and the ten-second countdown nobody moved. It was a perfectly timed strike, in the finest French tradition, and in front of the local bigwig too. Oh, how I laughed!

Once we got going I switched my brain to neutral so successfully that the first ten miles were a blur and I arrived at the first checkpoint in a bit of a daze. I felt absolutely fine, totally fresh, and tried to tell myself that the stage was only starting now and the previous section had been a dream. It felt like that anyway, for how else could one account for the presence of random groups of children out here, miles from any obvious human habitation, and even at one point a man in flowing robes on a bike? It was all most peculiar.

By the second checkpoint I had to change brain gear. I'd decided this would be the point where I took stock of everything, performed a quick body check-up and service if necessary, and broke the rest of the run down into manageable chunks. Drifting along in neutral would only get me so far; to get through 50 miles I needed to properly manage both effort and fuel.

I had a fuel *injection* to look forward to as well. I'd decided to keep a couple of treats until late in the race, so had been dangling caffeine and music in front of myself like the proverbial carrot since day one, holding off until I felt I'd really earned them and needed a lift. I'd brought a couple of the caffeine tablets that worked so brilliantly on the Race Around Ireland, and washed one down alongside the salt tablets.

After four days and no cramping or muscle pain I was beginning to feel quite attached to the salt. How I wished I'd had these on the Étape and the Lough Erne swim! If it had taken me all those events to learn that a lack of salt was my Achilles heel, perhaps I should go back and do them all again, but better? No thanks. I'd always believed the marketing hype from various sports drinks about replacing the correct balance of fluids and minerals, so it was hard to accept that actually all I had to do was eat some common or garden salt chunks. They did seem to work a treat though ... I strapped my iPod to my arm, picked the medium energy playlist I'd sorted before leaving Ireland, and within minutes the world was wonderful.

While millions of pounds are spent every year analysing and researching physical performance in endurance athletes, only a fraction of that is spent on looking into psychological performance. I have never understood that, because in my experience being in the right shape mentally is every bit as vital a component. Twenty minutes after taking a caffeine tablet and starting some music, I felt like I was floating. Pain free, with huge reserves of energy, I sailed along and felt I could run forever. Nothing had happened physically, but mentally I'd managed to put myself in a different place. I'd been telling myself all week how much easier it would be when I had some caffeine and some tunes, and I suppose now I was determined not to let myself down. Very strange, but our minds are an endless source of wonder and we really haven't a clue how it all works.

It probably helped that the ground was a lot firmer in this section; it was all compacted sand and stone paths, much easier to run along. I remember getting up and over a couple of hills and seeing one of the checkpoints in a valley a few miles below. The sun was setting and there was a weird orange and purple haze settling over everything; the MDS tents stood out against that backdrop and it really was quite beautiful.

I guessed I'd gone about 35 miles by this point but felt as fresh as a daisy. I couldn't begin to explain it. I was more than fresh, I was really happy. Grinning rather than grimacing, really enjoying the intensity of the whole experience, being in the moment, being in the desert, being fit, being free, running for an entire day and not being tired. It all made sense at last. The near four-year build-up, the admin, the frustrations, the struggles of the first few days, all counted for nothing against a stand-out moment like this, a once in a lifetime performance, a perfect snapshot captured and burned on the canvas of my mind forever.

*

Suddenly there were only five miles to go and it was almost completely dark. I was wearing my head-torch and picking steps carefully through the rocks. The route was lit by little glow sticks every few hundred metres and by the torches of other runners, bobbing like fireflies in the distance. I was ticking them off, one by one, seeing a new light and hunting it down as quickly as I could. I still had music banging through the headphones, and that, plus the fact that the only light was coming from my own head-torch, created a cocoon-like effect of being in my own little world. Everything was internal.

Eleven hours of focusing solely on the one activity had been good for me, this was mindfulness in the extreme, and even if it took a lot of money and a lot of effort to get it, it was worth it.

But the mental peace contrasted with growing disquiet from my guts. They weren't enjoying the ride as much as the rest of me. If they were empty and not being called into action they'd probably have accepted it, but in order to run for 11 consecutive hours in the desert I needed them to process gallons of liquid, handfuls of salt, and the weight of a human baby in energy bars, nuts and other very highly calorific foodstuffs, while jiggling up and down all day in 40°C heat.

I ignored the protests until finally they could be ignored no more. Loudly and forcibly my guts informed me that they were ready to evacuate. I was only a few miles from the finish, but they wouldn't wait, and I had to scramble off the track, dump my rucksack and answer the call. Fortunately it was pitch dark by this point, but *un*fortunately everyone was basically following the head-torch of the runner in front – even if that runner had foolishly

forgotten to turn the torch off before evacuating nois-
ily behind a bush. It was one of the most embarrassing
moments of my life, and the contrast with the purity and
peace of the previous few hours made me laugh out loud
as I heaved the rucksack back on.

As if the spell had been broken, suddenly I felt human
again, in fact absolutely knackered as I rejoined the track
and tried to regain the rhythm that had carried me to within
a few miles of finishing this epic day and breaking the back
of reputedly one of the hardest physical challenges in the
world. Little niggles started making themselves known.
My hips ached, I felt stiff, the terrain was rocky and treacherous in the dark, and I had to grit my teeth and suffer for
the first time that day.

I could see the lights of the campsite sending a glow to
the sky for miles around, and gradually they became more
distinct and I could make out shapes, outlines, and more
and more detail until I was in the last few hundred metres.
My heart was filled again and I hammered home. This was
the fastest I'd been running for months, this wasn't plodding, this was being athletic again, this was performing,
this was finishing a 52-mile race with a sprint.

I was dizzy as I staggered through a finish arch and
was met by a number of the race officials, some of them
looking into my eyes, which felt wider than saucers and
open for the world to see into my very soul. Whatever the
officials saw in the half-light, they were happy I was OK
and let me wobble past them through to the tent village.

My heart was slamming, my head spinning a bit, and I
was focused determinedly on going straight to the tent, as
if I was afraid to let go until I was safely returned to where
nothing would matter for all that night and all the next

day. By doing the 52 miles of stage four in one go, in one crazy 12 hours, I had bought a massive chunk of recovery time. The cut-off for that epic stage was something like 36 hours, but finishing in less than 24 gave you the whole of the following day and night to rest.

I found tent number 84 and collapsed. I barely had the strength to take off my rucksack and couldn't bring myself to sort the recovery drink and food. My heartbeat took ages to settle as I lay on the ground, spent. I grew cold, and eventually found the energy to get my extra clothes out of the pack and curl my sleeping bag around myself. I don't know how long I lay there, almost in shock. I had this weird sense of being somewhere between sleep and alertness, as if my mind was racing to places where my body couldn't follow.

Everything was swimming a bit, and as I started to feel even colder and slightly queasy I knew I needed to sort myself out and get some food in. My hands were trembling slightly as I mixed the recovery shake but within minutes of drinking it and eating the Peperami and a bag of nuts I felt better. I got the stove going, ate the awful freeze-dried grit I was now beginning to detest, and waited for some strength to return. It was nearly 11 o'clock. In just over an hour it would be my birthday. That was a strange realisation, like a bit of a former life arriving in a new one. Then my guts brought me back to the here and now. Not again …

Shakily, but with as much haste as I could manage, I shuffled off through the darkness to the latrine cubicles. This inner turmoil would pass, I hoped; it was all part of the after-effects of the toughest unbroken strain I had ever put myself through.

Once far enough away from the tarpaulin cubicles I stretched straight and took a few long, deep breaths through my nose. The air was cold, and felt clear, cleansing like spring water. I thought we must have been absolutely miles from anywhere, as far into the absent centre of the Sahara as we would get. The stars and the moon felt so close I could touch them, so bright I could turn off the head-torch. I felt better, and by the time Piers arrived back I was full of hyper chat, going through my feet wash routine and then plummeting to sleep as soon as they hit the bottom of the sleeping bag.

One of the unique things about the Marathon des Sables is that you can do it more or less at your own pace. There are cut off times for each stage, but these are so generous it is possible to walk the whole thing slowly and still get within the limits, which are very leniently applied anyway. So among those who do it there are widely varying levels of athleticism, and it is much more inclusive than most other major endurance challenges of this scale. But finishing it slowly does not make it any easier.

I had slept for nine hours and had breakfast and lunch before many of the competitors even got back, so their effort was much greater than mine. I opted to get each day's effort over and done with as quickly as possible, whereas on this epic stage Rob was on the go for a full 24 hours, through day and night, a very long period of full desert exposure on shredded feet. He was pale when he limped in, a combination of the pain and the lack of sleep, but I knew by the look on his face that there was no longer any thought of giving up. He was past the point of no return, he was going on to the finish and there would be no more chat to the contrary.

This was a day of great camaraderie for our little tent group, the eight of us finally all back together when David stumbled in mid-afternoon. He'd slept for a couple of hours in a hut somewhere along the route and, though stiff and exhausted, his spirits were great. He'd bought himself a place on the MDS for his 60th birthday present and had set out to prove to himself and his ex-wife – who had recently divorced him – that he still had the courage and virility to come through a massive physical challenge. He confessed that he'd been in some pretty dark places since his wife left him a few years previously, and we all felt somehow responsible for him getting through what was clearly a transformative experience. Rob and he leaned on each other for the remainder of the race, and we all made a pact that everyone from Tent 84 would finish.

As if to illustrate the *esprit de corps* we had formed, Rob produced a birthday card signed by the whole tent. I couldn't believe it. It wasn't like he'd hurriedly popped down to WHSmith's that morning. How he had the foresight to add a birthday card to the myriad of kit he'd packed in Ireland a week earlier was beyond me, but genuinely touching. Another few pages of emails arrived too, including birthday wishes from Claire telling me how proud she was of how I'd done so far, and also that Reuben was teething so badly he'd been gnawing at his wooden cot like a beaver. Suddenly the skinny sleeping bag and rock bed of my nights on the Marathon des Sables didn't sound so bad. It was likely that Claire was getting less sleep in an air-conditioned house than I was getting in an open-sided camel-hair tent.

It was by far the most unusual birthday I could remember, but in the afternoon it moved from unusual to bizarre.

It started to rain. The Sahara Desert, which in the last few days had almost roasted me alive, served up rain on my birthday, the only day of the week in which I didn't have to run anywhere and could sunbathe and relax. From nowhere, the weather was pissing on my parade.

There was a massive crack of thunder and suddenly the gentle, intermittent raindrops got angry. A storm of biblical intensity came roaring in. The rain came pelting down in sheets, turning the sand to mud, but not before it was whipped round us by freak winds. The sand stung our legs, arms and eyes as the pathetic camel-hair tent crumbled and blew apart. The stinking, musky, heavy sides collapsed on top of us and we ran out and tried in vain to secure them and shore it up. But the storm intensified and it was pointless. The only thing to do was climb inside a now mud-encrusted sleeping bag and hide.

It was horrible. The storm raged, literally kicking dirt in my eye, and I honestly felt persecuted. How could this be happening? We'd got this far, taken the record heat, the sand, the dunes, the mountains, the freezing nights, the freeze-dried food, survived it all, and now the Sahara had invited the worst of a British spring over when we were off guard to kick the shite out of us. It's hard to explain – it was just bad weather after all – but lying there as mud formed over all my stuff, this felt like a kick too far and I'd had enough. This whole thing was a shit idea from start to finish and in a few days it would all be over and I'd never mention it again. I yearned for the real world, with hot showers and washing machines and soft beds and coffee shops and fresh fruit and a change of clothes. I'd never be in a bad mood again! Just get me home.

It blew over in an hour and I found the resolve to climb out of my hiding place so I could huff in public. We all let off some steam, searching for something to blame. Cue Patrick. Or the loudspeaker anyway, to announce that the organisers had a little treat for us if we could all queue in the middle of the tent village. We were used to heading there for our rations of water but today we were being rewarded with a little tomato and pistachio nut bar and a can of coke.

I am quite sure that had it been offered at a drinks party back in the real world I'd have run a mile from the tomato and pistachio bar, but I devoured it in the desert, my first new taste for five days. For most of the others the leap was too great, not even those strenuous circumstances could make that bar palatable, so I hoovered up theirs as well. The can of ice-cold coke was the nicest I have ever had, oh sweet nectar of the real world! It wasn't the greatest birthday meal ever, but it remains one of the most appreciated. Everything is relative.

The sun came out again and everything was dry in minutes but covered completely in dust and grit. It was in our ears, our mouths and every orifice, all through the rucksack, in every pocket and in every bag of food. I would have given everything I had to jump in a pool of fresh water. Just to feel clean again. I set my sights on a shower in the hotel at Ouarzazate.

Stage 5 on Day 6 was a mere marathon. Half the distance of stage 4 but the last big test, as the sixth and final stage was less than ten miles and regarded as a victory parade, like the last stage of the Tour de France. I stood in the start group and took stock. My approach had changed. This one felt different. I was quite psyched up actually. The ruck-sack was only half the weight it was before, I was twice as strong, and I was going to charge round this marathon and get another day closer to the shower.

I let my mind drift during Patrick's ramble, getting keyed up for a big blast. Then he called out my name and I realised he was doing the birthday announcements for the previous day alongside this one. He misses nothing. I raised my hand in acknowledgement like a sprinter being announced to the crowd. Then we were on the countdown and I was off.

I gave myself the first hour to settle in, check everything out. Then through the first of the three checkpoints it was iPod time, and half a caffeine tablet. And off I flew. Three hours in, I was practically sprinting. I bombed past the Frenchwoman who was actually first female home overall. I felt fantastic, empowered and untouchable, hugely emotional after a week of blood, sweat and digestive confusion. Tears were streaming down my face.

It was easily the most exhilarating athletic performance of my life. I felt no pain, no fatigue, just strength – and, strangely, as if I had somehow connected to something inherent but previously hidden. Perhaps it was sunstroke. I'm assuming it was possibly akin to the surge of positive emotional clarity people claim they experience in moments of religious conversion. The years of preparation and the week of pain were entirely worth it, to feel like that for just a few hours. It was even better than the 52-mile day.

We passed through half-ruined villages and there were more kids along the route, shouting excitedly as we passed. Some held out their hands for shakes or high fives. I am ashamed to say that the intensity of my focus and my utter paranoia about finishing the event was such that I was scared of catching any bugs at this late stage, so from me they had to settle for a big wave.

Despite a deliberately slow first hour, then travelling over sand dunes and mountains and with slight delays at the checkpoints, I ran that marathon in four hours. I crossed the line in a tunnel of intensity. There was a photo of me finishing the stage posted on the MDS website that evening. I have this crazed, faraway look in my eyes. It was a moment of such emotion and clarity of purpose I'll never forget it.

I had promised not to switch my phone on for the full week, thinking the break from that omnipresent of modern life would be an essential part of the whole MDS experience, but I needed to talk to someone. I phoned Claire and cried down the phone. It must have sounded like I'd finally lost it, raving hysterically from the middle of the desert as she calmly went about her day back home, but she understood that it was almost over, and I was having a bit of a release.

Sadly the other releases of that day came relentlessly. The gut protest had got more vociferous and even violent. There was blood. It wasn't what Piers wanted to talk about, I'm sure, when he got back to the tent, but I was worried. What did it mean? Had I ruptured something, was this serious? And, the biggest conundrum of all, should I go to the medical tent and tell them, and risk them taking me out of the race – with everything done bar the parade lap?

I lay for a few hours feeling really queasy and then quite faint. How quickly the euphoria had disappeared. I lay dead still, apart from sipping water, and hoped against hope this was nothing serious. Slowly I began to feel a little better, walked off to take in some air and decided it was ridiculous not to go to the medical tent.

Talking about extreme diarrhoea is hard at the best of times, but trying to do so across a language barrier is even worse. The doctor I spoke to was eventually happy to let me go with some tablets and recovery salts, a bung and a refuel basically. I took a gamble and didn't tell him about the blood.

The paradox of the MDS and probably most other ultra-distance endurance events is that in actual fact it is a trial by inches and not miles. It is as much about overcoming a series of small discomforts and challenges as about covering enormous distances. Just like in life, we are defined as much by how we deal with the regular struggles as the irregular.

An hour into the final stage I was again in a dark place. My paranoid fear that something could yet happen to prevent me from finishing the race just miles from the end was now casting such a shadow that I couldn't settle. I was tense, concentrating all the time on not twisting my ankle on the uneven ground and cursing the organisers for what I saw as an unnecessarily cruel final route over some of the highest dunes and most shifting sands we'd experienced all week. This was no victory parade. Far from it.

This was the most irrational I'd been all week, and it stemmed from my impatience to have the whole thing wrapped up at last. For me the challenge had ended the day before, when I ran so hard I'd ended it shitting blood. This last ten miles was nothing but a pointless inconvenience, and the fact that we had to churn over these enormous final dunes right at the last, rather than coasting home in triumph, pissed me off no end.

It pissed me off so much in fact that I finally got into gear and hammered myself angrily over the last three miles or so. By the final section, when the destination town appeared in the distance, I was snorting fire and sprinting home through the growing numbers of locals and family members that were grouped on opposite sides of a dune pass, forming a stadium effect for the final 500 metres.

I ran flat out right to the line, where a tape was raised for each finisher to run through, and Patrick waited to hand over the medal. I raised my arms across the line and ran through the tape. I felt it slide down my thighs and a weight slide off my shoulders. It was over.

Patrick shook my hand and I bent my head as if to be crowned. 'C'était facile,' I told him. He looked shocked, almost hurt, but then I smiled, he laughed and I walked on. And then I was at a bit of a loss. I didn't have to find my tent, I didn't have to mix up a recovery drink, I didn't have to move all the stones from under a rug, sort my rucksack or light a stove. I sat down on a wall and was immediately set upon by locals trying to sell me bottles of Coke and Fanta, young kids begging for my gear, and then, memorably, one entirely delusional carpet salesman. Did he really think …

I bent over, with my elbows on my knees and my head down, and took it all in. There was all too much madness, noise, sand, heat and discomfort. I yearned for that shower, and this wouldn't be over until I was standing under it. Above all, I realised, there were too many other people. I yearned for a bit of privacy. I wanted a door I could shut, a time to just sit and reflect, just for a while. For more than a week the closest I'd got to privacy had been squatting over a plastic stool surrounded by tarpaulin walls that were blown open at the sides by any passing breeze.

I picked up the lunch box prepared for each finisher and found the buses that would bring us on the lengthy journey back to Ouarzazate. Another annoyance. We had run 150 miles but not back in the direction from which we'd come. It seemed silly, and a few hours later in the bus, when the first confined space for a week really brought home how badly we all smelled, it was quite sickening.

Over that long five-hour journey back to the hotel I reminded myself of the 'inches rather than miles' concept, how these final few irritations were merely small tests and part of the bigger examination, which would end in a matter of hours and required no further physical effort, only patience.

I couldn't find my suitcase at the hotel. Inches rather than miles. It was in the wrong hotel. Inches rather than miles. It was retrieved. I couldn't find my hotel room. Inches rather than miles. It was on a corner and not sequentially numbered. Up the stairs, couldn't turn the key in the lock. Inches rather than miles. Wrestled with it, and finally it gave. Locked the door, stripped off, turned on the shower, then looked at myself in a mirror for the first time in eight days. Jesus Christ, how skinny. Those inches sure added up. Then the water was running down my head and body at last. It ran brown, but I scrubbed until it ran clear. It all ran clear. And all things come to pass.

For the record, I finished 126th, in a time of 34 hours and 24 minutes. But on the MDS, for all but the top 50 elites, finishing positions and times are irrelevant. Being there at the start, and at the end, is all that matters.

The buses returned to Ouarzazate at sporadic intervals, each one setting off as soon as there were enough finishers to fill it, so it wasn't until the next evening that Tent 84 had a proper recap all together. The Scottish couple, Derek and Yvonne, were veterans of lots of long, long races, had smiled all the way through and didn't seem any different now that it was over. Derek produced a bottle of whisky and poured everyone a dram. Norman announced that he didn't really drink, then downed his dram in seconds without a flinch. Piers was as relaxed as ever, Rob was exhausted but happy to be off his lacerated feet, and poor old David, having proven all he had to and more, had picked up food poisoning in town that lunchtime. It was rotten luck, but having the iron constitution to survive the Marathon des Sables doesn't mean you should recklessly order a seafood pizza in a Moroccan café hundreds of miles from the coast.

There was a vague 'zombie' feel to the hotel next day; many of the guests had more bandages and tape visible under their sandals than skin. Others were being literally carried around by their mates, and a few were on crutches. Only 60 competitors hadn't finished, which out of nearly 900 starters is a very high completion rate – and testament, I felt, to the mad expense of having to come back and try again. One poor guy had collapsed in a coma and was airlifted to hospital. He later recovered.

I sat in the lobby waiting for the bus and watching everyone hobble around. What on earth was it all about? What was it for? Why were all these people on crutches smiling, having just forked out close to £4,000 to return home maimed and probably unable to work for a few weeks? Humans are weird, I decided. Weird, but also wonderful. In all the animal kingdom there is only one species that deliberately drives itself to exhaustion and personal injury for no tangible reward. But there is only one species that truly rules the world.

I wondered if everyone else had experienced the same manic euphoria that I had at times. I hadn't really shared much of those moments, and nobody else had revealed too many deep emotions either; they felt private somehow, even though we'd all been through one big shared experience. In a way, I was glad I'd come out alone. I thought Robster would have absolutely loved this, but running together perhaps would have precluded those intense, internal moments I'll remember and treasure for ever.

Those on crutches – and the one guy I saw being pushed through the airport in a wheelchair – were coming home happy because they had the evidence of how much pain they could endure for a cause that somehow was represented as noble. Everyone had been through a massive experience in one way or another, had a vault of memories that would sustain them through the drudgery of 'normal' life for a while. With moments as intense as those survived in the desert there are no such things as good and bad memories; the most painful experiences are usually the ones that live longest and most meaningfully. The pleasurable anticipation of re-telling and re-living the hardest week of their lives in the comfort of the rest of their lives was what had everyone smiling, and that was worth £4,000 of anyone's money.

The terrifying digestive mayhem had gone before I left Morocco, and it was fantastic to be at home eating and drinking whatever I wanted and passing it off as re-fattening my skeletal frame. I also tore into an unhealthy amount of drink on a couple of big nights out, celebrating throwing off the four-year MDS yoke. Everyone asked me how I felt, and I genuinely felt great. I never had any fatigue, lasting stiffness, feet problems or joint pain. I did wake up drenched in sweat most nights, but other than that I thought I'd made an immediate and complete recovery.

The human body sends messages incrementally. It whispers at first and then if you don't listen it shouts. And finally, if you still aren't listening, it throws a tantrum. I ignored the nightly sweats and too early began poisoning my system while it was quietly working hard to recover.

Some time after the first big night out I stumbled to the toilet completely soaked and both roasting hot and shivering at the same time. I'll spare you some of the details, but it all kicked off, and I was so weak I passed out and woke up on the cold tiles in a puddle of my own sweat. Almost two weeks later, exactly the same thing happened. The world's toughest footrace had the longest build-up, so I should have known it would have the longest recovery. I found out that other ultra-endurance people experienced similar nightly sweats and violent digestive reactions for weeks after each event, and when the sweats subsided, so did my concerns. I called it Patrick's revenge.

Eleven
BOB SMITH, IRONMAN

The best thing about having the Marathon des Sables in April was that I had all the following summer 'off' any major training or event preparation. I needed it, and Claire needed it too. She had been remarkably supportive over the years but had come under a lot of pressure with her family business. Now she was preparing to close the retail end of their furniture group, which she had run for the past decade. It was a big decision and a huge amount of work to get through with the sale of tons of stock. Not even my selective hearing could miss her gentle pleas that I knock the Man Tests on the head for a while.

It wasn't like I'd be idle in any case. I was producing and presenting a programme on ITV called *The Cycle Show*, worked ten weekends in a row through the summer, plus most days of the week as well, and of course the kids were still in need of full attention every waking hour. We had other friends whose children sat quietly in the one place or who had to be woken from sleep every morning, concepts that were completely alien to us. We had two little tornadoes. It was pointed out to me on many occasions that you get the kids you deserve, and that if my boys had been sleepy, meek or mild I should have been calling for DNA tests.

In August there was a big *Cycle Show* finale planned where I'd climb up the second highest paved road in the Alps, Italy's Stelvio Pass. At 2,750 metres high and over 20 kilometres long, it was a serious challenge, and the fact that I had to talk to camera and interview the British pro cyclist, Kristian House most of the way up made it considerably more difficult. So I had the perfect excuse to get back into training again – my job depended on it.

I loved it. I still had some endurance base from the MDS, and to be back on my bike more regularly was great. I felt really strong, and even though I did probably only a fraction of the mileage usually required to prepare for a big Alpine challenge, I coped OK with the Stelvio, finishing it in under an hour and a half. My heart rate had been through the roof – we measured mine compared to Kristian's and I averaged about 170 hammering beats per minute to his gentle 130 – but I enjoyed getting back to that kind of physical stress.

By the end of the year it was nine months since the MDS and people continued to ask me what I was going to do next. Claire had got the shop closed by then and although still very busy with other aspects of the business she wasn't enduring a long daily commute. The MDS glory had long since faded and although our lives were still pretty hectic, things were moving in the right direction. So clearly it was time to unsettle everything again. When asked what was next, I began mentioning – loud enough for Claire to hear – that there was really just one more big thing I wanted to do. I had plenty of ideas for challenges

I'd like to get round to eventually, but just one that constantly itched. I had to do an Ironman triathlon. If I ticked that off, there would be no more real 'burners', anything else could wait. Being a Marathon des Sables veteran *and* an Ironman would surely be enough. That's what I told Claire, and I did actually believe it.

I can trace my Ironman fixation back to my student years at Loughborough. English and Sports Science was the perfect degree for someone like me with a short attention span and an aversion to stereotypes. I could play the twin roles of learned poet with a hard sport edge and fit jock with a bookish sensitive side. The English half I hoped would add academic respectability; the Sports half I hoped would add fun.

One of the first sports lectures I went to was given by a Loughborough legend called Bob Smith, a strength and fitness tutor. While we waited in the big, steep-banked lecture hall for the main act to appear on stage, fellow students spoke in semi-hushed reverence of Bob the fitness freak, an ultra-endurance warrior and hard man who was ... lean in, widen your eyes ... 'an *Ironman!*'

Very few of us knew what exactly an Ironman triathlon entailed, but we all grasped the concept that it was a whole day covering enormous distances through water, on bike and on foot, and that the very few who had done it were near-mythical creatures of astonishing physical capacity and resolve. That one would shortly appear before us was indeed exciting and entirely in keeping with the mystique of Loughborough, which we still viewed as a centre of sporting amazement.

Bob bounced onto the stage and gave one of the most enthusiastic, energetic lecturing performances I have ever seen. He was about five foot six, completely bald, weather-beaten and ripcord lean. We were awe-struck. He finished his lecture with a lame joke about contra-indication and a picture of his Alsatian, at which we all guffawed obsequiously. As we filed out, the chat was not unlike that of concert-goers leaving a gig. 'That was fantastic. Isn't Bob amazing? An Ironman, you know …'

I never forgot the admiration bestowed on the Ironman. From that day on, an Ironman triathlon became for me the yardstick against which all endurance athletes would be judged. It was a stamp of honour, an achievement that generated lifelong respect and admiration. It had taken the past few years of ever-harder challenges for me to consider myself a candidate. Could I join the pantheon of Bob Smith-style hard men? Once I set out on the Man Tests journey it became obvious that I couldn't ignore the reality of a challenge I'd previously considered superhuman.

Of course, in the years since, I'd met dozens of Ironmen, and not all of them commanded the respect bestowed on Bob. There has been enormous growth in the numbers of people now regularly testing themselves at that level; there are now six official international Ironman events in the UK alone and the fact that the Ironman brand was recently purchased by a Chinese conglomerate for around $650 million indicates that it is now seen as a potential mass participation event of the future. Maybe it'll become the new marathon, a previously elite challenge now conquered by the majority of people in your office.

Maybe, but I'm not so sure. The challenge of each of the three sports individually is more than significant. Swimming two and a half miles, cycling 112 miles or running a marathon will probably remain beyond the reach of most people. Taking them all on one after another was a monstrous examination of fitness and fortitude that in my opinion was still the ultimate test of any endurance athlete. It was just something I felt I needed to do, and perhaps then, after that, there wouldn't be anything else with quite the same pull.

Looking at a calendar of Ironman events, I found one that was well over a year away, by which time I assumed things at home and at work would be on a more even keel. It was Ironman Barcelona, at the start of October. Having identified that as the next target, I forgot about it until the New Year, and knew better than to mention it too early to Claire.

I still had a big pile of mostly unread triathlon magazines in a cupboard, from the days before Tough Guy, and some of them had Ironman training programmes, tips and nutrition plans. In January, I dug them out and started reading. There were programmes for beginners, programmes for achieving specific times, programmes for every conceivable Ironman target or eventuality. I flicked through them, and felt nothing. They made me tired just reading them.

I looked at one of the weeks in the intermediate plan, and then looked at my diary. Hmm. I was away for two of the three days when cycling was booked in. And on that third day the weather forecast was for snow and strong winds. The plans required some form of training six days a week, and sometimes twice a day. It was way more than I'd done for the Marathon des Sables, which lasted a week. It was starting to make me feel a bit overwhelmed, so I ripped out one programme for a few training session ideas and dumped the rest of the magazines in the recycling bin, which felt weirdly cathartic. Fitting in that much training would be like a full-time job, and unnecessary, I felt. I now had the confidence that I could get through most things, and I knew how much training I needed, or rather, how little I could get away with.

I'd learned long before that the most essential aspect of all of these big challenges was the right psychological approach and the best motivation for me is fear. If the idea of the challenge scares the shite out of me, I'll do anything to try and reduce the expected pain levels by getting as strong as possible beforehand. In some ways then, paradoxically, training is for wimps. The real test would be to take on the challenge without preparation. Problem with that is – and I'd also learned over the years that this is another key motivator – you then pay a fortune to enter and travel to an event and run the very real risk of not finishing it.

One of the main reasons for picking the Barcelona Ironman was that it allowed me the whole summer to prepare. I could be cycling in the sun rather than on dark, freezing winter mornings. But that also meant that it was a long time coming around. Even doing probably the bare minimum in terms of training was a considerable commitment, and nine months was too long trying to focus on the one event. By the end of the summer I'd had enough.

One Saturday in late August an old school pal and I had finally managed to align our diaries, and we were taking our respective kids down to the Mournes for a boys-only camping weekend. Christian and Reuben were now four and two and I tried hard to fit in as many little adventures with them as possible. It was all becoming much more manageable and we had great craic together, but even so, a couple of days in a tent without any female common sense was ambitious to say the least. It wasn't that long ago that my old mate and I couldn't be trusted to look after *ourselves* on a weekend away, let alone five kids under seven years of age, but I was really looking forward to this big step on the ladder of life.

There was only one problem. For trainee Ironmen, weekends are sacrosanct. These are the days that training plans always highlight for long bike rides, double swim sessions, slow tempo 18-mile runs, etc. The fact that for most people weekends are also the time when you get to let your hair down or douse it in alcohol or whatever you like doing socially doesn't seem to count.

Although I'd sworn off training plans, I was trying to get at least one big training deposit made each weekend in the run-up to October, and as I was working quite a few of them, *non*-work weekends were even more important training-wise. There was no option but to start the Saturday with a 6am alarm call and a 90-mile cycle on an almost empty stomach, and to finish it knackered and stiff as a board lying on the ground between five restless small children. Increasingly, in moments of honesty, I admitted to myself that this whole Man Tests thing was becoming a complete nuisance.

The world's biggest online bike retailer, Chain Reaction Cycles is based in Northern Ireland and I was working for them occasionally at the time, presenting some product guides to run on their website. It was in their enormous Aladdin's Cave of a shop in Belfast that we did all the filming and I spent hours trying to earn money without immediately spending it.

I arrived one morning after a rough bike session in the hills the evening before and a Reuben special during the night. There has never been a child who teethed for so long nor so loud. One of the crew was setting up the lights when I arrived, yawning.

'Tired?' he asked rhetorically.

'Shattered,' I replied. 'Hopefully I'll not fall asleep on camera.'

'Kids?'

'Kids and training. I signed up for an Ironman at the start of the year, assuming that our youngest would be in a nice sleep pattern by now. He is in a pattern, but unfortunately it's a one-hour pattern. It's a nightmare.'

'When's the Ironman?'

'Few months yet.'

'You'll be grand.'

He is a pretty chilled guy normally, but even by his laconic standards he seemed a little underwhelmed by the prospect of an Ironman. This clearly wouldn't do. I had got used to – and was quite enjoying – the sharp intake of breath or whistle most people employed when 'Ironman' was mentioned, so I felt clearly he needed to know more.

'The training is pretty full-on, a big time commitment ...' I began.

'I know,' he interrupted. 'There's a guy working here who is doing ten Ironmen in a row, ten consecutive days, this summer. It's called a Decaman.'

This was annoying. Ten?! Why?! Also, what is the plural of Ironman? Ironmans or Ironmen? *Ten* full Ironman distance triathlons on consecutive days in a quiet rural part of County Tyrone. If he finished he would become only the 70th registered Decaman in the world, and hopefully raise a ton of money for charity.

But my instinctive initial reaction wasn't very charitable, I'm sorry to admit. I'd never heard of a Decaman before and felt a mixture of scorn and also something approaching despair. It wasn't that someone was stealing my thunder or inadvertently diluting the scale of my own ambitions, but rather a realisation that actually there was no endgame in all of this, that once we start this sort of carry-on of multiple marathons or Ironman races there will always be somebody somewhere doing one extra. Why stop at ten? Who will become the world's first Centaman?

If there had been a Decaman on campus during my days at Loughborough what would that have made Bob Smith? Some sort of wimpy *mere* Ironman? Was an Ironman not enough any more? My sniffy ambivalence towards the very idea of a Decaman deepened as I learned more about the forthcoming attempt. It was based around a small lake in the country actually owned by a friend of mine, and not an especially scenic or striking place.

The swim was six laps of the lake. Six laps, of the same lake, every morning for ten days. The bike sounded even less inspiring – 12 'laps' on an out-and-back course of 9.5 miles each. So out nearly 5 miles and then back nearly 5 miles repeated 12 times a day for 10 days. The run was worse. Laps of 1 kilometre, 40 times a day for 10 days. It sounded like a course of medicine, and would surely be just as unpalatable.

A few weeks later, I met the prospective Decaman in the shop. I couldn't believe the size of him. Andrew Hassard is six foot five and about 16 stone. How on earth he was going to put that massive frame through ten days of relentless rotating and pounding was beyond me. If he stuck it out, I'd be beyond impressed.

Andrew was far from the metronomic sports geek I had expected. He was almost apologetic when quizzed about the challenge. I got the impression that, like me, he couldn't quite work out why he was doing it. Also like me, he'd taken up extreme challenges after he quit playing rugby, and got into triathlon simply as a means of training for something else, adventure racing. But then he found he quite liked it, and was pretty good.

He moved from a sprint triathlon to a full Ironman within a year. He admitted he has what could be described as an addictive personality. He signed up for the Nice Ironman on the Côte d'Azur, one of the hardest on the circuit, and any other epic challenge he could find by way of preparation. He ran the Glasgow–Edinburgh Ultramarathon, a 55-mile run around the canals that link the two Scottish cities, which for Andrew finished with a sprint through an Edinburgh housing estate when local kids began hurling bottles and setting dogs on him. He was on a mission to learn how to cope with pain and to build mental resolve. We chatted about motivation and ambition, and the monstrous scale of his preparations.

'People say to me, oh you have the mental fortitude to do these things, but that doesn't ring with me,' said Andrew. 'You train your mind as much as your body. You don't train your mind sitting watching *EastEnders* on a Tuesday evening. You do it by going down to swim in the Irish Sea at six o'clock in the morning in April with the temperature between five and seven.

'Within two seconds of being in the sea you can't feel your feet and every single bone and cell and sinew in your body is saying, "Get out, just go back, just go back, nobody will know whether you went in or not, you can just say you did it." That's exactly where you get the fortitude and the resolve to say, "No, I'm in control here, I'll decide what to do."'

I'd come across this idea of a 'second voice' before. In 2011, Professor Steve Peters wrote a book called *The Chimp Paradox*, which did really well in the wake of his work with high-profile sports stars like Ronnie O'Sullivan and teams like British Cycling and Liverpool FC, and suddenly had people all over the country 'taming their inner chimp'.

His central idea is that there is a constant struggle for control between the different parts of our brains. The emotional, irrational part of our brain, which makes us anxious, excited, embarrassed, scared, etc., is dominant, and we have to accept that and try to work with it.

He portrays this emotional side as our 'inner chimp', which he claims is five times stronger than the more rational part of our brain, which he portrays as the human within. In sport, the belief is that this inner chimp can be harnessed or controlled, so top-level performers can deal with nerves and anxiety and make the right decisions at the right times.

But somewhere along the line I think this has got confused in some people's minds with the voices that scream 'Enough, enough!' when we put our bodies under the huge stress of high-intensity exercise. The key part about Peters's model is that the *chimp* is irrational. But surely someone voluntarily putting their body under the sort of immense stress that Andrew Hassard does on a regular basis is behaving irrationally, and when the 'monkey voice' complains, I would argue that he's the one being *rational*, and that ignoring all the pain alerts from the body is *irrational*.

'What you learn to do is normalise what other people tell you is impossible,' Andrew continued. 'You go through the point where you think this is completely impossible, nobody can do this, then you think actually it might be achievable, and then you get it in your head it's a perfectly normal thing to do.'

'At one point a Double Ironman was insane, but then when I was doing the training for it, it became normal to go out and do a 30-mile run on a Saturday morning before the Six Nations Rugby. Humans are creatures of habit. When you start to train for it, you normalise it in your head.'

I enjoyed talking to Andrew, and was inspired in some way to push a little further in my own sessions, but he was in a totally different place from me in terms of the commitment required to achieve his aims. He was also in a totally different place from me in terms of free time and independence.

I continued simply to do what I felt like in training and was blessed with the best Irish summer for years. The days were long and warm, conducive to getting out on the bike or into the sea, but it was another relentlessly busy summer and I began to think of how much more I would enjoy cycling and swimming if I only went out when it really suited and if it was just about gentle exercise and not hard-core training. Adding stress to my 'recreation' time started to make less and less sense in a hectic life. The second series of *The Cycle Show* on ITV was a massive stress from start to finish, and that coupled with my other roles in other programmes and business initiatives, plus everything at home, including an impending house move, put us all under a lot of strain. More than once I vowed that the following year would be about simplifying everything as much as possible. We'd been through a lot in the previous years and I was concluding that this constant chaos and pressure was not healthy. I was beginning to envy people I met who had spare time and weren't continually lurching between different commitments.

I didn't think I shared Andrew's addictive personality. I'd thought about whether some sort of addiction to endurance challenges was a factor for me in bouncing from one to another, but rejected the idea. If I was addicted to these tests, surely I would have been doing them far more regularly. But in fact, I was being highly selective about what I took on; between these big events I wasn't competing in anything at all. What I was actually doing was working through some sort of Man Tests bucket list. And now, as the Ironman got closer, I was beginning to feel a sense of relief that the bucket appeared to be full.

I hadn't previously been much given to introspection, but that summer had been so stressful I began to think a lot more about what I really wanted from life, what made me tick and why. I read more about adrenaline addiction and found different types of people displaying different characteristics. I read a blog post from an American 'Organisational Health' company called The Table Group, whose description of one personality type made me wince. They identified 'The Accomplisher', which they described as the 'classic' type of addict, with 'an almost innate need to stay busy and cross things off a list in order to feel productive. They like to be able to measure daily progress in terms of what they have completed, even at the expense of the bigger, long-term view.'

That was me to a tee. It was almost embarrassing to see myself laid bare like that as a 'type'. I didn't like it, and pondered more deeply on what I was all about. What was it that had been driving this need for continual epic tests, and was it now on the wane? Sports scientists have identified four main types of motivation, and again, one of them stuck out for me. People with high 'Identified Regulation' motivation levels perform activities out of choice, but without necessarily enjoying them. They recognise the *benefits* of the activity, and that is the main motivation for doing it. As the Ironman loomed closer, that summed up my attitude. And looking back, I felt it was ever thus.

I once read the full unabridged version of *War and Peace*. I hated it, but I loved the fact I had finished it. It fuelled my accomplishment addiction and also I recognised it was probably important mentally to struggle through a weighty tome every now and again rather than reading a series of 140 characters on Twitter. Equally, I now realised that when I said 'I want to go running', what I actually probably meant was 'I want to have the feeling of having been for a run'. I enjoyed the achievement of the activity more than the actual activity.

So as the event loomed closer, I felt that what was now actually important to me was just getting through it; then I could remove that pressure from my life and move on. I'd felt this one hanging slightly heavier than any of the previous challenges, had considered it an irritant rather than an inspiration much earlier during the build-up. It was probably a result of our ever more hectic and uncertain lives, but also there was this growing awareness or acceptance that after the Ironman, I was done. I had already 'normalised' endurance feats I had not that long ago thought impossible and achieved more than I'd ever considered, so after this was over I didn't feel much drive to explore again. Getting through an Ironman felt like some sort of endgame. Next stop was Barcelona.

In the queue at Belfast International I bumped into an old acquaintance from my hometown. She and her husband were heading to Spain for a short break, and had that pre-holiday glow of anticipation. 'Why are you going?' she asked. 'Business or pleasure?' Instinctively, I answered 'Neither.' It wasn't a business trip, but it certainly wasn't going to be pleasurable.

It was a bit of a lonely experience entering, training and travelling alone, but I'd been told about a couple of other Northern Ireland lads, Neville and Shane, who were racing, and we met at the airport. Neville had organised transport up the coast to Calella, the little tourist town hosting the event, and was generally much better informed than me on what was happening. There was precious little information from the organisers and I wasn't 100 per cent happy that I was definitely even registered. But neither Neville nor Shane had heard much more than I had, which was reassuring.

The hotel had a bit of a Seventies Brits Abroad feel and the lift was about the size of a small toilet cubicle, which was a bit of an issue for me with the cumbersome bike box. I gingerly turned it straight up on one end, hoping not to hear the tinkle of bike parts that had been damaged in the plane sliding loose within, and squeezed into the corner of the lift beside it. A large-bellied German with a walrus moustache tried to squeeze in as well and wouldn't take *nein* for an answer. Cheek by several jowls, we travelled together to the seventh floor, uncomfortably close and uncomfortably warm. Being the repressed Irishman that I am, I focused on anything except eye contact with a stranger just inches from me and stared at the badge on his shirt. It looked suspiciously like the badge of a band uniform. I'd seen similar colours and logos at the Munich Beer Festival, the Oktoberfest, years before.

When the lift doors eventually creaked open, seven long floors later, there was a great Bavarian harrumph as two more large-bellied Germans greeted my lift partner with a huge laugh and slaps on the back that would have shaken the internal organs of anyone else. They too were wearing white shirts with the band badge on the breast pocket. Surely not …

I wrestled the bike box free from the lift and found my room. As I was fiddling with the key (none of those awful plastic cards in this Hotel That Time Forgot), there came round the corner a sight that made my heart sink. A man carrying a huge brass instrument, one of those big tuba things with the wide funnel outlet that appears to grow out of the musician's shoulder. I was certain now. There was a German oompah band staying in my hotel, many of them on my floor, and they would be performing, probably long into the night.

This *was* actually the first week of October. Why on earth would a German oompah band be coming to Spain to celebrate a Bavarian beer festival? When the rest of the world is heading to Munich, why in the name of God would they be coming here?

There are some travel groups that go well together. But Ironman triathletes and brass bands celebrating a beer festival do not. This was like a plot device from a National Lampoon film or Benny Hill sketch. Except it was real, and a potential disaster for my preparation. I dumped all my stuff in the room and went out onto the little balcony. I had a sea view at least, which was nice. But a little table on the balcony next door was absolutely covered in one-litre bottles of San Miguel and at least 50 fag butts spilling out of the ashtray. And, horror of horrors, the case of some sort of musical instrument was lying in the corner.

I held my head in my hands. All this effort to get here and get this done as peacefully and as smoothly as possible, a 5.30am start for a momentous challenge, and I am room-ing next to some brass-band party animals. I couldn't quite believe it.

I dragged the bike box out to the balcony and began to open the little padlocks. May as well get all the bad news out of the way in one go was my thought; if any bike parts were snapped I'd want to know immediately. What a relief. Everything seemed to be intact. I'd wound and rammed so much bubble wrap, cardboard and old pillows round everything that it didn't look as if anything had moved so much as a millimetre.

I started to try and put it all together. Suddenly there was a great cacophony from next door that seemed to indi-cate that my neighbours had just arrived back. Oh God. It was two young fellas, already glowing unmistakably from too many steins in the sun, and already communicating at what I call alco-volume. You'll be familiar with the concept, I'm sure. They turned on some techno music (could this get any worse?) and came out on the balcony for a smoke.

'Guten abend,' I began anxiously, making a big show of lifting up my bike for illustration.

'Heh,' one of them replied between swigs of a new San Miguel. 'You are cyclist?'

'Yes, I am here for the big triathlon tomorrow.'

I nodded at the beer bottles and the fags. 'You aren't doing the triathlon?' I tittered falsely.

'No! We are beer festival! Oktoberfest!' They clinked bottles and grinned wildly.

'Ah yes,' I whimpered. 'Emm, we start very early tomorrow morning ... is it possible you could not be very loud tonight so I can sleep a bit? Please?'

'Ha ha ha, yes, sleeping. OK.' They both raised their bottles and nodded.

I wasn't convinced, but it was the best that could be done other than hurling them and their instruments over the balcony and into the swimming pool later that evening.

Neville and Shane wanted to go for a spin to loosen their legs and make sure their bikes were assembled properly and asked if I wanted to join them. Changing in my room, I smeared on my new chamois cream.

This is an essential element of cycling preparation. Chamois cream is basically a lubricant that protects the undercarriage from the inevitable rub of a saddle. It's applied liberally and gingerly and I suspected would be of vital importance in an Ironman, as the thought of running a marathon with a pre-existing chafing condition after six hours on a bike was too horrific to contemplate. That being the case, I'd bought a new tube especially for the race.

I had just run out of a brand that came in a red and white tube and had never let me down. Following the old mantra of never changing for a race what you have done in training I spotted some of the same brand in the Chain Reaction shop and grabbed a tube after finishing one of the presenting days. Someone had stuck a very large shop label over the front, over the product description, and later I would come to wonder whether that had been done deliberately. I'm not sure if I noticed at the time, but I didn't investigate further, either in the shop or after. Big mistake.

I was heading for the lift with my bike when I became aware of a growing warming sensation down below. 'Just the heat,' I decided, trying to ignore it. But the warming soon developed into a conflagration and in a panic I ran for the toilet and yanked down my shorts.

Jesus Christ, I was bright red. I was like a female baboon in season. Frantically I grabbed the hose end of the shower and tried to put out the blaze. I was afraid that vigorous rubbing would only irritate everything more, so I soaked a towel in cold water and began dabbing away like a fussy housewife removing red wine from a linen tablecloth. This was a potential disaster. The inside of my legs were getting redder but gradually the burning was fading to a dull heat and my panic subsided as I put on some cooling moisturiser.

I went in search of the tube and peeled off the offending label. 'Thermogel'. Oh my God. In exactly the same tube as the chamois cream? With the name obscured by a careless (or perhaps careful and malignant) shop assistant? I could sue! What a catastrophe that would have been had I not opted for the spin with the lads before the race. Self-inflicted third-degree burns of the crotch would have been a particularly ignominious way to end an Ironman attempt. Now late for our ride and still glowing down below, I gingerly John Wayned it down to meet the lads.

They were both 'proper' triathletes, members of clubs with training programmes and, unlike me, as professionally prepared as an amateur can be. There were no Bavarian brass bands in their hotel, no Thermogel on their scrotums, and no problems with their bikes. I was off mine within five minutes. Something was rubbing. This is a common psychiatric complaint among cyclists, I think. If everything appears more effort than it should be, there must be something wrong with the bike … But in this case, I could actually hear the back wheel whine.

I hopped off at the side of the road. We were on the route of the race bike leg, which seemed to have a lot more ups and downs than one would expect from what was advertised as a flat course. The back brakes were closed round my wheel. I'd had all this overhauled and sorted just weeks before, so it was a bit of a concern. I forced them apart, did a few test spins and squeezes and got back on to chase after Neville and Shane.

Neville was fast. He was already coming back the other way and I could hear the low hum of his rear disc wheel as he sped past, perfectly tucked in, smooth and aerodynamic with a pointed aero helmet and on a proper time-trial bike. He looked like a pro. I was wearing an ill-fitted, eight-year-old basic helmet and riding the same bog standard road bike that had got me up and down the Pyrenees and around the perimeter of Ireland, but which wasn't the best set-up for a triathlon. I had a cheap set of tri-bars screwed onto the handlebars to at least create the impression of an aerodynamic position, but it probably didn't fool anyone, least of all the wind.

And then, as I headed out along the road and the bike worked and the sun came out, warming my skin, I had a kind of small epiphany. It didn't matter that I didn't look as good as the rest, hadn't trained as much as the rest, wasn't in a triathlon club. In terms of perseverance, stickability and tolerance for discomfort, I was well and truly road tested. I might not have much triathlon experience or preparation, but I was battle-hardened from years of big events and epic challenges; I had great deposits of training and reserves of fitness and fortitude.

I could dig and dig to depths I'd never imagined; like Andrew Hassard I had normalised this madness and got through tests I'd previously considered superhuman. Yes, I'd bumbled through quite a lot of them, but I had yet to fail, and come hell or high water it wouldn't be any different tomorrow. If I'd been on a journey of self-discovery for the past few years, there was now nothing I didn't already know about myself, and the most important thing I knew was that when it got hard, I could get through it. I could shine light into the dark places, and that was absolutely key. With a smile I realised I was ready, I was there, and I was actually confidently looking forward to it.

The only cloud on the horizon, however, was the clouds on the horizon. A printout on the noticeboard beside reception made for uncomfortable reading. A little graphic of forked lightning seemed to leap out from the page, as if it was in 3D. Within hours it was a reality.

I have seen big weather all over the world, but I can't remember an electrical storm quite as vivid as that one. I watched from the balcony as colours collided over the sea. Dark blues, reds, purples flashed in turn as shards of light cascaded down from the sky, illuminating the seafront. It was spectacular, thrilling, unreal, and in any other circumstances a delight. But not if it continued until tomorrow, as was forecast.

I tore myself away from the light show and methodically went through all my preparations, pinning the race number to the little triathlon belt, lining up my kit and sorting out one food bag from another. My bike was already on the stand in the transition zone, probably getting absolutely drenched (could a bike rust overnight?) but I would have to bring my running kit and all the rest down in the morning. I tried to think through everything in order. Which kit had to go where, what food had to go where and when: the general logistics that make triathlon a bigger stress than most other sports.

Because of the Thermogel disaster I had no chamois cream. I had never, ever ridden a racing bike without it. Was I going to do 112 miles sitting on a pointed saddle with no protection? No thanks. Despite my aversion to pre-race Expos, I had hunted round all the stalls in the hall at the race registration, but every tub or tube that may have been chamois cream was labelled in Spanish or French, and I didn't trust my language skills enough to be sure of what I was getting. There was still a warm glow from the Thermogel and there was no way I was coating myself in anything that I wasn't absolutely certain would help and not hinder. I reasoned that Vaseline would probably do the same job and I had that for my feet anyway.

Apart from the lack of lubricant, I had no worries and felt pretty relaxed. I forced another of the porridge pots down, the last of my carb loading, and just chilled out watching CNN inside and the lightning storm outside. My phone buzzed. It was a text from my dad, an arrival rarer than Halley's Comet.

'I still think you are mad, but I hope it goes well.'

Coming from my father, not previously disposed to flowing encouragement of my extra-curricular activities, that message represented a Churchillian pep talk. It actually made me a little emotional.

The rain hammered down outside, churning the water in the swimming pool, and the sky continued to be lit periodically by vivid fork lightning, each one closer than the last. Were we expected to swim in that? Could you get electrocuted in the sea? Was there a metal zip on my wetsuit?

Just as I was getting into bed and trying to pretend I was tired and would sleep soundly as soon as my head hit the pillow, my German neighbours returned. I knew I'd never sleep if I got wound up, so just tried to stay calm and hope that they'd pass out. They must have been on the rip for over ten hours now. To be fair, they did manage to keep it down to a dull roar, the faint thump of techno music and the odd loud guffaw aside. There was no trumpeting or tromboning, thank God, and no mad party on the balcony. I drifted off at some point and faded in and out of the normal pre-event restless sleep until the alarm went off at half five.

As usual on competition day, I was wide awake in seconds. Adrenaline overrides the body clock, and every body *function* in fact. I can see how it could be a problem in a lot of sports, inducing a faulty tennis shot, an over-swing in golf or a careless lunge in football, but in endurance tests adrenaline must almost always be a positive. It can shake the lethargy from a shallow sleep; scratch the fuzz from a well-worn training routine; and lift the weight off heavy miles. I thought of the surge from seeing the rat on the Race Around Ireland, and the noise of the hounds on the hunt runs. There is an extra reserve of harnessable energy deep within us all. The only problem is that to use it, we have to frighten ourselves. And if that was a constant, we'd be exhausted.

At breakfast I added a shot of caffeine to the motivational mix, collected my stuff from the room, paused in front of the mirror to say 'I will be Bob Smith', and practically bounced down to the beach.

The storm of the previous night seemed to have passed for now, though more heavy rain and thunder was forecast for the afternoon. The morning was warm, with only a faint breeze and just a little chop to the sea. Pretty much perfect for a triathlon, in fact. Hundreds of black, rubber-clad humans walked, stood or stretched on the beach, like a colony of large penguins. After dropping off my bag and laying out both cycling and running kit, I wriggled into my wetsuit and went over to join them.

Different age groups had different coloured swimming caps and went off at different times. Like flocks of sheep in a market we were corralled into different pens, advancing from one to the next, getting closer to the front at ten-minute intervals as each start time approached.

It's hard to know how to warm up for a triathlon, especially an Ironman. If you were running a marathon or 10k race you'd know to gently stretch your calves, thighs and hamstrings, for example, and jog to loosen everything up. If you were competing in a swim you'd know to swing your arms and rotate your hips and swim a few lengths. But one warm-up routine for three different sports while wearing a wetsuit? Any movement is severely restricted, I thought I'd soon overheat in the morning sun without the cooling effect of the sea, and there didn't seem to be much point stretching for the run or the cycle since they were hours away, so I just swung my arms a bit and did a couple of silly little shuffle runs on the sand before joining my fellow 30-somethings in our pen.

I had a set of extra goggles in the small of my back under the wetsuit, which my more regular triathlon friends insisted was an absolute must in case the first pair got kicked off and I lost them. It was a little uncomfortable in such figure-hugging attire, but it would be OK once I was floating.

Slowly the minutes ticked away and we progressed at last to one pen from the front. I pulled on my goggles, tightened the straps and then stretched the blue cap over them and my head. It felt like something was squeezing the blood from my brain. I took the cap off and gave it a good stretch. Again, I reasoned it would be more comfortable once it got wet. Unfortunately my reasoning hadn't extended to actually trying this out when I was given the cap at registration the day before.

I took some long, deep breaths through my nose, stretched my head back and closed my eyes. It was the same routine I'd done at the start of the first stage of the Marathon des Sables, and without Patrick and 'Highway to Hell' I felt serene – completely at peace, which was bizarre given what I was about to take on. I'd experienced similar feelings just before starting some of the other big challenges: the Europe to Asia swim, the Man v Horse, Tough Guy. Perhaps it was relief at cracking the hardest part of the whole thing and making the start line. Perhaps it was what confidence felt like. Undoubtedly it was a form of mindfulness, and even if it took months of painful preparation to get there, it was worth it.

And then the hooter blasted and all was a whirl. We ran into the sea and my heart was thumping as soon as we hit the water. I dived under a wave, and everything was turmoil. Choppy water, deafening noise from the frantic strokes of hundreds of other swimmers, limbs thrashing in front, behind and to either side – I just stuck my head down and tried to close it all out. Two and a half miles, two and a half miles, I kept repeating to myself; this was a marathon not a sprint. It was a long, long swim, and the sooner I settled into a rhythm and could find my own pace, the better.

Just like at Windsor for the Royal Triathlon and at the Hellespont, there were swimmers beneath and on top of me. It was like being flushed down a drain with 200 others, and completely unnecessary since we had the whole width of the Balearic Sea to swim in. I veered off wide to the right to try and find some space and settle down.

After a few minutes it got a bit easier; I was able to put together more than a few consecutive strokes without banging into someone and I was soon slipping through the waves quite easily. I felt very strong and smooth, which was not always the case with my sometimes robotic swimming style. The water was warm, but by keeping things steady I was hoping not to over-heat, and soon everything was fine and dandy.

Fifteen minutes were up surprisingly quickly – normally I find time drags dreadfully when I'm swimming – and I was cheered by the thought that I was probably well over 800m through the swim already, leaving only 3k, which I'd covered in training lots of times. It was nice and quiet, nobody was swimming across me, in fact nobody seemed to be near me at all. Was I out in front of our age group without really even racing?

I stopped for a second, lifted my head to check, and swore loudly. I was way off course. I had drifted really far to the right, and the float I was heading for was not actually a yellow race marker, but a yellow fishing buoy. I lifted my goggles to check, and wiped the inside. When they were marking out the swim course the previous afternoon I had noticed that the big race markers were the same colour as the lines of buoys marking lobster pots or fishing nets. I thought that was pretty stupid, but reasoned that because they were a different size and different shape nobody would mix them up. But from low in the water, in between waves and swim strokes, and through misty goggles, it was very hard to tell. A yellow flash was a yellow flash.

Shit. This had lost me some time. I began to track back towards the proper course, swimming far too fast before giving myself a talking to. 'Calm down, it's only a few minutes, settle down, still another 3k or so to go. Settle down!' Gradually I brought myself back towards the frothing mass of other swimmers and decided to try and stay a bit closer to everyone else. This was nowhere near as pleasant as swimming peacefully in my own water and might hold me up a bit, but at least I wouldn't waste precious time and effort getting lost again.

I tried to settle back into the great rhythm I had before and got my breathing under control again, but now I had another problem. My goggles were leaking. I'd been trying to ignore it since noticing I was off course, but my right eye was drowning. I swam for a bit with it shut tight, but crinkling my face up loosened the rubber seal on that side and let even more water in. I had to stop. Again. Shit. Other swimmers coming from behind nudged into me like blind whales hitting a trawler. I moved off to one side again, emptied the goggles, wiped the lenses clear again and fastened them tighter. Too tight – I thought my eyes were going to pop out. I stopped again.

And so it continued. I would swim for as far as I could before the right eye filled again and I'd have to stop, empty, clean and replace. I was raging. This had never happened before with these goggles, why oh why would it be happening now?! I tried not to let my anger make me swim too hard but I couldn't help it. It was just so frustrating. I felt I was swimming very well, and going off course and now this goggles issue had spoilt what was probably going to be a really good swim time. But there was worse to come.

I'd noticed the strokes becoming heavier for a while, and thought it was just because I was overdoing it in an effort to claw back the time lost on the goggles. But when I decided finally to give the second pair of goggles a go rather than continuing with the leaky ones, and stopped yet again to undo my wetsuit and fish them out, I discovered the zip was already down and the top of my suit was trailing behind me. Jesus Christ. So I'd been ploughing along and for the last few minutes the rear shoulder sections of my wetsuit had been raised like big paddles holding me back? Nightmare!

Frantically I grasped around behind my back trying to find the little cord to pull the zip back up. I kicked and bobbed while using both hands to find and close it. It's bloody hard to do on land, never mind in the water after 40 minutes of sea swimming. Finally I got it sorted and, really pissed off now at this bizarre sequence of unfortunate events, pulled the goggle strap as tight as I could bear and set off like a madman to get the swim over. After a wild few minutes I'd thrashed out most of my anger and settled into a more manageable pace as I reached the last big marker before the turn for home.

This final stretch seemed to go on forever. I wasn't tired, just a bit pissed off with the swim and ready for it to be over so I could make amends for all the mishaps with a smooth bike ride. I knew I was definitely swimming well, given how I was catching and passing quite a few people, but with all the pricking about I also knew my time would have suffered.

Finally the beach got closer and closer and I thrashed on until my hands were grazing the sand on the swim strokes. Swimming in was quicker than wading, and by now the sea was quite choppy with a bit of an undertow. When the water was just over my knees I sprang to my feet and ran up the beach, ripping off my swim cap and the bastard goggles as I went. If I hadn't been paranoid about some officious triathlon rule relating to goggles on land I would have stamped them into the ground.

Fresh water sprinkled down from wide shower heads and I wriggled out of my wetsuit and had a quick rinse. Everyone else powered straight through, but wary of dried salt stinging my face on the bike I was happy to sacrifice a few seconds. And then from somewhere a voice of reason told me I should relax through the whole transition. What did I care if I spent an extra few minutes getting changed? What were a few minutes in the grand scheme of a whole day of strenuous competition? I resolved to take time to get things right, to make sure there were no more infuriating mishaps. Since I hadn't done any triathlons at all for four years, it made sense not to rush straight onto the bike and risk making some fundamental error, especially when I hadn't really any particular target time in mind.

Before I left for Barcelona, people kept asking me if I was aiming for a specific time, and I had always, truthfully, replied that I wasn't. But my standard answer, that I just wanted to complete rather than compete, wasn't entirely accurate. I was caught between two motivations. The principal one was to finish at all costs and not let anything jeopardise that, and the second was the idea that if I was only ever going to do one Ironman, it needed to be in as fast a time as possible. These two aims were almost like rivals, as the one didn't necessarily complement the other. It's a pretty common trade-off with major endurance events, but I had to keep reminding myself that the absolute key objective was just to finish, to become an Ironman, and never to have to bother with it all again.

I followed everyone along the red carpet and into the big changing marquee and dumped my wetsuit in the wet bag we were given at registration, all the time being ultra-observant of any rules I could remember. Triathlon officials are particularly fussy about the order in which you do things for some reason. All around me other competitors came flying through the transition zone like whirlwinds, wriggling out of clothes here and into clothes there, grabbing bags of supplies. By contrast, I was sitting on a bench drying my toes and eating a banana.

I wasn't deliberately faffing, just making sure I gave myself the best chance to finish everything in as much comfort as possible. Most people were heading for their bikes wearing just a thin tri-suit, but I needed a cycling top as well because I had a lot of food I wanted to bring with me, which I stuffed into the rear pockets, like a squirrel with its winter supplies. I had so much food and other bike equipment like inner tubes, pump and tyre levers that when I put the top on, it was actually quite heavy. It felt like I was going to war. I did one last check-through of everything in my head as I ran to collect my bike, and then I was off.

The first brief section of the bike leg was through the backstreets of the town, narrow little roads with speed bumps in places, so it was a bit of a neutralised start before we got out onto the roads I was on the day before with Neville and Shane.

We had to travel up and down the coast three times in all, on the same road out and back, which meant that I got to see the professionals coming back the other way. They looked and sounded fantastic. Bent low over their bikes, tucked in aerodynamically, and I didn't notice any of their pockets bulging with peanut butter rolls. That's what I was currently munching through. I was pretty pleased with how – after five years and one or two near disasters like the Welsh 1000m and Man v Horse – I'd finally learned to properly manage my fuel supply during a big challenge.

My basic plan was to eat loads. More specifically, I was going to eat the bigger stuff early, so that as I got progressively more tired I'd be asking my digestive system to do less and less. The early part of the bike ride I'd identified as a time when I'd be eating both to recover from the swim and also to store some fuel for the run, so that meant heavier, 'proper' food like my white rolls with peanut butter. From those I would progress to Nutri-Grain bars and oat crackers, then to bananas and sweets, and finally to gels, the least palatable but the easiest to swallow.

In the pouch of my race belt I also had a store of Nuun isotonic tablets to pop into my water bottles at each refill, the salt tablets that had worked so well on the MDS, a couple of caffeine tablets in case things got really tough, and a load of peanut M&Ms. Little and often was the key phrase for Little. Just like in the Marathon des Sables, I also planned to take a drink without fail every ten minutes, which helped break down the magnitude of the bike ride and gave me something else to think about. I'd swallow one salt tablet with each water bottle.

It wasn't the most interesting bike route I'd ever ridden. During the early part out of town the road hugged the coast and had a few short hills, with spectators and well-wishers lined up along the side, but after that it was completely flat and straight, past an occasional row of shops and cafés but mostly through a big deserted industrial area of warehouses, side roads and roundabouts.

I began to recognise the same people, either them overtaking me or me overtaking them. I wasn't sure if it was my pace that was variable or theirs. I was looking out for Neville and Shane. I hadn't seen either of them since the start, but once or twice I thought I saw Neville flying past on the other side of the road, which would mean he was a good bit ahead of me. Everybody on that side seemed so smooth on the bike, so low over the handlebars, that I was beginning to yearn for a few Pyrenean mountains to even things up. Aerodynamics weren't such a factor going up the Marie Blanque or the Soulor, and the landscape was a bit more interesting too.

A few hours in, I really needed to go to the toilet. This was a good sign, I reasoned, it meant I was taking on enough fluids. But I didn't know what the race etiquette was. I knew that in professional cycling and triathlon competitors often just pissed themselves while riding, or sometimes shot over the sides without getting off the bike, but the former was disgusting and the latter was beyond my cycling capabilities. Besides the general etiquette, I wondered about the race rules. Given that there were numerous points about removing clothes, surely there was bound to be something about removing waste?

With race officials in yellow hi-vis vests patrolling on the back of motorbikes and stationed at various points along the route, I really didn't know what to do. I hadn't seen any toilets on the route – or anyone else taking a leak. I pedalled on until it really became unbearable, and then up ahead I spied a couple of big commercial wheelie bins in front of a fence. That would have to do. It took ages, so obviously the ten-minute drink schedule was paying off and I certainly wasn't at risk of dehydration.

That felt a bit like half-time in the whole challenge. The swim was done and half the bike ride. I was still feeling pretty fresh and didn't think I'd really stretched myself too much. The prime motivator again was just to make sure I finished, so I kept a limit on my effort, tried to keep everything calm and methodical. It was boring, and quite strange to be constantly checking my vital signs, making sure I was lasting the pace.

I felt a bit like a hypochondriac but I was soon into the final third of the cycle and had been warned repeatedly by Ironman veterans to use the last stages of the bike ride to prepare for the run. They all recommended taking it easy in the final few bike miles to loosen the legs as much as possible before the marathon. One of them had also been adamant that it was wise to leave at least half your energy for the run, as it was at least as hard as the bike and the swim put together.

So it was a case of constant internal analysis. Running a full marathon while fresh was a frightening enough proposition, but taking it on after six or seven hours of prior exercise was a different story altogether. I was pretty confident I would get to the finish of the cycle in good shape if everything stayed as it was, and was on course for a time of about five hours for the bike leg, which I would have been very happy with. All things had to do was stay as they were …

I thought the Irish weather was unpredictable. It is, but you normally get at least half an hour or so of notice if it's going to turn nasty. Clearly that is not the case in north-east Spain. From out of nowhere, another massive storm exploded all round us. Big, thick drops of water splashed with an audible ker-plop on the road and off my helmet, accompanied by cartoonish thunder crashes. It seemed as if someone had turned down an enormous dimmer switch, for suddenly it was too dark for my sunglasses.

I was soaked in less than a minute. And a few minutes after that it was really difficult to see. The spray from the road, the cloud that seemed to have dropped to sea level and the slanted, heavy drops that stung my eyes combined to make this some of the most dangerous weather I'd ever cycled in, especially given my already perilous progress on the tribars, on which I was still a little wobbly.

It poured and poured, and soon rivers of rainwater were flooding down the road, joined by streams of muck coming off the higher ground above that deposited treacherous slicks at random intervals. At the bottom of each hill there was a flood of water at least a foot deep, which I presumed would wreck the brakes. It was all quite mad, but with each unforgiving minute ticking on, everyone continued to hammer along at top speed.

I heard sirens behind me and an ambulance went flying past in a haze of spray. A mile or so later I realised why:

someone had skidded off the road and down a steep bank perilously close to a cliff. It was a warning and I resolved to take it a bit easier even if nobody else did. I passed another few bodies on a corner a little further on, two bikes and two triathletes tangled together at the bottom of some railings. This was a time to keep one's head and one's balance when all about were losing theirs. It wasn't a painful crash I was scared of so much as a growing paranoia about having something happen that would prevent me from finishing. Having come this far, that would have killed me.

I pulled over at one of the feed points to fill my water bottles and add the Nuun tablets. My plan was to drain them before starting the run, which I reckoned was less than an hour away now. I opened the pouch, and my fingers sunk into a sticky, fizzing mass. The rain had reacted with the effervescence, and there was now just a single, horrible concoction of half-dissolved electrolytes, salt tablets, caffeine tablets and peanut M&Ms. And it was all fizzing perilously close to an area already infamously prone to agitation.

Quite apart from the terrifying prospect of an effervescent sting along the crotch for the duration of the marathon (I admit that I have an unhealthy paranoia about this area in connection with exercise), there was also the thought that I now had no electrolytes or salt tablets, and there was still at least four hours of the Ironman to go. I was sure I'd cramp up on the run if I didn't continue with my tried and tested re-fuelling programme, so the only option was to try and swallow small bits of the sticky, salty mess, washing it down with a load of water.

But that would mean a mix of undissolved, concentrated electrolytes, salt and caffeine hitting my stomach as it bounced up and down for four hours. It was disgusting, but, looking on the bright side, I thought the uncertainty about how this would play out would at least add a touch of arse-clenching jeopardy to the potentially boring marathon leg.

I came down the hill towards the town one final time and heaved on the failing brakes as I slid and veered through what was now a river running across a wide road junction in a valley. The water was easily knee deep by now and the rain continued to fall. Officials were out with whistles and flags, jumping up and down to be seen, holding up signs saying '10 KPH' and shouting 'Diez, diez!

They had neutralised the final three kilometres through the streets of the town, which was certainly the right decision given the awful conditions, but which would cost another chunk of time. With the water flowing over them the town streets were like glass. I could feel the bike sliding beneath me every time I went round a corner, even at 10kph. I just wanted to get back safely now and get stuck into the run. It hadn't quite been the fast finish to a reasonable bike leg that I'd wanted but it gave me a chance to shake my legs out a bit and rest them ahead of the marathon.

The very mention of the M word scared the shite out of me. Over the past year I'd preferred to call it 'the run leg' rather than mention that it was a marathon. A marathon was a massive undertaking in its own right and I'd been around enough people preparing for and finishing them to know that it hurt. Despite everything I'd been through over the previous few years, I'd never actually run a 'normal' road marathon. My previous experiences had all involved mountains, horses, red wine or sand dunes. The monotony of this one, as well as the fact that I already had over six hours of high-intensity exercise behind me, made it a bit of an unknown.

I decided that attitude was everything, and as I pedalled slowly round the last kilometre of the bike leg, my mind was racing. I got it into my head that I was super-confident, strong and fit, the swim and bike had been easy, and I was fresh, nicely chilled after an hour of torrential rain and just jogging home to finish another session. No more, no less important than any of the previous training outings at home.

I dropped the bike back onto the rack and had another look at the fizzing mess in the pouch. I scooped a couple of bits out, quickly shook them up in the water bottle, and gulped some down. Triathlon purists will be horrified to learn that my total transitions time – adding swim to bike and bike to run together – was nearly 13 minutes. That is pretty dreadful. But I wasn't the worst – there was a Frenchman who seems to have taken 20 minutes between swim and cycle. But he then absolutely flew round the bike course in just over five hours, one of the fastest times of the day. I'm not sure what he was doing in that 20 minutes but it clearly worked.

When I was finally ready, I set off slowly on the run, doing little more than jogging to begin with to shake the 112 cycle miles out of my legs. I didn't feel too bad, just a bit mechanical at first, as if I had to tell my legs how to run, and as if they needed a bit of grease round critical joints. I knew that they'd start loosening up eventually.

The rain had eased slightly but part of the run course, over compacted sand parallel to the beach, was now pock-marked with muddy puddles and little trenches. Part of the course ran in parallel lines up and down a wide path beneath some pine trees, and this is where most of the spectators gathered, sheltering from the rain and shouting encouragement in a range of languages. I shut most of it out and tried to get into MDS trudge-and-mind-numb mode.

I had broken the run leg down into 5k chunks, decreeing that I was only allowed to look at my watch and think about how I was doing when I hit a 5k marker. The 5k points were also going to be my feed stations during the first half of the run, one gel at each. For the second half I'd just be on water and the occasional half banana, available at the official feed points. That was the strategy, and I stuck to it rigidly. It definitely helped me to take an element of control over a major challenge like that, to feel that I had a plan to manage myself through the struggles, and short targets making up the whole.

At 10k in, I felt pretty good. I was in a solid rhythm, not fast but steady, with no pain and no real issues other than slightly heavy legs. I was waiting for this big wall to arrive and wondering how far I could get without a real fight and how far I'd have to go while really struggling. I told myself that every extra kilometre in this free-wheeling state was a bonus and pretended that the run wouldn't really start until I said so. This way I was able to motivate myself in the short term to get the first half out of the way as preparation for the real challenge, when the exhaustion kicked in, and also psyche myself up for the pain that must surely be coming.

The longer this went on without any real deterioration in my condition, the more frequently I started trying to calculate what my finish time was likely to be. I didn't want anything to alter this quasi-Zen state I'd managed to find, but playing with the numbers and struggling to add everything up gave me something else to concentrate on. I have always been appalling at maths, so it kept me occupied for ages before I decided it was probable that I'd have the whole thing finished in less than 11 hours, 10.5 if I upped the pace.

There was another reason for not setting a target time, apart from the fear that it could have encouraged me to go too hard too early and risk not finishing at all. I really didn't like the idea of finishing the event – a significant achievement – and feeling in any way disappointed. If I set a random target and missed it by minutes, I would feel I'd let myself down despite the fact that I'd just become an Ironman, something I had for years considered almost superhuman. To achieve something I'd previously thought impossible and yet feel disappointed just seemed ridiculous. But now, considering all seemed well … it was tempting to race properly. The next kilometre marker gave me a dose of reality. I still had 25 kilometres to run.

Neville was in a different place in terms of motivation. He had finished an Ironman before, so didn't really need the 'badge', or tattoo of the logo – *de rigueur* for most finishers – and had therefore set a very clear target of finishing in under ten hours. There was a certain amount of freedom, I felt, in being able to just go out and aim for as fast a time as possible. It was like a football team qualifying early for a major tournament and having the freedom to experiment in the remaining group games.

But there's always the risk that in blindly racing to a schedule, you don't listen to the clues from your own body. I was shocked to find Neville sitting down on the road about halfway through the run, with a pained look on his face that turned to something approaching despair when he saw me coming past. His girlfriend was bent over him with a water bottle and said he was OK but had been puking and cramping for the last few miles. He nodded that he'd be grand and I ran on.

It was a further reminder of how quickly it could all go wrong. I remembered my collapse at the Man v Horse, the amazing treadmill road on the Race Around Ireland, that horrible last leg of the Lough Erne swim. I was growing increasingly paranoid that a big collapse was coming or that I would twist my ankle in the last few kilometres, and started thinking about how far I could crawl if it really came down to it. This nonsensical line of thought actually made me smile. I knew it was just a symptom of the tumultuous combination of fatigue, caffeine and sugar processing going on inside my body.

The 30k marker appeared and I was on the final loop of the run. I'd been waiting for this, the chance to tick off all my little landmarks for the last time. It hadn't been the most inspiring run loop, it felt a bit like pointlessly running up and down in straight lines through suburbia simply to clock up the appropriate distance. But what a prize at the end of it! To become an Ironman. To join the legions. I thought about the tattoo on the calf. Would I get one? My neighbour at the time was actually a tattooist; I could get the obligatory Ironman stamp done as soon as I got home. Then I'd go to Club La Santa at Christmas and stroll around in my shorts ... the stroll was as good as a strut when that badge of honour was visible.

What time was I on for? It looked like under 11 hours easily if I kept up this pace. That would do very nicely, and despite all my prior self-lectures about targets and completing rather than competing, I did want to be able to say I'd finished in ten hours something. Towards the end of a full day of continuous, strenuous exercise probably wasn't the time to start making new plans, but suddenly I had a new focus, and I wanted history (or more specifically the obligatory finish-line photo) to record the fact that I was once a ten-hour Ironman man.

Then I remembered that on the way past the finish area before the final loop I'd noticed that the big race clock above the arch was ten minutes ahead of the time on my watch. It must have started when the wave before my age group began. Would that mean that in my official race finish photo, my finish time would be shown as ten minutes slower? So if I wanted that to declare a sub-11-hour time, I had to finish before 10 hours 50? Shit, I'd have to speed up to make sure.

But I was actually getting slower. My legs were getting heavier and heavier, my groin and hip joints felt stiff and ancient, my ankles hurt, my shoulders and neck ached, and I was weary, really weary. This was hard all of a sudden. I trudged on, avoiding any steps or inclines, trying to keep my feet as low as possible to the ground for fear of not being able to swing my hips into any action other than a flat forward shuffle. The upper part of my groin felt like it could snap into a rigid cramp at any moment. I was ruing not putting the salt tablets into a waterproof bag.

I swiped half a banana from the next feed station and started eating it as I shook out my legs on the way to the big bin at the end of the pit lane. I checked my watch again. The finish-line photo had become a fixation. I didn't want to be cheated out of ten minutes. The ten-hour thing had suddenly become hugely important, and I began to curse myself for drying my toes in transition. What an idiot! Every minute did count after all!

Fired up again, I started running harder and harder, suddenly desperate to finish and in a race against the clock. Inside two kilometres to go I was almost sprinting. The two-way path was narrow and I nearly smashed into a spectator who stepped out at the wrong moment to take a photo. The shock made my heart leap and unsettled me; there was still time for something awful to deny me becoming an Ironman. But I felt strong again, so strong, and the sub-11-hour photo was absolutely crucial! Get out of my way! I was perilously close to mowing people down, and if I hadn't gone slightly mad at this stage I would probably have been embarrassed at finishing like a demon, as if racing for an Olympic medal.

But my heart was thumping again, my pupils dilated as I raced towards the big floodlit finish stretch like a man possessed. Music blasted out of the speakers and people were cheering from a grandstand and on either side of the railings inside the last 200 metres. I tore round the last few corners and finally there it was, the finish arch, the big clock ticking remorselessly towards 11 hours, the giant red numbers changing every second, changing, changing – and I made it. Just. I almost collapsed over the line. My legs wobbled, I bent forward and almost piled into the ground. Someone put a medal around my neck and guided me towards a big marquee. I took in huge gulps of air, stood hands on hips, tilted my head back and looked up to the sky. My heart and my eyes felt swollen with the rush of emotion. I am an Ironman. I am Bob Smith.

The marquee was like an army field hospital. There were rows of tables laden with food and drink; beds with medics buzzing round semi-conscious triathletes; and massage beds where thick-wristed men in thin white tracksuits pummelled shattered muscles. I necked a can of coke in about 20 seconds flat and helped myself to crisps, nuts, pasta, anything salty that I could find. I had exactly the same sort of cravings as after each stage of the MDS, and the same aversion to sweets or recovery gels or anything of that ilk.

Within minutes of the finish, I felt totally fine. A little stiff, a little sore in the legs, but other than that, totally fine. I'd run the marathon in 3 hours 44 minutes and done the whole Ironman in 10 hours 49 minutes. I was chuffed, I was relieved, I was … well, one word that came into my head was capable. I was *capable* of doing this sort of thing. It didn't really faze me. I actually felt better after that than I had done after a lot of training sessions for some reason. I suppose that was the whole point of the training. Train hard, race easy is the old triathlon mantra.

Shane had finished about ten minutes after me, was carried onto one of the beds and given some oxygen and a bit of attention, but recovered quite quickly. Neville came in after him, having endured a horrible run. Pushing through and finishing, given that he already had one Ironman in the bag, took some guts. They went off to see family and girlfriend respectively, while I started the long process of rounding up all my stuff.

I was leaving first thing next morning so I had to mop up the logistics there and then and I had a feeling that all this positive energy couldn't last. The bike was at least a mile away, and there was so much crap to carry that I dumped my wetsuit and running stuff back in the hotel first and had a long, hot shower. I did my customary congratulations in the mirror, and grinned.

I phoned Claire, Mum and Dad, and good old Slippy on the walk back to get the bike. My knees groaned a bit and my lower back was pretty stiff but the walk did me good. There were still loads of people on the course, splashing heavily through the mud, desperately trying to eke out last reserves of energy to get across the line before the cut-off time as the rain came down again in sheets. That was a long, long day, and soaked to the bone, I began to wonder again about the sense of it all.

Business or pleasure?! I laughed as I repeated the question from the airport. It had come to define this trip, and perhaps the past five years or so. All around me there were people literally crying out in pain, limping to the finish. I was in for a long evening of taking apart a bike and packing stuff up and then getting up at the crack of dawn to fly home so I could present a match the following day. Three days in Spain on my own and this was how I spent it? Was this a holiday or what? I smiled again at the whole preposterous nature of this manic challenge chasing.

I felt better in the morning when I'd finally got the bike box checked through at the airport, after dragging it between two different terminals and up and down several aisles in a prolonged search for the right excess baggage chute. It made it back to Belfast, and I pushed it through the terminal where Claire was waiting with the boys. Christian had drawn a poster of me running, swimming and cycling, with 'Well Done Daddy' written by Claire but coloured in by him across the top. Reuben leapt up and gave me a big hug. Seeing those three filled my heart and I felt a little frisson of excitement about the coming months when I was determined to have more time for each of them. I also felt a sudden stab of pride at the thought that the boys in future years could tell their friends their Daddy is an Ironman.

In the car on the way home, I barely got a word in. A squirrel had been spotted in the garden, Eamonn from pre-school had made a Ninja Turtle out of plasticine, and Reuben had stolen sweets from Mummy's cupboard. These were the things that really mattered.

At home I hung my medal up with all the others. This had become a ritual, but this one felt more significant somehow. I suddenly felt like I didn't need to add any more. The rest of them were just hanging there, gathering dust, already forgotten: inanimate objects that I never looked at.

EPILOGUE

Years ago, I spent a week at UTV in Belfast as a 17-year-old work-experience student. I looked at some of the reporters and thought they must go round in a constant buzz of happiness and satisfaction, warm in the knowledge that they were local celebrities, that they had made it onto TV, they were 'somebody'. I thought that no matter what happened to annoy them that day, that week, that month, they had these achievements to fall back on. Six years later I was a TV reporter myself, and thought nothing of it. Very quickly it just became what I do for a living, it didn't change my sense of self in any way at all, and it certainly hasn't meant I walk around in some constant buzz of satisfaction, alas. We push, we reach, and we move on.

Have you ever asked a young child about their day? About what they did at nursery or at school? They can never remember, or if they can, they can't be bothered recounting it. But ask them what they're doing right now, or what they might do tomorrow, and chances are you'll still be listening five minutes later. Kids don't look back; they only look at the present and to the future. It's the right way to be.

I thought about the tattoo again a few days later. Barcelona already felt like a distant memory. I'd done the Ironman, but didn't feel I needed to be constantly reminded of it every time I went for a shower or wore shorts in the summer. I'd done other things that were probably harder, and as well as an Ironman, I was a dad, a husband, a son, a grandson, a brother, a nephew, a cousin and a friend. I believe that we are all the sum of many parts and advertising one achievement or facet above all others just wasn't for me.

I rang big Andrew Hassard to hear about his Decaman attempt. I knew he had finished it but wasn't expecting him to tell me that getting through it all was actually a disappointment.

'Crossing the finish line was one of the most unsatisfying experiences I have ever had in my life,' he said bluntly. 'In the six or seven months before it, out training, one of the things I thought about a few times was crossing the finish line, finishing this momentous challenge and the emotion of it and what it would be like. There were tears streaming down my face thinking about the emotion and the achievement.

'But I got to the finish line and, honestly, I was just waiting for it, waiting for this emotion, waiting for this total euphoric sense of satisfaction, but it never arrived. And I guess that's one of the things that drives you to continue on and do that little bit further every time.'

'But you can't possibly do much more than ten Ironman triathlons in a row, Andrew,' I said, suddenly concerned for him. 'I mean, where would it end?'

'Maybe you do get that sense of satisfaction if you do a double Decaman or even a triple Decaman!' Andrew laughed. 'Maybe there's no end to it. There's always another challenge but maybe it's about the expectation. You have to understand where the satisfaction comes from, it has to come from the whole journey. It wasn't just about that final five metres, it was about the ten days we'd gone through and lots of little achievements and gate posts and dark places that I was in but got through along the way.'

Chatting to Andrew made me think about what I had been through myself, about what I had wanted from it all, and what I had got. Unlike him, I had felt fulfilled on finishing the Ironman, the MDS, the Lough Erne swim and all the rest. I felt rewarded. It sounded like the *process* was the key for Andrew, whereas for me, I felt it was all about the conclusion, the closure, the ticking off of each target. I had this growing feeling that the Ironman was some kind of natural ending, and that now I needed to evaluate and reflect. Very few of us do enough of that, and I often think perhaps it's because we're frightened of what we will conclude. We are happier to be too busy, happier to be fully engaged with things that really aren't important at all than to begin a potentially tumultuous soul search. I filled the next few months with work, the house move, lots of family time, and put off further introspection until our customary Club La Santa Christmas break.

On the first day, Claire's brother Brian asked me if I wanted to do a few track sessions with him. I'd seen him puke doing these in previous years, so no, that wasn't attractive, thanks.

'So what *are* you going to do? What are you training for?' he asked.

'Not much, haven't decided what event I'm doing next, so I might just try out this concept of "relaxing" on holiday actually, Brian.'

He scoffed at the very notion, so I wound him up a bit more. 'We Ironmen have nothing left to prove, you see.'

But I was half serious. For the first time in five years I'd come out to Lanzarote without a specific challenge on the horizon and I felt a little adrift.

I'd brought my cycling gear and hired a bike for the week, but the first day I went out I got blown about in the wind so much that I came back shattered. This is par for the course out there, but this time felt different. I'd already been to all the places I cycled to, had already done all the climbs, already ploughed through the Canarian headwinds, so what was the point of suffering through it again?

I went out next day too, but my arse was so tender from not cycling in months that I was too uncomfortable to do more than an hour. I went swimming instead, but struggled to find any decent rhythm and was washed back by the wake of Belgian teenagers effortlessly overtaking me in lanes either side.

Something wasn't right. On the second last day of the trip I went for a run. Usually within 15 minutes of starting out running I get really into it and go pretty hard. This time was different. I was running along the coast, waves were crashing in over the black volcanic rock, the sun was shining and all was perfect. And then I stopped.

Suddenly I just didn't see the need to keep going. Bob Marley's 'One Love' had come round on the song shuffle on my iPod. Not exactly a song to inspire physical effort. Something just clicked, and I stopped. I had never ever stopped running before getting home or finishing a session. I sat on a bench and looked out to sea.

It had been three months since the Ironman, and normally I would have the next event long since lined up and the training under way. But this year I felt no pressing need to do anything. I remembered what I'd said to Brian at the start of the week. I think I actually meant it. Maybe becoming an Ironman was it for me and I need not do another Man Test for the rest of my Man Years. Whatever mad drive I'd felt to test or prove myself had been sated, at least for the time being. I'd explored and found the boundaries of my endurance, got a glimpse of the deep capacities of the human body and injected some real adventure into my sporting life. And I was proud of what I'd done. If this was all about testing, I felt I could stamp 'Pass' on myself, and carry on now with something else.

Some anthropologists identify two principal personality types among the earliest humans. There were sensation seekers, and sensation avoiders. The sensation seekers had proven more successful because their personality type encouraged them to explore more and to seek out new experiences – they were rewarded with new food and mating opportunities.

Fifteen thousand years later, most of us are descendants of these sensation seekers, which is why we challenge ourselves, explore limits and constantly strive to advance to build on what we have. But having spent years exploring *my* mental and physical limits, I no longer thought I needed to seek out or explore much more pain and suffering. I had found new horizons, thrown myself into situations of uncertainty and adventure, built up a reserve of stories and vivid memories to sustain the future fireside days. In years to come when I start to fall apart, I will know I was once able to run 50 miles in one go over sand dunes; swim, bike and run for nearly 11 hours; front crawl between continents; and of course, run a marathon fuelled by wine and cheese.

But there were plenty of other rewarding sensations I felt I could seek, and each unforgiving minute didn't need to be about physical growth or adventure. Conversations I'd had with the now four-year-old Christian had been as rewarding as finishing any race; watching and learning about he and Reuben's very different personalities absorbed me. Like any challenging activity, the more you practise parenting, the easier it gets. That's why a year later we took on another big test – a daughter. Baby Isla should ensure that the devil cannot make work with my idle hands, and there is still not another big endurance event on the horizon.

That said, from anthropology we also learn that although our everyday activities have changed dramatically in the past 15,000 years, the essential components of our anatomy and psychology have not. So we are essentially the same driven species we were way back then, just with different life circumstances and different pressures. So you see, as I always say to Claire, I wasn't being an idiot for all those years, I was just being a human. And like all humans, I can keep my true nature and instinct suppressed, for a time. But the endurance junkie drive is unlikely to stay suppressed for ever. Maybe just one more hit. There is always Everest.

THANK YOU

I didn't set out to write about my adventures in endurance; they were supposed to be purely extra-curricular. That the experiences now exist in some tangible format is due to the effort and support of Jonathan Marks of MTC, a titan of an agent. I am also greatly indebted to Andrew Goodfellow at Ebury for his foresight, and to Liz Marvin for her fortitude. She gently and expertly cajoled the words out, Steve Dobell cut them back, and Jo Bennett made sure people knew about them. Thanks all.

For the fact that an unbridled restlessness became harnessed to 'Man Tests' I am indebted to Graham Smith and Tyvian Temple. Thanks also to each of the athletes, adventurers and joiner-inners that helped when a challenge required a team. The wonderful men of Team No Prior Experience on the Race Around Ireland are a special bunch of people, and the wonderful men and one woman of the Lough Erne relay team are made of stern stuff.

To my parents, Peter and Melanie, I am thankful for the genetic cocktail that created the blend of romantic naïvety and pig-headed stubbornness required of the endurance adventurer; and to my wife, Claire who has to live with the consequences of that cocktail every day, my eternal gratitude and devotion. I am so glad you didn't die on Kilimanjaro. It would have quite spoilt the honeymoon.

ABOUT THE AUTHOR

GRAHAM LITTLE has been a TV sports reporter and presenter for 13 years, appearing on all the main UK broadcasters and also working as a freelance features and travel writer contributing to national newspapers and magazines. He is best known as a Sky Sports football and cycling anchor and recently featured as presenter of ITV's *The Cycle Show*. An accomplished sportsman and keen adventurer, he has finished a series of tough endurance challenges and has competed internationally in sports as diverse as elephant polo, camel racing, body-building, and sumo wrestling. He lives in Bangor, Northern Ireland with his very understanding wife Claire and their three children.